PUBLIC CHOICE AND PUBLIC POLICY

PUBLIC CHOICE
AND
PUBLIC POLICY

Seven Cases in American Government

edited by

ROBERT S. ROSS

Chico State College

MARKHAM PUBLISHING COMPANY / Chicago

MARKHAM POLITICAL SCIENCE SERIES
Aaron Wildavsky, Editor

Axelrod, *Conflict of Interest: A Theory of Divergent Goals with Applications to Politics*

Barber, *Citizen Politics: An Introduction to Political Behavior*

Barber, ed., *Readings in Citizen Politics: Studies of Political Behavior*

Cnudde and Neubauer, eds., *Empirical Democratic Theory*

Coplin, *Introduction to International Politics: A Theoretical Overview*

Coplin, ed., *Simulation in the Study of Politics*

Coplin and Kegley, eds., *A Multi-method Introduction to International Politics: Observation, Explanation, and Prescription*

Dolbeare and Dolbeare, *American Ideologies: The Competing Political Beliefs of the 1970s*

Dvorin, ed., *The Senate's War Powers: Debate on Cambodia from the Congressional Record*

Greenstein, *Personality and Politics: Problems of Evidence, Inference, and Conceptualization*

Greenstein and Lerner, eds., *A Source Book for the Study of Personality and Politics*

Lane, *Political Thinking and Consciousness: The Private Life of the Political Mind*

Lyden and Miller, eds., *Planning Programming Budgeting: A Systems Approach to Management*

McDonald, *Party Systems and Elections in Latin America*

Mitchell, *Public Choice in America: An Introduction to American Government*

Payne, *The American Threat: The Fear of War as an Instrument of Foreign Policy*

Ranney, ed., *Political Science and Public Policy*

Ross and Mitchell, eds., *Introductory Readings in American Government: A Public Choice Perspective*

Ross, ed., *Public Choice and Public Policy: Seven Cases in American Government*

Russett, ed., *Economic Theories of International Politics*

Sharkansky, *Public Administration: Policy-Making in Government Agencies*

Sharkansky, ed., *Policy Analysis in Political Science*

Strickland, Wade and Johnston, *A Primer of Political Analysis*

For Mother and Pop

Acknowledgments

Much of the credit for this venture must go to David Woolston and John Applegath of Markham Publishing Company. They performed more than the normal duties of publishing executives. David provided the initial inception for publishing such a book; John displayed an unusually sophisticated appreciation of political science. Hopefully their contributions have led to a better book. Jenny Gilbertson provided the editing skill. My thanks go also to Mrs. Billie Harris, who by now must think that all typing must be done within a 24-hour turnaround deadline. Douglas Detling provided many services, not the least of which was to help me in proofreading. For their many helpful suggestions I owe thanks to Professors Charles Price, George Greenberg, and William C. Mitchell. My colleague Edward J. Bronson deserves special mention for his consistent open-door policy toward those who wish to discuss their problems and for his constant stream of innovative and novel suggestions. Finally and foremost, my thanks to my wife Sharon, whose sharp pencil and keen insight have helped me immeasurably.

The Authors

LEWIS CHESTER, GODFREY HODGSON, and BRUCE PAGE are reporters and editors for the *London Sunday Times*. Each has written award-winning articles and authored or co-authored books in addition to their major study of the 1968 presidential campaign, *An American Melodrama*, from which the case for this book was chosen.

JOHN H. DENTON is a lawyer and real estate appraiser who until recently headed the Business Administration Extension of the University of California, Berkeley. He is now an Urban Projects Counselor in Berkeley. Among his other publications is *Race and Poverty*, which he edited.

CALVIN B. T. LEE, Executive Vice President of Boston University, is a lawyer and also author of *Chinatown, U.S.A.* and *Improving College Teaching*.

GRANT MCCONNELL is Executive Vice Chancellor and Professor of politics at the University of California at Santa Cruz. Among his numerous publications are: *The Decline of Agrarian Democracy, The Steel Seizure of 1952,* and *Private Power and American Democracy*.

DANIEL M. OGDEN, JR., is Dean of the College of Humanities and Social Sciences at Colorado State College, Fort Collins, Colorado. From 1964 to 1967, Dr. Ogden was Assistant Director for Planning and Research of the Bureau of Outdoor Recreation, United States Department of the Interior, and was directly responsible for the preparation of the Administration's Redwood National Park proposal.

ROBERT S. ROSS is Associate Professor of political science at Chico State College. Among his other publications are: *Introductory Readings in American Government: A Public Choice Perspective* (co-editor with William C. Mitchell) and *American National Government: An Introduction to Political Institutions* (forthcoming).

IRVING SCHIFFMAN, a lawyer, is an Assistant Professor of political science at Chico State College. His publications include chapters on Howell E. Jackson and Melville W. Fuller in *Justices of the United States Supreme Court: Their Lives and Major Decisions* and a bibliography, *The Politics of Land-Use Planning and Zoning.*

BERT E. SWANSON is Professor of sociology at Sarah Lawrence College and Coordinator of its Institute for Community Studies. Among his numerous publications is *The Rulers and the Ruled* (co-author).

Contents

ROBERT S. ROSS

Introduction: The Case Study

Selection of works to be included in this book has been both professionally stimulating and personally exciting. I have for some time felt that extensive provision for the use of case studies in introductory American government courses is beneficial. Case studies offer the student an excellent vehicle for amplifying the hypotheses and concepts of a standard text. A case study is a detailed account of a particular event or institution. It explores in depth the interplay of various individuals within the context of institutions they are associated with as they confront the objective situations and forces of the broader political context.

A case study, in its detailed exploration of an event, permits the student to view political phenomena as more than cold, recorded facts; it enables him to survey the intricacies of politics and to observe the complexities facing the makers of public policy. Furthermore, the wealth of detail allows examination of the event from differing perspectives, depending upon the interests of the student. For example, one might take the first case study on the Presidency and approach it from the perspective of institutional analysis—concerning oneself with the established and patterned behavior of the President. The case could also be approached from a perspective of the personalities involved—how various people perceived their own actions and how these actions were shaped by personal characteristics. Another approach would be to study the case from the perspective of describing a particular administration, in this case that of John F. Kennedy. Finally, the student might be concerned with the actual substance of the decision or event itself. He may be interested in the President's relationship with the economy or with the response of big steel to political pressure.

The case study approach does have a number of specific limitations that students should recognize. Most case studies are quite narrow in their substantive concern; they are limited in time and in theoretical perspective to the single event they are studying. In looking at events and situations in such detail, authors usually find it difficult to generalize or to suggest that what transpired in their particular study is of value to the study of political science. Indeed, it is for the reader to determine the applicability of various events and situations mentioned in a case study to the broader perspective

1

of the operations of American government. Do the events and situations found in the case correspond to or illustrate the generalizations found in the textual material? Do these events and situations conform to the readers' intuitive grasp of the field of American government? If they do, then the case does not *prove* the generalization, but rather adds further credence to its acceptability as an accurate portrayal of American government.

If the case does not conform to the intuitive perspective of the reader, to the perspective developed by the instructor, or to the generalizations found in the textual material, then the student is faced with an interesting and sometimes perplexing problem: to fathom the real significance of the events being discussed and to fit them into some coherent scheme concerning American government. The case may represent a unique occurrence that, while interesting and perhaps enjoyable to read, does not in any way detract from the generalization concerning American government or, in all likelihood, would occur so infrequently that it need not be entered into a classificatory scheme describing the American political system. Alternatively, the perspective held by the student or the instructor, or represented in the text, might need revision. The student should seriously consider this possibility as he attempts to take the events described and fit them into an understanding of the American system. Finally, of course, the case might develop some event and situations leading to a broadening or expanding of the generalization held by the student. In his previous conception of the system, the student may have failed to take into account the situation or the conclusions to be derived from the present case, and while his perspective is not inaccurate it is incomplete and needs refinement.

Cases should first be read for the story portrayed and as an enjoyable exercise in the real world of American politics. But the reader should not stop at this level. Cases can be invaluable in allowing him to better understand the American system, to select those portions that illustrate general phenomena in American politics, to recognize the unique, and to use the events and conclusions of cases to improve and broaden his own perspective on the workings of the political system.

A PUBLIC CHOICE PERSPECTIVE

The cases in this text have been chosen to illustrate several values concerning political science. They cover a broad array of *political institutions:* the Presidency, Congress, the courts, the bureaucracy, local government, political parties, and pressure groups; the cases can be read purely from this institutional perspective. These cases also represent a broad array of *functional areas of policy* in the American system—conservation, reapportionment, desegregation, and so on. Most important, these cases illustrate a *particular perspective* on American government held by the editor—a perspective that might be described as a concern with how *public choice* is made in the American system.

Each of us is faced daily with making choices, from minor concerns such as where to cross a street and what to wear, to major questions such as how to spend our income or determine our career objectives. It does not stretch reality to assume that choices are being made by our political leadership as well. These choices, however, must be considered as categorically different from the choices made by individuals. Collective choice is not the summation of individual choice, though certainly some of our decisions, such as elections, are made through a summation process. Choices made by the collectivity are sometimes concerned with producing goods and services that are indivisible—they cannot be sold individually on the open market. Defense is such a public good. One cannot maintain exclusive possession of certain amounts of defense as he does his food or clothing.

Governments, of course, produce goods that can be divided and distributed. Since, however, many goods are produced that cannot be distributed directly to the individual, we have had to find ways to determine what to produce and how to pay for it. In all likelihood, individuals differ as to what goods and services government should provide and who should bear the costs. The difficulties of operating a political system on voluntary contributions should be manifest. Collective choice, then, involves imposing the wishes of some on all. It involves the element of coercion because, in many instances, choices are made with which an individual might not agree and, given the option, might not obey. For example, to achieve most goals governments must raise revenue, yet few of us voluntarily give our money to the federal government (though surprisingly few of us refuse to pay what we owe to our government). We have, of course, an elaborate apparatus to handle evasion and we spend considerable energy socializing citizens to convince them that they should indeed pay what is owed to the government in the form of taxes. Coercion prevents freeloading and forces compliance with government decisions.

An examination of public choice includes the determination of the costs involved in arriving at decisions and the costs imposed as a result of those decisions. Public choice is also concerned with the benefits derived from particular decisions. A major component of the public choice perspective, therefore, is cost-benefit analysis. This approach to the study of American government—or any other political system for that matter—is starkly realistic. Emphasis is placed upon the actual configuration of power, the actual making of choices, and the most accurate assessment of the costs and benefits of those choices. "With costs and benefits in mind, attention can easily be directed to those areas of policy-making most relevant to our interests and the relative importance of governmental decisions can be assessed."[1] Formal institutions are considered only secondarily. Institutions are certainly important, but their importance derives from their impact upon the policies that emanate from the decision-making framework. Most case studies focus upon particular institutions or particular decision situations. This does not mean, however, that the student cannot grasp the real situation of decision-making as he looks at specific institutions.

In public choice analysis, institutions are viewed as the setting for decision-making. "Americans . . . conduct their public choice through bargaining within a set of fairly stable political institutions (sometimes called political markets.)"[2] The use of the term "market" implies, for us as for the economist, a place where exchanges are made. "Men seek their advantages by offering to confer advantages on others; in doing so they seek, establish, and attempt to maintain favorable exchanges."[3] Exchanges are arrived at primarily through bargaining; once decisions are reached they become binding and coercive. As individuals engage in bargaining, they choose viable strategies for securing their goals. Since individual political resources—the means at one's disposal for influencing policy—vary depending upon the policy area and the institutional and constitutional position of the participants, appropriate strategies also vary. Public choices —the markets involved, the bargains struck, the strategies employed, the costs incurred and benefits received—can be illustrated by a careful reading of the case studies that follow. Each case clearly points to the interplay of a variety of forces—personality, constitutional requirements, institutional setting and the context of the particular event—as they co-mingle to produce the situation described. To illustrate the relationship of the various approaches to politics that have been discussed, the seven cases are descriptively categorized in Table 1, indicating the institutions involved, the constitutional questions being considered, the policy area under discussion, and the major components of a public choice framework that are involved. Clearly, the cases present a broad spectrum for the student to consider.

PUBLIC CHOICE AND PUBLIC POLICY IN AMERICAN GOVERNMENT

American government is frequently referred to as a system of "separation of powers." One must, however, look at the particular institutional arrangements closely to gain a real appreciation of the workings of American government. One author, Richard E. Neustadt, has indicated that we "created

TABLE 1

Chapter	Institution	Constitutional questions	Policy area	Component of public choice
1	President	Presidential powers	Economic regulation	Costs and Strategy
2	Congress	Advise and consent	Court nomination	Markets
3	Courts	Equal protection of laws and national supremacy	Reapportionment	Markets
4	Bureaucracy	Separation of powers	Conservation	Costs and benefits
5	Local governments	Equal protection of the laws	School integration	Bargaining
6	Political parties	Federalism	Party nominations	Strategy
7	Pressure groups	Equal protection of the laws	Housing	Markets

a system of separate institutions *sharing* power."[4] We might also describe our system as separate institutions competing with one another for the responsibility of defining issues, of delineating alternatives, and of ultimately choosing from those alternatives. However, the ability to actually choose one alternative from several is not the major power one might possess in the political system. The emphasis upon formal choice, such as the enactment of a law, the promulgation of a policy by the President, or the handing down of a Supreme Court decision, all of which might be found in an American history text, leaves us with an unrealistic picture of how decisions are reached.

Decision-making is a continuous process. One political scientist has indicated that there are three major stages of decision-making: (1) searching the environment for problems in need of resolution; (2) framing alternative solutions to solve the problem; and (3) the selection of a particular alternative.[5] While texts tend to concentrate unduly upon the third stage, Herbert A. Simon suggests that the first—the searching of the environment for questions in need of resolution—is the most significant.

The primary power of an American institution, such as the President, is not in his formal ability to sign laws, but rather in his ability to set the agenda of government. Modern American politics is dominated by the President because the President is the one who defines the major issues that face us and sets the tone by which these issues are considered. Grant McConnell's study of "Steel and the Presidency" describes how the ability to determine the agenda of government and to approach problems with a particular tone gives the President considerable power in influencing decisions in the American system.

The ability to determine that actions by private corporations are to be dealt with through the political system and by what types of government action constitute the basic ingredients of the modern President's power. Congress plays a much less significant role primarily because it takes the major questions facing our system as they are defined by the executive branch.

A single individual holding the position of President obviously cannot become familiar with or concerned about all of the issues that face our political system. He has around him a number of advisers who occupy both line and staff functions. These line and staff agencies provide much of what is issued in the name of the President. Also important in defining issues and policy for the Chief Executive is the professional bureaucracy composed of the professional civil servants in line agencies. Line agencies have a particular proclivity for assuming that due to their expertise and longevity with particular problems they should be the primary source of policy concerning those areas. Not surprisingly then, much of the President's program stems from this source. Daniel Ogden's study of the Redwood National Park illustrates the sources of policy that find their way into presidential programs. In this case the bureaucrats in the Department of the Interior, the Secretary of that department—a political line officer—and Presidential staff located in the Bureau of the Budget (now the Office of Management and Budget) became the chief source of the government's proposal. In the professional bureaucracy, political appointees housed in the Executive Office of the President, and the higher ranking line officers, we have the source of most of the issues presented for resolution in the American system.

Congress in most instances responds to the initiative of the executive by accepting, rejecting, or modifying requests in some manner to conform more closely with congressional perspectives on the issue. Such is the case in the study by Irving Schiffman, where the Senate refused to advise and consent to the President's nominee for a federal judgeship. Although this case is an exception to the above stated generalization, since by senatorial courtesy the nominee was proposed by a Senator, the most important fact to remember is that in most cases the issues being debated have been defined by the executive branch and not by the legislature.

Another reason for the importance of the executive in the formulation of policy in the American system is that the executive is charged with the implementation of established policy. We might conceive of decision-making concerning particular policies as a rather continuous making of choices; that is, policy begins with the determination by someone that there is a problem in need of resolution. Numerous decisions and choices are made as to whether, in fact, this particular problem will be placed on the agenda of government and how it will be defined when so placed. Once it has been determined that it will be considered by government there are numerous decisions from various components of the government in an attempt to formulate particular alternatives to the problem. There is considerable competition among both formal and informal decision-making groups, such as executive bureaus, the President's political appointees, interested Congressmen, especially those located on the relevant committees, and the clientele effected by a particular policy, represented by what we usually call interest groups. The ability of interest groups to secure policy objectives and their attempts to control a policy by keeping the issue off the agenda of government is described by John Denton in his case study of the National Association of Real Estate Boards.

Competition among these institutions produces decisions concerning the formulation of policy and once enacted, the policy must be applied. It is in the application, of course, that the real meaning of the policy is manifest and it is in execution of policy that the executive has primary responsibility. Thus the executive dominates the making of policy in the American system both in its inception and in its implementation. Congress has recognized this particular aspect of legislative dominance and has responded with a role shift to legislative oversight. "In performing these activities [oversight], Congress is acting where it is most competent to act: it is dealing with particulars, not general policies."[6]

The other major component of a "separate institutions" system, the Supreme Court, is in a much less advantageous position with respect to the formulation of policy. On one hand the Court operates under the rule of an adversary process. Questions must be raised by concerned groups or citizens, or by governmental units, and only after being heard by other components of the court system are the questions brought to the Supreme Court. Certainly the Court has sizable discretionary powers as a result of the 1925 Judiciary Act, giving it the right to pick cases it considers most significant with respect to American Government. But the case has already been initiated by someone else at some lower level of the court system and the Court seldom refuses to accept the facts as they are established by the trial court. On the other hand, the Court, having made a decision, does not have the means to carry out or to enforce that decision. Furthermore, in most cases, once the Court has ruled on a particular matter, the case is remanded or sent back to the court of origin—that is, the trial court—for implementation, thus allowing considerable leeway by various lower courts in interpreting what has been said by the Supreme Court. New cases must be brought to the Supreme Court questioning the implementation by the lower court, else the Supreme Court has little ability in influencing these lower court decisions. The case by Calvin Lee on New York's Apportionment Acts is illustrative of just such a series of cases where the courts were involved in attempting to insure compliance with their directives.

American government courses are concerned with a sizable number of issue areas, and the groups, individuals, and political markets involved in the formulation of policies for each area varies. However, many of the political combatants—the President, congressmen, leading political figures of the bureaucracy—are intimately involved in a number of issue areas; hence the necessity for such individuals to handle a diversity of conflict in the American system. Each political actor has a number of goals that he seeks to maximize, and these goals are somewhat different from the goals other actors seek to maximize. A more detailed account of these activities can be found in William C. Mitchell's *Public Choice in America: An Introduction to American Government* (Markham, 1971).

The actors in the political system must be willing to trade or exchange their support for particular issues about which they are less concerned in return for support on those issues in which they are vitally concerned. Trading across issues is usually referred to as logrolling and is not only a basic part of decision-making in the American system but an absolutely essential one. Unless we are willing to opt for a system in which decisions are made by command, we must find some manner of reconciling the differences we have as a people.

Bargaining, exchanging individual advantages or assets for more desirable advantages or assets for which someone else is willing to trade, is the heart of political activity in the American system. This aspect of the American system is portrayed in the case study of the New York schools' program for school integration by Bert E. Swanson. Swanson provides insight into the bargaining that ensued between pro-integration forces and the school administration, as well as carrying the analysis further in also assessing the consequences when bargaining breaks down as it did between the anti-integration groups and the administration. The strategies available to these groups in differing situations and the resources at their disposal provide insight into how one might influence policies adopted in the American system.

A concern for various strategies is the major focus of the case by Lewis Chester and associates studying the attempts by two candidates to secure the presidential nomination of their party. Elections are important in our system as a means of choosing who will make decisions for us during their tenure in office. Strategies available to prospective candidates are in large measure determined by the electoral system in the United States—one resulting largely from the federal system; with individual states responsible for most of the institutional arrangements of elections. The electoral market must therefore be dealt with on a state-by-state basis. The attempt by McCarthy in 1968 to secure his party's endorsement was unsuccessful primarily because of the institutional advantages of his opponent.

This brief overview of the American system illustrates the relationship of the case studies that follow to the basic components of the American system. At the same time, the use of a public choice perspective was shown to fit well with traditional institutional study and particularly well with the cases described herein. Students will, of course, have other frames of reference for the study of these cases and will have no difficulty in integrating them into the perspective chosen. This fact can be restated by returning to the opening theme; cases are excellent supplementary material for the study of American government.

NOTES

[1] Robert S. Ross, "Public Choice in American Politics," in Robert S. Ross and William C. Mitchell (eds.), *Introductory Readings in American Government: A Public Choice Perspective* (Chicago: Markham Publishing Company, 1971), p. 7.

[2] William C. Mitchell, *Public Choice in America: An Introduction to American Government* (Chicago: Markham Publishing Company, 1971), p. 113.

[3] *Ibid.*

[4] Richard E. Neustadt, *Presidential Power* (New York: John Wiley & Sons, Inc., 1962), p. 33.

[5] Herbert A. Simon, *The New Science of Management Decision* (New York: Harper & Row, 1960), p. 1ff.

[6] Samuel P. Huntington, "Congressional Responses to the Twentieth Century," in David B. Truman (ed.) *The Congress and America's Future* (Englewood Cliffs, N.J.: Prentice-Hall, Inc., 1965), p. 25.

The Presidency 1

Much of the commentary concerning the President is based upon his clearly defined constitutional roles, such as his actions as Commander-in-Chief or his primacy in the area of foreign affairs. The case by Grant McConnell points to the growing importance of the Presidency in areas not specifically delegated to him by the Constitution. While the President was not able to directly alter the decision by a private firm, U.S. Steel, to increase its prices, the vast array of powers he brought to bear on the crisis was impressive. The case concerns itself with these powers and the speed with which the Kennedy Administration mobilized its opposition to the actions of U.S. Steel. The end result was a rescinding of the price increase that would lead one to believe the President was directly responsible. The author of this selection points out elsewhere, however, that market forces, such as the generally weak demand for steel at the time of the price increase, may have been a more significant factor. Our concern, however, is with the Presidency rather than the conditions of the market in 1962.

This case, therefore, illustrates the growing concern of modern Presidents with the conditions of the economy. Responses of Presidents have varied from mild expressions of apprehension about the activities of various industries to more intimate attention in attempting to produce a desired outcome, be it a wage settlement or a price increase. Seldom has the government been mobilized as rapidly and as dramatically as during the steel crises of 1962.

The case might also be viewed from the standpoint of strategies open to various competing institutions in attempting to influence public policy. Of particular importance, the student of the modern Presidency should note the President's ability to mobilize opinion on his behalf through the mass media. Some commentators have gone so far as to suggest this might be his most effective power.

The necessity of attempting to mobilize public opinion resulted from a breakdown in the normal processes of bargaining and exchange that had led to the earlier agreement between industry and labor at the behest of the President. Students might, therefore, give serious thought to the conditions that make bargaining and compromise unworkable.

GRANT McCONNELL

Steel and the Presidency

Mr. [Roger M.] Blough [President of U.S. Steel] was ushered into the President's oval office, and the President settled himself in his rocking chair while Mr. Blough took a seat on a sofa close by. Mr. Blough handed the President a four-page mimeographed document. It began:
"For A.M. Papers
Wednesday, April 11, 1962
     "Pittsburgh, Pennsylvania, April 10—For the first time in nearly four years, United States Steel today announced an increase in general level of its steel prices. This 'catch-up' adjustment, effective at 12:01 A.M. to-morrow, will raise the price of the company's steel products by an average of about 3.5 percent—or three-tenths of a cent per pound."
     The President glanced at the rest of the release and then called for Mr. [Arthur J.] Goldberg [Secretary of Labor]. Mr. Goldberg arrived from his office on Constitution Avenue within a few short minutes. The President handed Mr. Goldberg the statement he had just read through. Mr. Goldberg read it hurriedly and then asked Mr. Blough what the purpose of the meeting was if the action had already been taken. Mr. Blough explained that he felt it was a matter of courtesy for him to give the news to the President in person. The Secretary of Labor, an unusually voluble man under any circumstances, heatedly began to lecture Mr. Blough: This threatened the government's economic policy, it would damage United States Steel, it would undermine responsible collective bargaining. And it could only be seen as a double cross of the President.
     Mr. Blough defended himself quietly and shortly left the White House. In New York the news release was sent out to the wire services at 6:10, a few minutes before Mr. Blough finished his talk with the President and Mr. Goldberg.
     This news release had been drawn up several weeks before. Its preparation accompanied a debate of some standing inside the Corporation. An increase of prices had been much discussed before the actual day of de-

     Grant McConnell, *Steel and the Presidency, 1962* (New York: W. W. Norton and Company, Inc., 1963), pp. 77–95.

13

cision. It had been passed by the Corporation's Operations Policy Committee, a body consisting of the Chairman of the Board, the General Counsel, the Chairman of the Finance Committee, the President, and the Vice-Presidents for Operations, Research and Engineering, International, Accounting, Personnel Services, and Commercial. The Chairman himself represented Public Relations. During the labor negotiations it was apparent to this body that profits were such that it was necessary to test the market (as it was later described). The public relations department and the labor relations experts in the Corporation had been consulted. The commercial people were doubtful whether the price increase would stick, but their doubts were overruled. The principal question was timing. An announcement during the negotiations might be disrupting; further delay was chosen. After the labor settlement, no point existed for waiting for what was long overdue. While there was no expectation of a response from President Kennedy anything like what came, there was no illusion that the price increase would release a great wave of popularity for United States Steel.

Several days before the public announcement a decision was made that Mr. Blough should go to Washington to deliver the news to the President. This was, as Mr. Blough later explained to Mr. Goldberg, a matter of courtesy. The nature of the interview that took place on April 10, an official of the Corporation explained some time later, was not foreseen. Mr. Blough had felt that President Kennedy understood the industry's problems. Moreover, it was thought in United States Steel that it was clear there could be no participation by Mr. Blough in any negotiations that involved a commitment on prices. Prices could not be discussed among the companies since a matter of law was involved in any agreement on prices in the bargaining with the union. Moreover, the Corporation official explained, Mr. Blough felt that prices should not by their nature be discussed with the union. And he had no idea what the rest of the industry would do.

So far as the notion of an implied commitment not to raise prices if a moderate settlement were achieved with the union was concerned, Mr. Blough indicated that he felt his position had been made clear long before. In his report to the stockholders at the Corporation's annual meeting on May 7, when the tumult had subsided somewhat, Mr. Blough recalled the letter he had written in reply to that of Mr. Kennedy of September 6, 1961. Mr. Blough told the stockholders his exact words in one passage of that reply: ". . . we in United States Steel cannot forecast the future trend of prices in any segment of the steel industry and have no definite conclusions regarding our own course during the foreseeable future. . . ." Mr. Blough described how he had further discussed the profit squeeze, the need for healthy industrial units in America, and the responsibility to maintain the economic freedom of the country. He added, "I do not see how anyone who read those letters could fail to understand clearly three things: first, that we had declined to enter into any commitment—express or implied—regarding future price actions; second, that we believed a substantial improvement in our cost-price relationship to be necessary not only in the interest of the company, its owners and its employees, but in the interest of the entire nation; and third, that any price decision we might make would be—as it inevitably must be—controlled by competitive forces that govern the market place."

Nevertheless, there were a number of people who had not caught the meaning of the passage that Mr. Blough quoted to his stockholders and as he explained it at the annual meeting. To one puzzled observer who asked a Corporation official some time later how it happened that the position of United States Steel was so misunderstood before it took action, this explanation was given: United States Steel had had to exercise some caution in expressing its intentions. The theory advanced by Mr. Eisenhower's antitrust chief before the Kefauver Committee, that steel-company executives communicated with each other by newspaper stories, had forced a discreet manner upon the Corporation. This had permitted some people, including many in the administration, to misunderstand Mr. Blough's intentions.

Despite the confusion in outsiders' minds before April 10, it is now clear that United States Steel's leadership had made preliminary plans for the price increase some time in advance of the announcement. It did not require a long meeting of the Executive Committee in the early afternoon of that Tuesday to make the formal decision to announce the general price rise. Three of the twelve members were absent, but Mr. Blough, Mr. [Robert C.] Tyson, Chairman of the Finance Committee, and Mr. Leslie B. Worthington, President of the Corporation, were present. The action was agreed upon and Mr. Blough went to Washington.

In the White House, after Mr. Blough had departed, a period of furious activity began. The members of the Council of Economic Advisers were summoned from their offices across the lane in the old State Department Building. The Chairman, Walter W. Heller, arrived first, Kermit Gordon arrived three minutes later, and James Tobin came somewhat later. Secretary Goldberg, with Mr. Kennedy's assistants—McGeorge Bundy, Theodore C. Sorensen, Kenneth O'Donnell, and Andrew T. Hatcher, acting White House press secretary—joined the emergency meeting. Mr. Kennedy had kept his temper under control during the time that Mr. Blough was in the White House, but now was the time when he is reputed to have uttered the profane comment about businessmen (or steel men, as the case may have been) that struck such terror into the heart of the business community.

There is no doubt whatsoever that the President was exceedingly angry. At this moment it would have been very difficult to convince any-one in the White House that the explanation by United States Steel as it has been given above was a fair statement of the situation. What had occurred was a betrayal, a double cross. The administration had gone out of its way to indicate that the White House would use its influence with labor in return for the exercise of forbearance by the steel industry on prices. A low-cost labor settlement had been obtained, and it had been achieved early and without a strike. Now the implicit agreement had been repudiated.

There had been no explicit agreement by United States Steel—this was readily conceded. So far as the argument that it would have been illegal to agree in this manner, United States Steel was the acknowledged price leader of the industry and price leadership had never been found to be contrary to the antitrust laws. One member of the group that worked with the President during this period has described the events this way: It was as though a young man had asked a girl to marry him. She replied, "Oh, I'm so glad you asked me." Together, they then set a date for the wedding. He gave her money for her trousseau, arranged for the invitations, the church, the flowers, and the preacher. The day of the wedding arrived, and everyone but the bride came to the church. The groom phoned her and was told, "Yes, you asked me to marry you, but I didn't say I would." Whatever the merit of the analogy, the supposed bridegroom exhibited a fury equal to that of any woman who has ever been spurned.

The problem that confronted the little group in the White House that evening was exceedingly difficult. Abstractly two choices were open: the President could accept the action by United States Steel, perhaps thanking Mr. Blough for informing him personally and expressing a wish that other companies would exercise greater restraint; alternatively the President could seek to obtain a reversal of the action. To attempt the first might have been simpler if the part played by the administration had not been generally known. If it had been thoroughly secret except to industry and labor lead-ers, presidential prestige might not have received a damaging blow, except in the eyes of the labor leaders. This would have been serious, and the President could have looked forward to a period of difficult relations with those leaders, but, assuming that the story did not get out to the union membership, this period might have been passed.

However, the part played by the administration in the earlier nego-tiation was well known. The President's letter to the steel-company execu-tives was public, and the other activities of the administration had been discussed in the press and praised on the floor of Congress. However great the personal good will of labor leaders might have been, they would have come under great pressure from their members, who could have been urged by union rivals to repudiate an official leadership that had settled for less than might have been obtained by more determined bargaining, enforced by a strike perhaps, and by a leadership not disposed to listen to the blandishments of a government that could not, as it now appeared, deliver on its promises. To accept the action, then, would vastly increase the determination of everyone in conflict with the administration in any way and would harden all opposition. Acceptance would have had the result of forcing the administration to abandon any hope of dealing actively with economic issues, which was, of course, one of the chief desires of many business leaders. In administration eyes, this would have been exceedingly serious economically, particularly in view of the relationship of the steel issue to the uneasy problems of the balance of payments, unemployment, and growth. Moreover, the reverberations of such a capitulation would have reached beyond economic affairs—how far, it would have been impossible to say. Certainly, the effects would have been felt in indefinite ways in the conduct of foreign affairs. Ultimately the very power of the presidency was at stake. There is no evidence that this course was considered.

On the other hand, if the President chose not to accept U.S. Steel's action, what could he do? No legislation authorized him or any part of the government to control prices by command. To seek legislation would be time-consuming and probably futile. Moreover, this was not a power that anyone desired. Short of such action there were some possibilities, but they were of so miscellaneous a character as to be out of scale with the problem that had so suddenly materialized.

The most obvious possibility was quickly decided on. The President had his regular press conference on the following afternoon; the President would make a statement on steel then. The power of persuasion and publicity was ultimately the greatest power any President had. A fund of information was necessary for this statement and for the longer pull ahead. The members of the Council of Economic Advisers returned to their offices. Secretary Goldberg reached his chief of Labor Economics whom he asked for an emergency crew, and three men soon joined the Economic Advisers at work. Mr. Heller broke off to go to a dinner given by the German Ambassador for the President of the Common Market. A guest told a reporter that Mr. Heller arrived midway through the meal looking like Banquo's ghost in a tuxedo. He was back at his office by midnight, bringing with him another guest, George W. Ball, Under Secretary of State. At 2:45 the men from the Labor Department departed; Mr. Heller and Mr. Tobin worked on until 4.00. Mr. Gordon did not go home but took a few hours rest on a couch in his office.

At the White House, the President, after seeing the staff work organized, called three other members of his cabinet, Attorney General Robert F. Kennedy, Secretary of Defense Robert S. McNamara, and Secretary of the

Treasury Douglas Dillon. The last had just arrived in Florida for a vacation. Next, the President telephoned Senator Kefauver, who was on the
point of going out for the evening. The Senator readily agreed to issue a
statement expressing his "dismay." The Senator would also consider calling
an investigation of the affair. The President then changed to formal clothes
for the annual reception he and Mrs. Kennedy were giving for members of
Congress and their wives. The President chatted lightly with his guests, perhaps slipping out to survey the battle preparations from time to time, until
a few minutes after midnight. Lights had been burning in various offices of
the White House Staff, the Council of Economic Advisers, the Departments
of the Treasury, Defense, Justice, Commerce, and Labor. Some of them
continued to burn on into the night.

At breakfast on Wednesday morning President Kennedy brought together Vice President Johnson, Secretary Goldberg, and a group of the
White House staff. These were Theodore Sorensen, who held the title of
Special Counsel to the President, but whose tasks were exceedingly varied
and who often worked on the drafts of presidential speeches; Myer Feldman, Deputy Special Counsel; Mr. Hatcher; and Mr. Heller.

Later during the morning, the President talked with Secretary Dillon
in Florida and reportedly discussed one of the most drastic ideas that had
occurred in the crisis. This was for a change in the Treasury Department's
plans for a liberalization of depreciation allowances on taxes. This liberalization had been a goal of many industries, of which steel was one, and the
Bureau of Internal Revenue had been working on the details for some time.
Although the idea of a change in these plans was presumably rejected in
the discussion between the President and the Secretary, Mr. Kennedy later
hinted at his press conference that there might be a review of the plans.

By midday it seemed as though things were happening all over Washington. Secretary Hodges spent most of the day telephoning businessmen in
different parts of the country. Other officials were doing the same wherever
they had well-placed friends in business. Things were noisy on Capitol Hill.
In the House of Representatives, Mr. Celler announced that his subcommittee would begin hearings on the increase on May 2. He wanted to know
whether the antitrust laws needed amendment. Senator Kefauver directed
the staff of his committee to prepare recent data on steel. He would co-
operate with Mr. Celler. Senator Gore suggested that there should be court
orders for cooling-off periods on the analogy of the Taft-Hartley provision
in national emergency strikes, before prices in "monopoly-controlled basic
industries" could be increased. Senators Mansfield and Humphrey, House
Speaker John W. McCormack, and Representative Henry S. Reuss all made
statements denouncing the price increase with varying degrees of anger.
Perhaps the most striking statement in the Capitol came from Representa-

tive John W. Byrnes, who felt the action was unfortunate because it could "set off another wage-price increase." Mr. Byrnes was chairman of the House Republican Policy Committee.

However, things were happening elsewhere also. Bethlehem Steel announced a price increase equaling that of United States Steel. Similar announcements quickly came from Republic Steel, Jones and Laughlin, Youngstown, and Wheeling. The hope that perhaps the industry would not follow the leader was fading. Some telephone calls had gone to the executives of these firms, but that game seemed to be lost now. Nevertheless, there was a group of companies whose leaders indicated they were still "studying" the problem. These included Inland, Kaiser, Colorado Fuel and Iron, Armco, and McLouth.

What the administration had feared since the previous evening seemed to be taking place. The steel industry was in the process of lining up behind its leader. The largest companies after United States Steel were paying no attention to the pleas that had been directed to them. The forlorn attempt on Big Steel itself, via a call from Under Secretary of the Treasury Robert V. Roosa to the Chairman of Morgan Guaranty Trust, a call that was based upon the presence of a Morgan representative on the U.S. Steel Finance Committee and the well-advertised influence of Wall Street in the Corporation, failed. In his press conference, President Kennedy would give little impression that he held any further hope in persuasion.

As for Mr. Goldberg, he composed a letter of resignation. He felt, as he told a few of his associates in the Labor Department, that his usefulness was ended. He considered that he had taken his government post to bring about a different pattern of labor-management relations. The action by United States Steel had undermined his entire campaign. In reality, Mr. Goldberg was at this point the most exposed member of the administration, more so in some ways than the President himself. Mr. Goldberg had carried most of the burden of persuading labor and management everywhere to engage in "responsible" bargaining, and to reach an early agreement in steel. Many of the initiatives had been his. In a more general way, he had been talking about the creation of a different atmosphere in industrial relations for a number of years before he became Secretary of Labor. He had carried his message into vigorous action by his very dramatic and successful interventions in the disputes of the New York tugboatmen, the flight engineers, the Metropolitan Opera, and others. But the biggest coup of his governmental career had seemed to be the early steel settlement. Now he could reasonably expect that those leaders in the labor movement who had been lukewarm to his appointment would become outspokenly critical and that his influence with labor would sharply diminish. On this very day one labor leader said. "I can't imagine any wage restraint now by unions when industry exercises none. Unions will thumb their noses at it." Fortunately, however, Mr. Goldberg did not send his letter and few people were aware of it.

The tone of the President's press conference was harsh. His language about the steel industry has been described as the harshest used against businessmen by any President since Franklin D. Roosevelt delivered his 1936 speech accepting renomination. However, that assessment ignores President Truman's radio speech just before he seized the steel mills in 1952. The topic of steel seems to have a very particular quality for presidents. When he stood before the television cameras at his conference that afternoon, Mr. Kennedy denounced the price increase as "wholly unjustifiable and irresponsible." He said that "a tiny handful of steel executives" were seeking "private power and profit" at the nation's expense. They were showing "utter contempt" for the interests of 185 million Americans. He contrasted the behavior of the steel executives with that of the reservists called from their homes and he cited the soldiers dying in Vietnam. He said that he had asked no commitment from the industry, but emphasized that in his talks with Mr. Blough and Mr. McDonald the thread ran throughout that the labor settlement should not lead to a price increase. He also spoke bitterly of the manner in which he had learned of the price increase, after it had occurred.

The alternative to persuasion, some form of compulsion, seemed to be foreshadowed in the President's conference. Threats of Congressional investigations seemed to be in the process of being made good by Senator Kefauver and Congressman Celler. Late on Wednesday, the Chairman of the Federal Trade Commission announced that the Commission was beginning an informal investigation of the price increase in the light of the consent decree of 1951. All this activity was headline material, but those who had followed the history of antitrust ventures in steel—and this presumably included leaders of the industry—were familiar with its record of futility. The President phoned the Solicitor General, Archibald Cox, who was just arriving in Tucson, Arizona, for a pair of speeches he had been scheduled to give. The President wanted to know what ideas Mr. Cox had for restoring prices to their previous level. Mr. Cox was convinced that experience had shown the inadequacy of the antitrust laws for dealing with steel. He believed that special legislation would be necessary and sat up all night working on the problem. After he had made his speeches he returned to Washington, where he stayed up most of a second night drafting the law that he thought would be necessary.

Antitrust legislation clearly was not an approach on which the administration was placing great hopes. Nevertheless, after the President had made his personal appeals to the steel executives, after a multitude of calls had gone from administration figures to whatever friends in business they had, and after the President had spoken directly to the public, there was not a great deal more that could be tried. There was hope that some kind of evidence could be found in the parade of similar price announcements by the big companies during the day. On its face, the pattern of price increases by a number of steel companies was nothing new; it demonstrated price leadership, and that was a very familiar thing. However, a statement attributed to the President of Bethlehem Steel at a stockholders' meeting on Tuesday seemed significant. The statement as it was reported read, "There shouldn't be any price rise. We shouldn't do anything to increase our costs if we are to survive. We have more competition both domestically and from foreign firms."

Since this statement was supposed to have been made before United States Steel's announcement, and since Bethlehem had increased its prices the day afterward, it might be evidence in a government attempt to prove that United States Steel exerted undue influence over other companies. Late on Wednesday Attorney General Kennedy gave orders to the Federal Bureau of Investigation to get the exact words of the Bethlehem President. Mr. Lee Linder, an Associated Press reporter in Philadelphia who had reported on the stockholders' meeting in Wilmington, Delaware, was awakened by a phone call at 3:00 A.M., Thursday. It was from the FBI. Mr. Linder thought he was the victim of a practical joke, but the call was serious. Agents were coming right out. He was questioned about the story he had given on the Bethlehem meeting. Another reporter in Wilmington was met by FBI agents when he arrived at his office at 6:30 A.M.

This activity of the FBI attracted widespread attention the next day and afterward. An inquiry at the Department of Justice about it after the excitement had subsided brought this explanation: The agents involved had been "eager beavers" and had rushed off thoughtlessly on receiving the orders, and the nocturnal aspect of their behavior had been their own idea. Neither in substance nor in manner was this explanation convincing. The implicit repudiation of the Department's subordinates and the agents' behavior combined to make the incident a very unsavory part of the government's activity in the entire affair.

The Department of Justice learned only that Bethlehem Steel considered the reported statement inaccurate, and that Mr. Linder stood by his report. However, the Department did take action. In the evening of Tuesday it announced that it was ordering a grand-jury investigation. The District Court in New York had been asked to impanel a special grand jury for this inquiry. The investigation implied the possibility of more than civil action. Seemingly, at least, this was a strong measure by government. An antitrust official, when asked about the step, stated that it was "routine," and that any administration faced with the fact of similar price actions by different firms in the same industry would have ordered a grand-jury investigation as a matter of course. It was, nevertheless, remarkable that this particular price increase received such prompt consideration from a division whose pace has often been measured if not stately.

The FBI's part in the Justice Department forays finally shook the Republican party out of a stunned lethargy. Mr. William E. Miller, Congressman from New York and Chairman of the Republican National Committee, compared the FBI activity to the behavior of the Gestapo in Hitler's Germany. This was too lurid a comparison, for in the present circumstances it was a reporter who was awakened at 3:00 A.M. and not the supposed victim. The Republicans were having other difficulties in getting moving. Congressman Halleck made a public statement that the issue was economic and not political. To add to the confusion, Congressman William W. Scranton, then Republican candidate for governor, and Congressman James E. Van Zandt, Republican candidate for senator in Pennsylvania, joined in signing a telegram to Mr. Blough. It began: "The increase at this time is wrong—wrong for Pennsylvania, wrong for America, wrong for the free world."

Already the complex issues of the affair were being reduced to simple black-and-white moral categories. Secretary of Commerce Hodges, in a speech at the Drexel Institute in Philadelphia, dwelt upon the controversy at some length. He illustrated his evaluation with a personal experience: "Night before last, Mrs. Hodges heard me up during the night talking on the telephone, and she asked me the next morning what was going on. I told her I had been conferring on the announced rise in steel prices. Then she exclaimed, 'But they said they wouldn't.' I believe the reaction of most people was that." Editorial opinion across the country began to line up on one side or the other. One paper called the industry's action "one of the dirtiest business tricks of the century on the President of the United States and on the people of the United States." A different paper asked, "Can the steelmakers of this country still fix the prices at which they will sell their product, or must they yield to government fiat?" Most of the comments betrayed strong feeling. That ultrasensitive indicator of business morale, the stock market, declined sharply. The market-commentator priesthood seemed agreed that this indicated a general belief that steel's action had insured an antibusiness campaign by government.

Mr. Blough held his press conference at 71 Broadway at midafternoon. Although some observers felt the tumult of the reporters somewhat rattled Mr. Blough, the evaluation made in United States Steel was that the conference had been a success. Certainly, Mr. Blough's temperance of language and his relative calm contrasted favorably with the temper of President Kennedy's remarks the day before.

On this same Thursday several attempts were made to restore diplomatic relations between the two powers. The President asked Clark Clifford, whose legal practice had brought him in contact with many corporate officials and who knew Mr. Blough, to help Secretary Goldberg in his talks with United States Steel. Mr. Clifford flew to New York and was received by Mr. Blough. Mr. Clifford explained the President's feelings of betrayal. He left with assurances that further discussion would be welcomed. There were also some indications of a more mysterious attempt to mediate between the two principals.

A large part of the President's day was devoted to the steel crisis. He began with a meeting of some of the key officials in the struggle, the Attorney General, the Secretary of Defense, the Under Secretary of the Treasury, the Secretary of Commerce, the Chairman of the Federal Trade Commission, the Chairman of the Council of Economic Advisers, and his assistant, Mr. Sorensen. A plan evolved for Mr. Hodges to hold his own press conference where he would attempt to refute Mr. Blough's statements at the United States Steel conference. The actions that came out of this strategy meeting became clear later in that day or the following day. After a long series of consultations the President concluded his day with a state dinner for the Shah and Empress of Iran at the Iranian Embassy.

In actuality, this was the day on which the outcome was decided, if, indeed, the outcome was not inevitable from the beginning. A meeting took place in an appropriately new and shining stainless-steel-sheathed building in Chicago's Loop. At the meeting were a number of members of the Board of Inland Steel Company. The Chairman of the Board, Mr. Joseph L. Block, was on vacation in Kyoto, Japan. His relative, Mr. Philip D. Block, Jr., Vice Chairman of the firm, was the senior officer present. Already the officers of the company had been receiving calls from regular customers of Inland asking them not to follow the lead of United States Steel in raising prices. Through Wednesday the directors had delayed the decision that they knew must be made.

Inland was not one of the real giants of the steel industry, but it was perhaps one of the most to be envied. Its plants were by the general standards very modern. Its combination of products was well adapted to the state of the market in the second half of the century. Moreover, the relationship of the firm with its customers was close and friendly. A reputation had been established that any substantial customer could telephone the firm and talk not just to a salesman but to the Chairman. And Mr. Block was eminently a man who was on top of his job. The firm was to some degree a family organization, but the supposed disadvantages of one-family influence had not appeared. Inland held approximately a quarter of the market for steel in the Chicago area, one of the most important in the country. The profit record of Inland was consistently the best or one of the best in the industry. In the past, Inland had repeatedly demonstrated a considerable degree of independence within the industry, a trait that reflected not only the character of its officers, but the firm's own efficiency and strength.

This record and the position of Inland had come early to the thoughts of the economists who were advising the President in Washington. Perhaps Inland could be persuaded not to raise its prices, and perhaps if Inland didn't, several others also wouldn't. Together these firms might account for as much as a quarter of all steel production, and this force would be massive enough to force Big Steel to back down. A telephone call had been made early on Wednesday morning by Mr. Edward Gudeman, Under Secretary of Commerce, to Mr. Philip Block, with whom he had been in school years before. Mr. Gudeman asked for Mr. Block's view of the steel price increase. Mr. Block said that he had been surprised. The call had awakened Mr. Block, for Mr. Gudeman had apparently overlooked the difference in time between Washington and Chicago. Mr. Block later emphasized to Chicago acquaintances that he was not particularly close to Mr. Gudeman and that they had only seen each other a few times since they were in school. Later on Wednesday other calls were made to Inland from Washington. Mr. Henry H. Fowler, Under Secretary of the Treasury, called Mr. John F. Smith, Jr., Inland's President, and Secretary Goldberg called Mr. Leigh B. Block, an Inland Vice President. Inland officials have been very firm in stating that none of these were "pressure calls."

At the Thursday meeting in Chicago, the directors of Inland decided to recommend that the firm's prices not be raised. A telephone call to Mr. Joseph Block was arranged with some care (the arrangements involved the personal attention of the President of the Illinois Bell Telephone Company). Mr. Block concurred in the decision.

This was probably the crucial decision in the final outcome. Its reasons have been the source of some speculation. In late 1961, Mr. Block had said publicly, "Profits can be improved either by raising prices or by lowering costs. Of these alternatives I would much prefer the latter." Retrospectively after the contest was over, he said that probably Inland would have gone along with the price increase if the government had done nothing. However, he added to this statement an explanation of the meaning of a remark he had made to a reporter in Japan at the time of the crisis, that a price increase "at this time" was not in the national interest. His reasons were, first that the time was too close to the labor settlement, second that most of the smaller companies were still negotiating with the union, and third that "the order book was disappearing." Of the three reasons, the third was, in his eyes, by far the most important: it is the worst possible time to increase prices when orders are running out.

The events of Friday followed. The Secretary of Defense did add one new feature to that which had been determined already. He told a news conference just before noon that the Defense Department had directed contractors to make their purchases of steel from companies that had not raised prices. Mr. McNamara also said that the price increase would increase the cost of national defense by more than 1 billion dollars. His Department gave a 5-million-dollar contract to Lukens Steel Company for special steel to be used in the Polaris program. The announcement of this award came later in the day and was perhaps the unkindest cut, for that particular steel had been developed by United States Steel, and had been made available to other companies at the request of the government.

Several meetings were held in the White House on steel before the President departed for Norfolk to inspect the fleet. The Inland announcement arrived before noon. The President's advisers saw its meaning but feared the effect might take time to arrive. The announcement by Kaiser that it would not raise prices arrived while the second meeting in the White House was under way. And Armco was now definitely holding. In New York the meeting of Mr. Goldberg and Mr. Clifford with the officers of United States Steel was going on in a mood of general gloom. The Bethlehem announcement reached that meeting at 3:20.

At 5:28 the Associated Press news ticker in the White House impersonally wrote out the message that United States Steel had rescinded the price increase.

Congress   2

Congress is composed of such a baffling array of rules, procedures, and idiosyncrasies that one case could not possibly shed light on them all. As its major emphasis the selection chosen describes the limits of certain norms in the U.S. Senate. In so doing, the selection also clearly indicates the importance of committees, the clienteles associated with committees, the skill and resourcefulness of individual participants in congressional proceedings, and the norms that customarily prevail.

In addition to its rich illustration of the workings of Congress, the Morrissey case was significant as an issue; as a precedent for handling unqualified nominations and as an episode in the phenomenal story of the Kennedy family in American politics. When the Senate was considering the nomination of G. Harrold Carswell for appointment to the Supreme Court both Senators Kennedy (D., Mass.) and Bayh (D., Ind.) used it as a noble precedent that President Nixon should follow, that is, withdraw the nomination. Much of the hostility to the nomination was clearly a result of attempts to discredit and frustrate the Kennedy family, both in the initial opposition of the Massachusetts Bar Association, which the author of this study, Irving Schiffman, indicates was hostile to the political power of the Irish, and the later hostility in the U.S. Senate, where the minority leader seized the opportunity to discredit the Democrats and the Kennedys. In viewing bargaining within this particular market (Congress), students can find illustrations of a wealth of strategies and of the unequal resources available to participants.

IRVING SCHIFFMAN

Senatorial Discourtesy: The Nomination of Francis X. Morrissey

"Senator Edward M. Kennedy, in a suprise retreat, abandoned his fight today to win Senate approval of Francis X. Morrissey's judicial nomination." So began the lead story on page one of *The New York Times* of October 22, 1965. The article went on to report that Kennedy had moved "to send the Federal judgeship nomination back to the Judiciary Committee thus heading off a Senate vote."

Kennedy's retreat ended a severe strain on the tradition of senatorial courtesy; a strain that might have brought that tradition to its first major test on a federal judgeship in fourteen years. Since 1951, the Senate had not voted to reject a judicial nominee; and there were few instances in which it had turned down a nominee who had the strong support of a senator of the President's political party.

The custom of senatorial courtesy has been generally described as an unwritten agreement among senators that requires the President to confer with the senator or senators of his party from a state before he makes a nomination to fill a federal office in that state. Should the President send to the Senate a nomination that the senator of his party does not approve, the offended senator will declare that the President's nominee is "personally obnoxious" to him. Consequently, the Senate will reject the appointment. This custom arose from the Senate's constitutional role of "advise and consent" concerning Presidential nominations for federal posts and has been practiced since the early 1800s. The net result of the practice is that the Senate has expropriated the President's power in so far as it concerns local appointments of interest to senators of the party in power.

A lesser known aspect of the tradition permitting senators of the President's party to approve appointees for federal offices in their states is the Senate's practice of not questioning the selections made by its members.

Irving Schiffman, "Senatorial Discourtesy: The Nomination of Francis X. Morrissey," Research Report No. 1, Institute of Governmental Affairs, University of California, Davis, 1968.

The fact that appointments are sponored by one or both senators from the state, and appointees' qualifications and records have been investigated by the department concerned prior to nomination, is ordinarily taken as sufficient indication of their fitness for the office. Although the Senate is aware that the qualifications for appointment to federal district courts are actually determined by the senators sponsoring the nominee, it rarely chooses to sit in judgment on the adequacy of those qualifications; to do so would, in effect, mean sitting in judgment on the individual senator responsible for the appointment. Further, having won from the executive the right of "eligible" senators to select the nominee, the senators have no desire to have the patronage and political benefits of this prerogative limited by the necessity of justifying each appointment to a scrutinizing and possibly critical body.

Thus, the tradition of senatorial courtesy has two sides: on the one hand it allows an "eligible" senator to blackball a nominee to federal office in his state and, conversely, it decrees that the nominee desired by the "eligible" senator will receive unquestioned confirmation by the Senate. This latter aspect of senatorial courtesy formed the crux of the "Morrissey affair."

THE APPOINTMENT

Francis Joseph Xavier Morrissey was a 55-year-old Boston politician who, through the benefaction of Joseph P. Kennedy, became a minor member of the Kennedy entourage. When young John F. Kennedy set out on his political career in 1946 the elder Kennedy asked Frank Morrissey to steer his son through the maze of Boston politics. Morrissey became John Kennedy's traveling secretary, confidant, and mentor and for a time was employed in Kennedy's Boston congressional office. In 1962 Morrissey watched over the political debut of Edward (Ted) Kennedy, helping to manage his first campaign for the Senate. For the Kennedys, Morrissey was always on call, and his nonpolitical duties with the family included playing in the celebrated touch football games at the summer colony in Hyannisport and on occasion shooting golf with Joseph P. Kennedy. Although he had been a member of the Massachusetts bar since 1944, Morrissey had never had any private practice worth mentioning, having made his living from political jobs. In 1958 the senior Kennedy arranged to have him appointed a municipal court judge in Boston and even for that judicial post his legal qualifications were questioned.

Placing Judge Morrissey on the federal bench had been a long-standing ambition of the Kennedy family and particularly of its patriarch, Joseph Kennedy. The passage of the 1961 omnibus judgeship bill with a provision therein for an additional judgeship in Massachusetts offered President Kennedy the chance to do so, thereby, as many saw it, repaying Morrissey for long and faithful service to the clan.

In 1961, following a procedure initiated during the preceding Eisenhower administration, Attorney General Robert F. Kennedy, upon receipt of the Morrissey name from the President, submitted the name to the American Bar Association's Committee on Federal Judiciary for a preliminary and informal investigation as to the candidate's qualifications for a federal judgeship. The Committee, through its representative in Boston, Robert W. Meserve, conducted a low-keyed investigation consisting of private interviews with a few lawyers and judges having knowledge of Morrissey's ability and character. Meserve then rendered an unofficial report to the Attorney General stating that upon full investigation the Committee would probably find the candidate unqualified for the proposed appointment.

Upon receipt of such a negative report, the Attorney General usually relays the information to the senator involved and suggests that he submit a different name. Often, if the senator had been unaware of his nominee's lack of qualifications, he thereupon submits a new name. However, the senator can insist that the Attorney General stick with his original candidate and unless the Executive Department wishes to stir up trouble with that senator or the Senate, the Attorney General will go along. In this instance there was, in reality, no Democratic senator who had to be consulted. The Democratic Senator from Massachusetts, Benjamin A. Smith II, an old school friend of John F. Kennedy, had been appointed to the President's vacated Senate seat; it was not expected that the President's former Harvard roommate would take his legislative cues from anyone but the Kennedys.

Within a few months of receipt of the unofficial report, a request was made to the Committee on Federal Judiciary for a "formal" report. An investigation of the nominee was conducted in depth, after which the Committee filed a statement concluding that Judge Morrissey was lacking in the experience and intellectual capacity necessary to become an efficient judge of the United States District Court. Faced with these adverse assessments and with bar association warnings that the nomination would be fought in the Senate, the President set the appointment aside. He considered submitting Morrissey's name to the Senate again in 1963 but backed off when the bar associations again raised objections.

The death of John F. Kennedy did not deter his family in their efforts to reward Judge Morrissey with a place on the federal bench. Immediately prior to his resignation from the cabinet in September, 1964, to run for the Senate from New York, Robert Kennedy petitioned new President Lyndon Johnson—his old adversary—to nominate Morrissey to the still vacant judgeship in Massachusetts, explaining that his late brother had planned to do so after the November elections. The President was noncommittal. The request was made again the following year by 32-year-old Ted Kennedy, the junior senator from Massachusetts. Johnson pondered the matter and on September 26, 1965, from his ranch in Johnson City, Texas, issued the announcement that the nomination of Francis X. Morrissey had been sent to the Senate for confirmation.

Adverse Reaction

Rumors of the impending nomination had circulated a few months earlier and the Boston Bar Association had immediately gone on record reaffirming its earlier objection that the nominee was "entirely lacking in the qualifications of training and education." When the nomination became official, the Chairman of the ABA's Committee on Federal Judiciary announced that he would fly from Chicago to fight the appointment before the Senate Committee on the Judiciary. Newspapers and magazines across the country criticized the appointment. Opposition came from the conservative David Lawrence, who denounced the nomination as displaying "a lack of ethics and a disregard for the public interest," and from the liberal *New Republic,* whose editors warned that the work of a federal district court judge "is intellectually demanding and judges who cannot cope with it are not harmless. They have a great deal of independent power, which no one can exercise for them. With the best will in the world, they are liable to injure private interests and the public interest." Law professors and attorneys protested the appointment, as did judges and members of the House of Representatives.

On September 29, additional fuel was added to the fire when a 1,400-word letter written to the Senate Judiciary Committee was released to the press. The well-known, outspoken, and highly regarded Chief Judge of the U.S. District Court for Massachusetts, Charles E. Wyzanski, Jr., who would be Morrissey's superior if the nomination were approved, informed the Committee members that "those who know Judge Morrissey as a judge, as well as in his earlier role as a practicing attorney, rate him at the bottom of each of these callings." The highly unusual and sharply worded letter further declared that the nominee "has neither familiarity with the law nor the industry to learn it," and concluded that the "only discernible ground" for the nomination was Morrissey's "service to the Kennedy family."

In the Senate, minority leader Everett McKinley Dirksen of Illinois let it be known that the Judiciary Committee of which he was a member would take a long, hard look at the nomination. Senator Ted Kennedy was shaken at the intensity of the opposition and the speed with which it had coalesced. On September 28, he addressed the Senate and spoke of his concern that the derogatory news stories and editorials might prejudice the minds of senators "before they have an opportunity to exercise their congressional function of considering the nomination":

If Frank Morrissey were as unqualified a man as these stories have made him appear, I would never have recommended his nomination and President Johnson would never have made it. . . . I would suggest that before Judge Morrissey is accused, tried and convicted in absentia, he have an opportunity to appear before the Senate and answer to his qualifications.

The Role of the Senate Judiciary Committee

The Senate Committee on the Judiciary is the last essential participant in the process of nominating and confirming judges. While the decision by the Committee to report favorably or unfavorably must be followed by Senate approval and then by the nominee's receipt of his commission from the President, these are no more than formalities and, in fact, are virtually automatic upon a favorable recommendation by the Committee. Before the Morrissey affair the Senate had last rejected a judicial nomination on October 9, 1951, refusing by a unanimous voice vote to confirm two Truman appointees to judgeships in Illinois after Senator Douglas of that state voiced his objection to both men.

The Committee's role in the processing of judicial appointments is unlike that of most other committees in the Senate. In the usual course of events a bill that passes the Senate is, to a large extent, similar to the bill reported out to the floor by the relevant Senate committee. In the words of Woodrow Wilson, "Congressional government is committee government," and the major decisions as to the form and passage of a specific bill are made within the committee having authority over that area of legislation. The main reason for this state of affairs is that time is short, hands are few, and there is much legislation to consider. Senators, unable to concern themselves with each piece of legislation, defer to the recommendations of the subject matter committees whose members are deemed to be better informed, if not "experts," in the specific area.

But neither the Senate nor the members of the Committee on the Judiciary perceive the task of the Committee—insofar as its function of advising the Senate whether or not to confirm a nominee for a federal judgeship is concerned—as making material decisions that can affect the chances of confirmation of the nominee. Rather, and in conformity with the tradition of senatorial courtesy, the Committee's role is seen as making sure that all the rules of the game regarding judicial selection have been complied with, for example, that the "eligible" senators have been consulted to the extent they desire. Nominations that are not in accordance with the rules of the game rarely get past the Committee. Similarly, once the Committee determines that the "eligible" senators approve of the nomination, its role becomes one of conferring legitimacy on the appointment by going through a perfunctory hearing and then recommending confirmation by the Senate. Nominations meeting the senatorial courtesy test are sometimes delayed but virtually never denied. Between 1951 and 1962 the Committee on the Judiciary recommended the approval of 301 of the 307 nominations received for consideration.

There are instances, to be sure, wherein the Committee becomes the focal point of a group drive by a bar association or other special interest to defeat a specific nominee. These attempts are rarely successful, primarily because the impetus to confirm is so strong that a very heavy burden of proof is placed upon those who oppose confirmation. It is not sufficient merely to show that the nominee is not "qualified" because the Committee has never set up objective standards by which to measure the competence required for the federal bench. Furthermore, as previously discussed, to turn down a nominee because of his lack of qualifications would mean sitting in judgment of the senators who, under the custom of senatorial courtesy, have the right to set the qualifications. According to Joel B. Grossman,[1] "In order to block confirmation it is almost always necessary to prove that the nominee has been guilty of conduct which contravenes accepted norms of legal or personal conduct."

The Subcommittee

Upon receipt of the Morrissey nomination, it became incumbent upon the Judiciary Committee Chairman, James Eastland, to appoint a subcommittee to hold hearings on the appointment. Ordinarily, the subcommittee hearings and deliberations would be *pro forma* and the makeup of the subcommittee would be of little account. But where a nomination has become controversial (as this one had) and where adverse testimony is expected (as several bar associations had made clear there would be) the membership of the subcommittee becomes very important. Members of any committee are disposed to give great deference to the recommendations of their subcommittees whose members have attended the hearings and are more familiar with the matter than almost anyone else in the Senate. Although a select subcommittee would not be awarded the deference a permanent subcommittee would command, the full committee might place great reliance on the view of the subcommittee members as to whether it had been shown that the nominee had indeed been guilty of unacceptable legal or moral behavior.

There was a second reason why the membership of the subcommittee was important—the hearings were going to be conducted under close public scrutiny. Committee or subcommittee members usually approach matters in their area of congressional interest with some preconceived ideas, including whether or not they wish specific legislation enacted or specific nominees confirmed. The respect accorded the witnesses, the questions asked of them, and the statements made by subcommittee members all can play a large part in shaping public and senatorial response to the proceedings and ultimately to the question of confirmation. Suppose, for a hypothetical example, that hostile questioning of the spokesman for the Boston Bar Association should reveal that his organization, which opposed Morrissey, had not seen fit to back an Irishman for the federal bench in its 125 years of existence. The public would then probably greet with rightful skepticism the spokesman's testimony that the present nominee was grossly unqualified.

Eastland chose Thomas J. Dodd of Connecticut for subcommittee chairman. Dodd was fourth in seniority among majority committee members and Eastland's selection of him over two Southern Democrats (one of whom subsequently voted against confirmation while the other failed to vote) indicated that the Mississippi Democrat was not going to put roadblocks in the way of the nomination. Having no personal or sectional interest in the dispute, Eastland, a friend of President Johnson since their Senate days together, could play the facilitating role expected of his Committee. Dodd was known as a friend both of the Kennedys and of the President; had he felt the slightest doubt that he would be able to support confirmation he could easily have avoided the assignment. The second Democrat assigned to the subcommittee was Quentin N. Burdick of North Dakota, then in his fourth year in the Senate after serving for two years in the House. He was not expected to act in any way hostile to the nomination. The Republican member of the panel was Everett M. Dirksen. Dirksen wanted membership on the subcommittee, and as ranking Republican on the full Committee his request was acceded to by the Chairman. A skillful and crafty politician, his presence on the subcommittee made necessary the appointment as chairman of a pro-Morrissey senator (Dodd) if the opposition were not to dominate the hearings.

THE HEARINGS

The hearings were especially important to the American Bar Association. Over a period of many years the ABA had sought to obtain a voice in the process of selecting federal judges, believing that fellow lawyers were best equipped to pass upon court nominations. In 1947 the Association had established its own committee, the Committee on Federal Judiciary (not to be confused with the Senate Committee on the Judiciary), and empowered it

on behalf of the Association, to promote the nomination and confirmation of competent persons for appointment as judges of courts of the United States and to oppose the nomination and confirmation of persons deemed by it not to be sufficiently qualified.

During the Eisenhower Administration, the ABA Committee entered into an arrangement with the Attorney General whereby the names of prospective nominees were forwarded to the Committee for investigation and evaluation. This arrangement was carried over into the Kennedy and Johnson Adminstrations but the Committee soon found that the two Democratic Presidents were often merely going through the motions of checking with it. President Kennedy had appointed nine men the Committee found "not qualified" and Morrissey was Johnson's fifth such appointment. Furthermore, and for the first time since 1956, a President had been making appointments without first even submitting the names to the Committee. Johnson was known to feel that the Committee had a built-in bias in favor of conservative lawyers and that as a result the system produced too many conservative judges. Thus, the Committee was looking for a *cause celebre* to call attention to the harmful consequences of the Administration's neglecting its advice on judicial appointments. Judge Morrissey's nomination fitted its needs very well. Not only were the nominee's intellectual capacity and experience questionable, but the ABA officials believed that they could produce the kind of detrimental evidence sufficient to require his rejection even under the harsh standards imposed by the Senate Judiciary Committee.

Support and Opposition

From the outset of the hearings it was obvious that Dodd was going to support and defend the nominee's right to be confirmed and that Dirksen was going to concentrate on bringing out the nominee's lack of ability and experience. Neither senator seemed interested in drawing out all the facts so that a balanced and objective determination could be made. Rather, the questioning of witnesses was designed to bring out information and arguments supporting viewpoints to which the senators already subscribed. If evidence elicited by one senator proved harmful to the other's position, it was immediately attacked or challenged. Similarly, if testimony offered was deemed helpful to either senator, it was aided and encouraged.

Dodd's position throughout was consistent with the self-effacing role

expected of the Judiciary Committee in its consideration of judicial appointees. His attitude seemed to be: why shouldn't this man be confirmed?
Why is he so different that we should depart from our usual practice of
recommending confirmation of almost every name that is sent to us? Thus,
Dodd carefully guided the testimony of the pro-Morrissey witnesses, came
to their aid when they were pressed by Dirksen, interjected personal opinions on the nominee's merits, closely examined and disputed bar association witnesses, lapsed into silence when the detrimental "Georgia episode"
was revealed, and sought to help the nominee in his explanation of the
incident. His Committee role supported his pro-Administration role of de-
fending an executive appointment. Both positions were reinforced by the
anti-bar association stance taken by Dodd, who expressed himself as
critical of the bar's qualification criteria and taunted ABA witnesses with
the names of successful judges whose confirmations had been opposed by
their organization.

Dodd's critical treatment of bar association witnesses perhaps stemmed
from an incident in his life; this incident may also have promoted the
senator's sympathetic feeling for Frank Morrissey. One reason for the
ABA's assessment that the nominee lacked the intellectual capacity to
become a federal judge was that he had twice failed the Massachusetts bar
examination. Dirksen took the position that as far as he was concerned
this was not very important since he himself had once failed the Illinois
bar exam, and jocularly referred to that fact several times during the
hearings. Dodd had no comments to make on this matter and certainly
none to make in a humorous vein. He had failed the Connecticut bar
exam that he had taken upon his graduation from Yale Law School. He
then joined the FBI and in 1945 sought to be admitted to the Connecticut
bar on motion, contending that his ten years of federal service was
equivalent to ten years of practice in another state, valid criteria for such
admission. Dodd's application was challenged through the local bar association and the matter was fought all the way up to the state's Supreme Court,
which held that Dodd should be denied admission. His motion for admission was not granted until two years later, after serving as an assistant to
Justice Jackson at the Nuremberg trials. Thus, Morrissey's plight may have
touched the Senator and made him determined not to allow the bar association another victory.

The role most obviously played by Dirksen was that of the concerned
bipartisan legislator seeking to protect the integrity of the federal judiciary.
He did not use the hearings for a general attack on Johnson Administration policy or for drawing specific conclusions detrimental to the Administration. Such a maneuver on his part might have compromised the impression he was trying to create of nonpolitical fidelity to the principle that

only "qualified" people should be appointed to the federal bench. He never criticized the practice of senatorial courtesy, however, but merely reminded the witnesses that in his exercise of the prerogative he had always chosen highly competent individuals.

Dirksen nevertheless played a pro-bar association role, leading ABA witnesses in their testimony and accentuating the importance of their statements. The ABA headquarters are located in Chicago, part of the Senator's constituency. He has always received support from the conservative members of the organization and that body forms an important reference group whose opinions Dirksen would be expected to consider.

Senator Burdick played a passive role in the hearings, occasionally helping the nominee and witnesses favorable to him out of tight spots, but generally leaving the questioning to Dirksen and Dodd.

The Witnesses Come Forth

The case for the nominee was made by nine witnesses led by Ted Kennedy. They insisted that Morrissey had made an excellent record on the Municipal Court where he had received the experience required for the federal bench, that he was highly thought of by his fellow judges and by the lawyers who practiced before him, and that he possessed the character and temperament necessary to a federal judge. Kennedy placed into the record a list of over fifty Massachusetts judges who had endorsed the nomination, as well as endorsements by such organizations as the American Trial Lawyers Association and the Massachusetts Trial Lawyers Association.

An unexpected witness for the nominee was Speaker of the House John W. McCormack. It is a rare enough occasion when the presiding officer of one house of Congress testifies before a committee hearing held by the other branch, but the Speaker's appearance was even more surprising in light of his past relations with the nominee's sponsors. The McCormacks had frequently warred with the Kennedys in Massachusetts politics and, except for the Speaker, they had usually lost. The latest loser had been McCormack's favorite nephew, Edward, whom Ted Kennedy had defeated three years earlier in a bitterly contested senatorial primary. During the Kennedy Administration a distinct coolness existed in the relations between the old and unscholarly Speaker and the youthful and erudite Chief Executive. Morrissey, however, had the strong public support of the head of the Catholic Church in Massachusetts, Richard Cardinal Cushing, an important personality in the ethnic and religious politics of that state. The Speaker's attendance at the Morrissey hearing could thus be viewed as either an effort on his part at a political reconciliation with the Kennedys or as a necessary response to pressures generated in his home constituency, or both. In any event, McCormack's testimony was brief. He praised Morrissey as a faithful and loyal friend to the Kennedys and a fine family man and brushed aside criticism of the nominee on the ground that he had twice failed the Massachusetts bar examination: the fact that he took the exam the third time spoke well of "his courage and ambition to become a member of the bar."

The opposing positions of Dirksen and Dodd were apparent in their questioning of the pro-Morrissey witnesses. Dodd used his questions to bring out and highlight facts advantageous to the nominee while Dirksen sought whenever possible to belittle the nominee's skills and accomplishments, as indicated by the following exchange.

Senator Dirksen.   How do you account for the fact that (Morrissey) was not endorsed by the Boston Bar Association?

Senator Kennedy.   I would let those who are here representing it respond on that. I am not prepared to answer that.

Senator Dirksen.   That is all.

Senator Dodd.   Judge Morrissey was endorsed by the Massachusetts Bar Association?

Senator Kennedy.   That is correct. The Massachusetts Bar Association, The Massachusetts Trial Lawyers Association, the country organizations of Middlesex, Worcester County and a number of other cities and towns in the Commonwealth. . . .

Senator Dodd.   Well, is it fair to say that he was certainly endorsed by these organizations representing the majority of lawyers in the state?

Senator Kennedy.   I think it would not only be fair and accurate to state that but I think it would be fair to say that those who know him best and appear before him most often, are those who have endorsed him.

Dirksen was exceptionally critical of attempts to make Morrissey appear an experienced trial judge able to take on all matters dealt with by federal district courts. Thus this colloquy with Harold W. Canavan, an Associate Justice of the Boston Municipal Court, on the criminal trial experience of the nominee:

Judge Canavan.   Now, the caseload of the Boston municipal court on the criminal side, and this covers a period from July 1, 1963, through June 30, 1964, total criminal complaints 76,693. This represents about 20 per cent of all criminal complaints issued by the 72 district courts of the Commonwealth. I must admit that this 76,000 figure does include automobile traffic violations.

Senator Dirksen.   Well, in fact, about two-thirds of all the cases on the criminal side deal with drunks, violation of paroles or violation of parking regulations, speeding and things of that nature?

Judge Canavan.   I will go along with that, Senator; two-thirds of 76,000.

By the time Dirksen finished questioning the pro-Morrissey witnesses, Morrissey's Municipal Court, which Ted Kennedy had described to the subcommittee as being, in reality, a county court handling the same type of cases as that handled by a federal district court, turned out to be a forum without equity jurisdiction or provision for jury trials, whose litigants could appeal its decisions and obtain a new trial automatically, and which could impose a maximum prison sentence of only five years.

The Attack on the Nominee

The critical and supportive positions taken by Dirksen and Dodd toward the pro-Morrissey witnesses were quickly reversed when the ABA spokesmen made their appearances. The role of investigator and prosecutor was not new to Dodd: as Vice-Chairman of the Senate Internal Security Subcommittee he had raked many witnesses over the coals in his search for Communists and "fellow travelers." He was, however, stunned into silence by the revelations of the ABA's first witness.

Albert E. Jenner, Chairman of the Committee on Federal Judiciary, had what he no doubt believed to be the type of evidence needed to discredit the nominee in the eyes of the Senate Committee on the Judiciary. He testified that after Morrissey had failed the Massachusetts bar exam in 1933, he went to Athens, Georgia and quickly obtained a law degree from Southern Law School, a nonfaculty diploma mill. At that time, a resident of the state could be admitted to the bar "on diploma." Morrissey thereupon swore that he was a resident of Georgia and on September 8, 1933 was admitted to the bar. On September 9, according to Jenner, Morrissey returned to Boston. The only inference to be drawn from this testimony was that the nominee had committed perjury in swearing that he was a resident of Georgia.

This revelation was followed up by the testimony of Robert W. Meserve, the ABA Committee member who had conducted its investigation of the nominee. He testified that Morrissey had never informed the Committee of his Southern Law School degree nor had he listed it on his three applications for the Massachusetts bar. As for Morrissey's judicial experience, Meserve introduced into the record a letter from a prominent Boston attorney who had recently tried a case before Judge Morrissey and compared the experience to "an unbelievable fantasy extrapolated from the Mad Hatter's Tea Party." He concluded by stating that throughout his investigation of the nominee he could not find a single lawyer or judge who had ever seen Morrissey try a case in court as an attorney.

The final ABA witness was the former chairman of the Committee on Federal Judiciary, Bernard G. Segal. He reviewed the importance of trial experience for a district court judge and Morrissey's lack of it and spoke of Morrissey's spotty academic record that included the attainment of his Massachusetts law degree at a nonaccredited law school at which institution he had failed four courses. Segal said that the facts forced him to conclude

that from the standpoint of legal ability and legal learning and legal experience we have not had any case where these elements are less adequate than in the case of Judge Morrissey, and I say that with deep regret.

As the adverse testimony continued, Dodd's anti-bar association role became more pronounced. He sought to get the witnesses to admit that their Committee had approved nominees with judicial experience equal to Judge Morrissey's. The replies he received were, in effect, "Yes, but they had brains." Dodd then changed course and sought to get the witnesses to admit that the ABA had in the past opposed nominees who had gone on to make good judges; he finally gained the admission that the organization had made "some mistakes." Finally, Dodd charged the witnesses with holding back information from the subcommittee and demanded that the subcommittee be supplied with all of the letters received by the ABA Committee that were favorable to the nomination.

Dirksen pretended to greet Jenner's Georgia revelations with surprise (it is hard to imagine that he was unaware of the ABA's case) and acted as though he were astonished as he had the witness carefully retrace his testimony concerning Morrissey's arrival in Georgia and subsequent departure and the type of law school from which he received his degree. His theatrics continued as he brought the question of perjury back into focus with his questioning of Segal:

Senator Dirksen. You see, if you allege that you live in one state for the purpose of being admitted to the State bar, when in fact you are not, there is a rather unpleasant word for that, as you know, I will not use it but it bothers me a little.
Mr. Segal. It bothers me Senator. It bothers me.

Morrissey Testifies

The final witness was the nominee. At this point Senators Eastland and Tydings of the full Committee joined the subcommittee. Morrissey began his testimony with an attempt "to clear up the Georgia situation." He testified that the age of 22, after failing the Massachusetts bar, he had gone to Georgia with the intention of practicing law in that state. He spent three months undergoing a review course in Georgia law under the tutelage of the three-man faculty of the Southern Law School. After his admission to the bar, Morrissey continued, he remained in Georgia for six months and left when he "could not get any cases." Morrissey protested that he had never attempted to capitalize on his Georgia bar admission in Massachusetts and could not have since he would have needed several years of experience in Georgia before Massachusetts would admit him to practice without his taking the bar exam. (He finally passed the exam on his third attempt in 1944.) He ascribed the entire situation to immaturity and poor judgment. He also protested the failure of the ABA witnesses to mention the fact that he had subsequently received a master of law degree from Suffolk Law School in Boston.

Senator Dirksen had been called away from the hearings to the Senate floor and as a result the nominee was subjected to no unfriendly questioning. Senator Eastland, in his few moments, displayed an attitude hostile to the ABA. He recalled Jenner and demanded to know the basis of his testimony that Morrissey left Georgia the day after his admission to the bar in light of Morrissey's testimony that he had remained for six months. When Jenner sought to deny that he had made such a categorical statement, Eastland persisted until finally Dodd stepped in to calm the exchange. Both Eastland and Dodd engaged in sympathetic questioning of the nominee that allowed him to explain many of the damaging statements affecting his character made by the ABA witnesses.

The next day's newspaper accounts of the hearing played up the contradiction between Jenner and Morrissey over the Georgia episode. Morrissey's "quickie" law degree from a southern diploma mill, his flunking of four courses in law school, his two bar exam failures and the assessments of his ability made by the ABA witnesses were all reported and made it appear that not only was the nominee spectacularly unqualified but that his character was questionable as well.

THE COMMITTEE VOTES

In a departure from usual procedure the subcommittee did not deliberate and vote on the appointment. Instead, the following morning the full Committee held a two-hour executive session at which its members went over Judge Morrissey's testimony in detail seeking to establish whether, in fact, perjury might have been committed. At the end of the meeting, Dirksen was still not satisfied. At Dirksen's request, Morrissey was asked whether he would consent to appear before the full Committee and submit to further questioning. Judge Morrissey agreed and that evening a meeting was held behind closed doors in Dirksen's office. The nominee was questioned for about an hour, mostly by Dirksen, and then the committee voted. Dirksen and fellow Republican Hugh Scott of Pennsylvania were joined by Democrat Sam Ervin of North Carolina, a former judge, in voting to oppose recommending confirmation. Senators Ted Kennedy, Eastland, Dodd, Burdick, Philip Hart of Michigan and George Smathers of Florida, the latter a former close friend of John F. Kennedy, all Democrats, voted in favor of the nominee. Seven senators failed to show up for the meeting.

A Conflict of Roles

The actions of two of the members of the Judiciary Committee illustrate the conflicts brought on by the Morrissey affair, conflicts that many Democratic senators were forced to resolve one way or another. Actors in the legislative system are susceptible to role conflicts because their congressional positions constitute not one, but a multiplicity of roles, defined for each congressman by varying expectations of the groups that he represents or with which he identifies. These roles frequently conflict because incompatible demands are placed upon an actor by the different groups with which he has relationships. The individual congressman must then find some way to reconcile these conflicts or, perhaps, withdraw from a conflict that he cannot resolve.

Senators Birch Bayh of Indiana and Joseph Tydings of Maryland, two Democratic members of the Committee on the Judiciary, did not appear to vote on whether or not to recommend confirmation. Both men were close personal friends of Ted and Robert Kennedy and their friendships transcended the halls of Congress. A year and a half earlier Bayh had dragged Ted Kennedy out of a plane that had crashed while carrying them to Massachusetts where Bayh was to address the state nominating convention. Tydings and Robert Kennedy were both elected to the Senate the same year and the socially prominent Marylander immediately became friends with the Kennedys.

Within the Senate the four young northern liberals formed a friendship clique, often discussing various issues and reaching common decisions. An analysis of 258 roll call votes reported in Congressional Quarterly for the 1965 Senate term reveals that the four senators either declared themselves or voted alike in 208 instances. Taking into account that on eight occasions the only defection consisted of one of the Kennedys voting apart from the group, the quartet held together on 84 percent of the roll call votes. Thus, these legislators had come to perceive their congressional roles as including a social role and the friendship clique had become an important source of voting cues.

The role conflicts arose for two reasons. Both Bayh and Tydings were under constituency pressure to oppose the appointment (this in itself might not have been sufficient to cause them to desert the clique on this issue). Of equal, or perhaps greater, importance was the fact that Tydings as Chairman of the Subcommittee on Improvements in Judicial Machinery, and Bayh, as Chairman of the Subcommittee on Constitutional Amendments, worked very closely with lawyer groups, especially the ABA, and had excellent relations with these groups. Tydings had previously stated his belief that an independent body in the government should be established to assist the President and the Senate in the selection of judges, and Bayh had received much bar association support in getting his presidential disability amendment through Congress the previous month. Both senators were sensitive to the views of the organized bar that did not expect them to oppose its position, especially after such a strong case had been established as to the lack of qualifications of Ted Kennedy's nominee.

Normally a legislative actor may reduce role conflict by compromise or bargaining. An amendment to a bill or some other modification may serve to remove some of the elements that brought on the difficulty. The question of confirmation, however, does not ordinarily lend itself to modification or to amendment. The nominee is either accepted or rejected (officially or unofficially). A congressional actor may also avoid diverse demands by invoking a legislative norm that supposedly has a higher claim on his loyalties. But here the custom of senatorial courtesy was likely to be repudiated by over a third of the Senate. Protestations that a senator was bound in good conscience to support this tradition would ring hollow. In addition, the norm itself was under attack by the organized bar. Unable to resolve the conflict in any other way, Bayh and Tydings withdrew from the field.

To the Senate Floor

Following the vote of the full Committee, Dirksen refused to commit himself about taking his fight to the Senate floor. He claimed to be dissatisfied with the Georgia episode and questioned Morrissey's trial experience. He informed Attorney General Nicholas D. Katzenbach that he would object to a floor vote on the appointment until he had an opportunity to brief the Republican Policy Committee on the case.

More on Morrissey's Past

Between the Judiciary Committee's vote on October 13, 1965, and the scheduled meeting of the Policy Committee on October 19, some new developments occurred. First came a disclosure by the *Boston Globe*: Morrissey had run for the Massachusetts Assembly in September of 1934 but he could not have legally qualified for the office unless he had been a resident of that state for the previous year. The *Globe,* which had zealously sought to discover everything it could about the man whose nomination it opposed, then turned up information that Morrissey had registered to vote in Boston on July 26, 1933, at which time, according to the nominee's testimony, he was undergoing a review course in Georgia.[2] On October 16 it became known that the FBI had reopened its investigation into Morrissey's background. On October 18, however, the Attorney General reported that the results of the investigation supported "Judge Morrissey's recollection that he attended classes at the Southern Law School in Athens from June until September, and remained in Georgia for some months thereafter." The statement said nothing about Morrissey's Assembly race or his Boston registration nor how many "months thereafter" he had remained in Georgia.

The report was obviously a whitewash but Dirksen did not wish to attack the FBI or charge that J. Edgar Hoover's organization had been used for political purposes. This reluctance did not extend to the House, where Republican Representative H. R. Gross of Iowa made exactly that charge. Instead, Dirksen switched his attack to concentrate on Morrissey's lack of fitness for the federal bench, informing the press that he would have to agree with the testimony of Bernard Segal that the nominee's qualifications were the worst he had encountered. He also declared a legitimate representational interest in the controversy, reminding the press that federal judges are often temporarily dispatched to courts with overloaded dockets and there was a chance that as a federal judge Morrissey might be assigned to sit in Illinois. Such being the case, it was his duty to make sure that the lawyers of his constituency were spared the burden of having to practice before an unqualified judge.

Saltonstall Retreats

The first inkling that the nomination was in real trouble and that senatorial courtesy might not prevail came on October 18 when Senator Leverett Saltonstall, Republican of Massachusetts, announced that he had withdrawn his "no objection" position on Judge Morrissey. After the nomination had been referred to the Committee on the Judiciary, following customary procedure, the clerk of the Committee notified the two senators from the nominee's state that the appointment had been made. This was done by sending a blue slip or form to the senators asking for their opinion and any information they might have regarding the nominee. Both Saltonstall and Kennedy had indicated their approval of the nomination by returning the slips to the Committee without noting any objection thereon. Although Saltonstall was not a member of the President's party, he could have delayed the hearings under informal Committee rules by failing to return the slips, explaining that he was investigating the qualifications of the nominee. A formal notice of objection from Saltonsall would probably not have prevented the Committee from recommending confirmation although there have been instances where such an objection has been sustained by the Senate.

In withdrawing his approval, Saltonstall explained that he had not previously raised objections because "this has been the customary procedure in the Senate when an appointee is not well known to the Senator from his state." He was careful to point out that he was withdrawing his approval not on the basis of the nominee's lack of qualifications (which would have been a direct slap at Ted Kennedy, a personal friend) but because he believed the inconsistencies in Morrissey's testimony required that the matter be referred back to the Judiciary Committee for further investigation.

Saltonstall's initial refusal to oppose the nomination had dimmed Republican hopes of creating an effective opposition, as Republicans could not very well oppose a judicial nominee when their senator from the nominee's state had declared that he had no objection to the appointment. Saltonstall's withdrawal of approval, however, provided Republicans with new impetus to oppose confirmation.

The Policy Committee

The Democratic and Republican Policy Committees were established in 1947 to formulate policies of senatorial parties on legislative issues. Both Committees are well staffed; they share a yearly appropriation of over a quarter of a million dollars. But the Democrats can seldom agree on a single policy, and as a consequence the only way in which Democratic Policy Committee establishes policy is its recommendation that certain legislation be scheduled for floor action. The Republican Policy Committee is generally more faithful to the original conception of the Committees and has managed to adopt policy statements subscribed to by the entire senate membership of the party.

As Republican floor leader, Dirksen was an ex-officio member of his party's Policy Committee. He met with the fifteen-member Committee on Tuesday morning and reviewed the Morrissey case. With Saltonstall having withdrawn his approval of the nominee and with Jacob Javits, on one end of the ideological spectrum, and John Towers, on the other, both opposing confirmation, Dirksen had little trouble getting the Committee members to agree to take an anticonfirmation position and call on all Republicans to oppose the nomination. Here was a fantastically easy way for the Republicans to make political capital at the expense of the President and the Kennedys and to score some political points at the end of a congressional session that had been highly favorable to the Democrats. An overly sufficient case had been made in the press to justify the refusal to follow senatorial courtesy in this instance. The Policy Committee also agreed that Dirksen should make the motion to return the nomination to the Judiciary Committee when it was laid before the Senate. This may have been slightly upsetting to Senator Javits, who had earlier assured the press that *he* would make the motion. After Dirksen, Javits was the most vocal of Morrissey's Senate opponents and his strong fight against confirmation was obviously intended to embarrass Robert Kennedy, whose political timing and excellent press relations had badly upstaged the senior senator from New York.

The Kennedys' Search for Votes

To a great extent, senatorial action can be explained by implicit bargaining wherein senators provide assistance to one another with the expectation that they will be repaid in kind. A senator's search for votes is often a process of cashing in on credit he has built up with his colleagues or allowing his colleagues to build up credit at his expense. A senator seeking assistance expends more credit on highly controversial issues. No legislator being solicited wishes to sell himself and his constituents short. Both Kennedy senators, especially Teddy, expended a great deal of credit trying to gain confirmation for Frank Morrissey.

Ted Kennedy was elected to his brother's Senate seat in 1962 at the age of 30, and was reelected two years later receiving 75 percent of the vote. In line with his party's policy of assigning new members to at least one prestigious committee, he was given a seat on the Committee on the Judiciary. Kennedy's first two years in the Senate were spent in the manner expected of freshman senators, making sure to be "seen and not heard." He came out of his custom-imposed shell in the first session of the 89th Congress and gained the respect of many of his fellow senators by his professional attempt to include a state poll tax ban in the 1965 Voting Rights

Act. He scored still further in the eyes of liberals with his work as floor manager of the immigration reform bill. In fact, by the middle of the year there was considerable talk about Ted being the Kennedy to watch rather than his more popular elder brother, Robert.

Ted Kennedy's newly won prestige and reputation, together with Robert Kennedy's popularity, no doubt constituted strong inducements for some senators to play ball with the Kennedys in return for later assistance. But many others felt that as much as they might enjoy building credit up with the Kennedys, this was one thing they could not do. They would have been willing to accommodate the two senators to the extent of voting for a candidate who was poor or mediocre, but with the press hammering away, they refused to stick out their necks to confirm an apparently unqualified nominee who had become a *cause celebre*.

The younger Kennedy strove diligently to convince his fellow senators to support confirmation. He pleaded with his colleagues not to allow the sensational press stories to influence them. His office reproduced the Katzenbach statement and FBI report supporting Morrissey's version of the Georgia episode and circulated them to the other 99 senators with a covering letter offering further elucidation on request. He accused the ABA of "setting itself up as a prosecutor" of Judge Morrissey and reminded the senators that bar association leaders had also opposed the appointment of Louis Brandeis to the Supreme Court. He issued a statement accusing Senator Dirksen of "attempting to use the Morrissey nomination for partisan political purposes." Then, in a final show of bravado aimed at convincing reluctant senators that they were not committing themselves to a lost cause, Kennedy told the press that the FBI report had impressed some wavering senators and that he now had enough votes to confirm the appointment. But many retained doubts on the matter because an important element of support was missing.

No Help from the President

Two weeks earlier, on October 8, shortly after announcing the Morrissey nomination, President Johnson had entered Bethesda Naval Hospital for a gall bladder operation and had remained there quietly recuperating throughout the controversy. For a while no indications of Presidential interest or support emanated from the White House or the hospital and it seemed the President had decided to let the Kennedys fight this one out on their own. Indeed, there was some speculation that Johnson knew the nomination would involve the Kennedys in a fracas and therefore made the appointment to damage them. But it was the President who had officially made the appointment and had, in effect, pronounced Morrissey qualified to sit on the federal bench. A defeat in the Senate could not help but cause him some loss of public esteem. The President no doubt appreciated that he was protected from a more serious public reaction by Ted Kennedy's vigorous sponsorship of the nominee, and that Kennedy would absorb most of the adverse political backlash. This may have been the reason the President felt he could make the appointment, whereas his predecessor held back. President Kennedy would have received the brunt of any negative feedback without the benefit of a sponsoring senator to cushion the blow. It is also probably true that neither Johnson nor the Kennedys realized the full extent of Morrissey's handicaps or the storm of opposition the nomination would arouse.

Unfortunately for the Kennedys, the President's illness left him weak and in constant pain. He was unable to make use of his intelligence network and persuasion operation that had been so efficient and so vital to the Johnson system. This very personal system built up in his majority leadership days and continuing into the presidential period, was dependent upon direct communication with the legislators either in person at the White House or by telephone. Had the system been in working order, the President would have been informed how each Democratic senator was preparing to vote. If he wished, he then could have applied the famous Johnson Treatment to any recalcitrants. Instead, as the day of confirmation drew near, Johnson called on Vice President Hubert H. Humphrey to help the Kennedys round up the needed Democratic votes.

Humphrey found the task rough going. First, the senators to whom he was appealing had already heavily supported the Administration, making the 89th one of the most successful Congresses for a President since FDR's honeymoon with the 73rd. There were few debts the Administration could collect and, in fact, the credit may have been running strongly the other way. Second, with newspapers at home headlining Judge Morrissey's Georgia episode and editorializing that the nomination was "irresponsible," and with the senators perceiving constituent pressure to oppose the nomination, the Vice President found it difficult to get his party's members to think as "Democrats." This issue, despite the President's noninvolvement, had come to involve the prestige of the Administration. Normally, such an issue will bring about a high degree of cohesion within the President's party, especially among those sympathetic to the goals of the Administration. But any foresighted congressman does not, on the mundane issue of the nomination of a Boston Judge, disregard the feelings of his constituency and vote the party. They are either delegates on such an issue or they withdraw from the field, returning to their party and "trustee" roles when the matter is one of more principle or of less concern to their constituents. Thus, Humphrey was constantly confronted with the responses of "Sorry, not this time." Senator Gruening of Alaska replied that he "couldn't vote for (Morrissey) if my brother asked me." A personal note penciled by Humphrey to his protege Senator Walter Mondale of Minnesota, was returned with the marking "Addressee Unknown."

Defeat

The vote for confirmation was originally scheduled for October 19 but protracted debate on the sugar quota bill caused the majority and minority leader to agree to reschedule it to October 21. On the evening of October 20 Ted and Robert Kennedy counted heads. They checked with Majority Leader Mike Mansfield and with the Vice President. They went over their scorecards. At least ten Democrats were going to vote "No"; fourteen Democrats including such liberals as Bayh, Muskie, Church, Hartke, Bass, Gore, Moss, McGovern and Anderson had withdrawn from the conflict by returning to their states; and other Democratic senators who had originally planned to vote "Yes" now refused to commit themselves. Because attempts to persuade some Republican senators to abstain from the voting had been unsuccessful, there would be at least forty-two votes cast against confirmation. Odds were high that if the nomination were brought to a vote it would be defeated. The Kennedys would have expended much political credit in vain and the press would have a field day heralding the defeat. The next step was inescapable. Ted Kennedy telephoned President Johnson, described the situation, and told the President that he had decided to move to recommit the nomination. On the following day the White House would issue a statement announcing that the President had replied to Kennedy that although he was willing to stand behind the nominee, it was a Senate matter and he would abide by the Senator's wishes. To some the White House would appear to be helpless trying to get itself off the hook by pleading that it was a helpless middleman in the game of senatorial courtesy.

On the morning of October 21, fifty-four Democrats and thirty-two Republicans answered the clerk's roll call. As Senator Dirksen sat upright at his desk on the Republican side of the Senate aisle ready to offer his motion for recommittal, Ted Kennedy walked across the aisle to speak to him. The acting President pro tem recognized Senator Mansfield. The Majority Leader moved that the call of the Executive Calendar be commenced "by laying before the Senate the nomination of Francis X. Morrissey to a U.S. district judge for the district of Massachusetts." The legislative clerk read the nomination and the chair recognized the senator from Massachusetts.

In a voice choked with emotion and embittered by defeat, Ted

Kennedy asked the Senate for "unanimous consent that the nomination of Francis Morrissey be recommitted to the Committee on the Judiciary." He had determined, he said, "that a majority of the members of the Senate are prepared to support Judge Morrissey's confirmation," but he recognized that some senators maintained honest doubts about the nomination that should be cleared up by the Committee "in a climate free from the press of adjournment, the pressure of partisanship and the atmosphere of controversy." He lamented the wrong he felt the ABA had rendered the nominee and caustically implied that Judge Morrissey's education at a local law school at night rather than a national law school during the day had been a factor in the Association's opposition to him. Kennedy's greatest scorn was reserved for the Chairman of the Committee on Federal Judiciary, Albert Jenner, who had brought up the Georgia episode at the hearings. Declaring that the subsequent FBI investigation "showed that on every controverted point, the testimony of Judge Morrissey was correct and the testimony of the ABA witness was wrong," Kennedy warned the Senate that

Those of us who put our faith in the past, in the reliability of the investigating technique and judgment of the American Bar Association, must think carefully what weight to give their future judgments. . . .

The next speaker was Everett Dirksen. Senators tend to be sympathetic with another man's political problems, and now that the battle was won Dirksen had nothing but praise for the young Senator. During the entire controversy he had never attacked Ted Kennedy personally or publicly stated what was commonly believed—that the appointment was a political payoff. He reminded the Senate again, as he had throughout the controversy, that his only interest in the matter had been his "devotion to the integrity of the Federal Judiciary system" and in mellifluous tones saluted Kennedy as rising "to the highest tradition of the U.S. Senate."

Kennedy, of course, could not have risen "to the highest tradition" had not Dirksen led his colleagues in the Senate in the rare act of negating one of its oldest traditions—senatorial courtesy.

POSTSCRIPT

Under the law the Morrissey nomination expired thirty days after the Senate adjourned. The unanimous consent required to carry the nomination over the second half of the congressional session was not requested. The President had the option of making a recess appointment, which would require a new appointment and confirmation in the next session of the Senate, or he could resubmit the original nomination for confirmation in the next session. A recess appointment would mean that Morrissey would have to give up his $20,000 a year position on the Municipal Court with no guarantee of later confirmation by the Senate.

In a letter received at the White House on November 5, 1965, Judge Morrissey asked President Johnson to withdraw his nomination so as "to prevent further anguish to my family and further harassment to you and to those who have supported me so loyally." The President replied that he would respect the nominee's decision.

BIBLIOGRAPHICAL NOTE

The primary published sources for this study have been the daily editions of *The New York Times* of October 13 through October 23, 1965 and the transcript of the proceedings of Senator Dodd's subcommittee, U.S. Congress, Senate Committee on the Judiciary. Hearings on the Nomination of Francis X. Morrissey, 89th Congress, 1st Session, 1965. Joseph P. Harris, "The Courtesy of the Senate," *Political Science Quarterly* 67 (1952): 36–49 and the same author's "The Senatorial Rejection of Leland Olds: A Case Study," *American Political Science Review* 45 (1951): 674–92, provided brief and lucid explanations of the two sides of senatorial courtesy. The role of the American Bar Association in the selection of federal judges and the mechanics of that role is detailed in Joel B. Grossman, *Lawyers and Judges* (New York: Wiley, 1965). The nature and work of the Senate Republic and Democratic Policy Committees is reviewed in Daniel M. Berman, *In Congress Assembled* (New York: Macmillan, 1964), p. 217, and the implicit bargaining that takes place among senators is discussed in Donald R. Matthews, *U.S. Senators and Their World* (New York: Vintage, 1960), pp. 100–1. Ted Kennedy's September 28 speech to the Senate in support of the nomination and his October 21 speech in which he moved to recommit it are reported in 111 Cong. Rec. 25313 and 111 Cong. Rec. 27935 (1965) respectively.

NOTES

[1] See Bibliographical Note

[2] For its campaign to prevent confirmation of Morrissey, the *Globe* was awarded a 1965 Pulitzer Gold Medal for public service.

The Courts   3

The Supreme Court has chosen for its review a rather narrow range of topics, primarily related to individual liberties. One such liberty is equal protection of the laws, which when applied to representative government has been interpreted by the courts to mean one man, one vote. Reapportionment has thus become one of those areas where the courts have directly engaged in controversy with other components of government. The present case is taken from a larger study that traced the efforts of WMCA (a New York radio station) to secure equal representation in the New York Legislature. Having secured favorable court rulings on the necessity for New York to redistrict, WMCA was forced to continue its court battle when the Legislature, controlled by the Republicans, passed several reapportionment measures that were felt by most observers to be unconstitutional. The courts as a market for policy making becomes readily apparent in this case as opposing sides of the controversy attempt to define the specific court in which the decision will be reached. Since this also involves state court actions opposing those of national courts, the case is illustrative of the constitutional problem of national supremacy. However, the major emphasis should be upon the strategies and resources available to various participants as one moves into different decision-making markets. This has great relevance for current American government since state legislatures are now beginning anew the process of reapportionment based upon the 1970 census.

CALVIN B. T. LEE

New York Apportionment Acts and the Courts

PART I

Rockefeller and the Republican-controlled lame-duck legislature had won the apportionment battle in the political arena. Whether their victory would be sustained by the courts was another matter. Albin Krebs, in the New York *Herald Tribune,* reported that "the immediate challenge to the apportionment bills will come from Nassau County Attorney Jack B. Weinstein, who has been working feverishly over the Christmas weekend to draw up legal papers to submit to the three federal judges." On December 31, precisely one week after Governor Rockefeller signed Plan D into law, Weinstein filed a "Notice of Motion" in the District Court, asking the Court for an order invalidating the four apportionment acts on the grounds that: (1) the laws provided voting figures rather than citizen or resident figures; (2) the laws provided for fractional voting within the legislature; (3) "the laws provide[d] districts which are not compact and contiguous and depart in a substantial and unreasonable manner from natural geographic and political subdivision boundaries"; (4) the laws were adopted at a special session of the legislature; and (5) "the deliberate adoption of four separate and different laws to apportion and district at one session of the legislature with the intent to permit the judiciary to choose from among the four laws constituted an abdication of legislative responsibility to adopt a single law for apportionment and districting. . . ."

On January 4, Leonard Sand and WMCA joined Professor Weinstein in his challenge of the new apportionment. The following day R. Peter Straus explained to the public the reason for this latest litigation.

One man, one vote. That's fair. But the voting power of a man in a rural county upstate was equal to eight Manhattan votes or twenty Nassau votes. That's unfair.

Reprinted by permission of Charles Scribner's Sons from *One Man, One Vote: WMCA and the Struggle for Equal Representation,* pp. 146–76, by Calvin B. T. Lee. Copyright © 1967 Charles Scribner's Sons.

So in 1961, WMCA asked the federal courts to make it fair by declaring that all votes must be equal in state elections. Three years later, the United States Supreme Court itself said we were right: You were being cheated outrageously in Albany.

But then, Governor Rockefeller and a lame-duck Republican legislature pulled a fast one. They passed four different reapportionment laws, pretending to comply with the "one man, one vote" decision of the Supreme Court.

The trouble is, each of the four laws continues to cheat city and suburban voters out of full and fair representation in Albany.

WMCA is back in Federal Court and we are asking the Court to declare all four laws unconstitutional. A victory for WMCA will mean a victory for you and your voting rights.

In a publicity release issued the same day, Straus charged that the apportionment act gave "all of New York State an unhealthy dish of gerrymandering, or lame-duck pie." He also accused the legislature of using a "pie-slice technique to cut into the representation" of every metropolitan area in the state. "In Buffalo, Rochester, Syracuse, Albany and Greater New York," Straus explained, "you find the same slicing into metropolitan voting rights: A slime wedge of cities and suburbs, filled with voters, is attached to a wide chunk of rural territories, all crust."

Straus also announced that an experimental computerized districting of the city of Syracuse and the surrounding counties of Onondaga, Madison, and Oneida would be submitted to the Federal Court by WMCA. "We are going electronic," Straus said, "not because we think machines can draw sound districts for people, but simply to contrast the biased, gerrymandered lines drawn by the legislature with lines laid out by an impersonal non-political source."

The Syracuse region was selected, Straus pointed out, because: "(1) it is essential to demonstrate that upstate cities and suburbs are as badly underrepresented, and worse, than New York City; (2) Greater Syracuse, at the geographical center of New York State, is typical of the more heavily populated metropolitan areas which have been gerrymandered by the legislature; and (3) in Greater Syracuse—as much as in any metropolitan region in the state—apportionment is already a live public issue whose significance is widely recognized and understood."

On Thursday, January 21, 1965, Judges Waterman, Ryan, and Levet began hearings on the challenge to New York's apportionment. Before listening to the attorneys, Judge Waterman issued a statement with which his colleagues concurred. After noting that wherever possible federal courts should abstain from interpreting state constitutions and laws, the judge noted that it was *"not the function of this Court to supervise the perimeters of districts, even though allegedly in violation of the New York State Con-*

stitution, if there are no invidious comparisons between the districts as to
the populations or numbers of voters or numbers of citizens therein."[1] The
districts did not display, Waterman continued, "any invidious discrimination relative to any person's race, color, creed, national origin or sex. . . ."
The Constitution required the Court, Waterman asserted, only "to ascertain
whether a vote for Assemblyman or Senator in one district is debased or
diluted in relation to a vote for Assemblyman or Senator in another district,
and to ascertain whether these districts are so constructed as to contain
within them as nearly equal populations as is possible." "Hence," the judge
concluded:

. . . [A]ttacks upon the constitutional validity of these districts grounded
upon alleged peculiarities of their shapes, alleged departures from claimed
accustomed criteria for the fixing of electoral district perimeters and like
allegations—in short, claimed legislative gerrymandering—we believe do
not raise questions under the federal Constitution, and consequently we
request of you that you devote none of your time in addressing us with
reference thereto.

The Court's refusal to hear testimony on the question of whether New
York's apportionment constituted gerrymandering clearly stunned the lawyers for the plaintiffs, for they had planned to use the gerrymander issue as
a major argument in their challenge of the Republican apportionment acts.
Not surprisingly, Waterman drew laughter from the audience in the crowded
courtroom when he noted that "some of you may be dissatisfied with this
statement from the bench" and "some of you may have your arguments sort
of maladjusted or reapportioned."

Orrin G. Judd, representing New York State, argued that the use of a
voter base, rather than a citizen or resident base in apportioning seats was
consistent with the demands of the Equal Protection Clause. He pointed
out that under New York's apportionment system, "each vote shall have
the same force and effect."

Fractional voting was justified by Judd on the grounds that it enabled
the state to continue to recognize counties as the basic units of government.
"Fractional voting," Judd noted, "has a considerable background in New
York law. We have weighted voting in various branches of municipal government. The County of Nassau . . . has a system of weighted voting on
its Board of Supervisors . . . New York City has had a form of weighted
voting in its Board of Estimates, and . . . in the New York Democratic
County Executive Committee, everybody has fractional votes, varying from
a half down to a sixth, and that is considered democratic, and I believe
that the varied use of weighted and fractional voting successfully over a
period of years shows that it is in conformity with sound principles of gov-

ernment, and there is nothing in the Constitution, the United States Constitution, which would require that it be set aside."

In answer to Judge Waterman's question of whether a special session of the legislature had the power to reapportion the state, Judd pointed out that "this Court having invalidated the Constiutional provisions governing reapportionment in New York, the requirement that legislation be enacted at a regular session would not affect it."

Leonard Sand began his argument by asserting that, as expressed by the Supreme Court: "State constitutional provisions should be deemed violative of the federal Constitution only when validly asserted constitutional rights could not otherwise be protected and effected. Clearly, courts should attempt to accommodate the relief ordered to the apportionment provisions of the state constitutions insofar as possible." The use of a voter base was therefore impermissible, Sand argued, because the state constitution provided for a citizen base. Fractional voting, Sand reasoned, was invalid because it required a double standard: One method of apportioning seats for densely populated counties and a different one for those in which fractional voting was to be employed.

After a fifteen-minute recess, Professor Weinstein began his argument for Nassau County. Weinstein pointed out that the major objections to the apportionment scheme were based on the assumption that the acts violated New York State's constitution. Since a challenge under state law had been filed in New York's own courts the previous day, proper federal-state relationships required the Federal District Court to defer action until the state court had an opportunity to decide the state questions.

Shortly before 5 P.M. on Tuesday, January 26, the Court handed down its decision: Plan A was held to comply with the implementation decree of July 27; Plans B, C and D were ruled invalid under the Fourteenth Amendment. The Court gave no reasons for its action but announced that an "explanatory" opinion would be filed shortly.

Reaction to the Court's decision was uniformly favorable, reported Ronald Sullivan in the January 27 *New York Times:*

Republicans and Democrats alike declared here [Albany] tonight that a federal court's approval of a Republican plan for legislative reapportionment was a victory for their party.

.   .   .

Governor Rockefeller, expressing pleasure with the decision, said in a statement issued by his office here:

"As I have said all along, our objective at the special session was to enact an apportionment law that would comply with the Supreme Court decision and the order of the Federal District Court, and I am pleased that the Court has so ruled.

"As to the full scope and effect of the decision, no further comment is possible until the full opinions are handed down."

.   .   .

However, a spokesman for William H. McKeon, Democratic state chairman, said the ruling merely opened the door to further Democratic attacks on the Republican plan. . . .

.   .   .

The man who originally challenged the constitutionality of New York's legislative apportionment, R. Peter Straus, president of radio station WMCA, said he looked forward to further court action.

In a statement issued in New York City, he said: "We are gratified that the Federal Court has upheld the principle of one-man, one-vote, striking down the most offensive evasions of that rule. We also are pleased that the Federal Court has retained jurisdiction, awaiting results of the fight that remains to be fought in the state court."

.   .   .

Justin Feldman, secretary of the New York County Democratic organization and a leader of the party's reapportionment drive, said tonight that he would ask the state's courts to rule the Republican plans invalid on the ground that they violated the state's constitution in several respects.

He said that according to the constitution, district lines must be "contiguous" and "compact."

However, he went on, the lines were gerrymandered under Plan A, towns were split, and the 150-member Assembly was altered. These were all, he said, in conflict with the state constitution.

.   .   .

Democratic legislative leaders said the decision would have no effect on plans to introduce their own formula, which calls for reapportionment by a non-partisan commission or a referendum.

In a thirty-two-page "explanatory" opinion filed on February 1, the District Court sought to bring order to an essentially chaotic situation. Judge Waterman, who emphasized that he was judging New York's apportionment exclusively under the provisions of the federal Constitution, generously noted that "under the unique circumstances of this case, it was not an abuse of our order for the legislature to enact four alternative plans rather than only one. At worst, insofar as the legislature's response to our order manifests its doubts about the validity of the plans which have been enacted, the presumption of constitutionality ordinarily accorded to legislation is weakened to some extent."

On the question of the validity of fractional voting, Judge Waterman's reasoning was more political than legal:

If voting were the only important function of a legislator, the scheme of fractional voting in Plans D and C would probably not offend "the base standard of equality" among districts. But legislators have numerous important functions that have nothing directly to do with voting: participation in the work of legislative committees and party caucuses, debating on the floor of the legislature, discussing measures with other legislators and executive agencies, and the like. The Assemblyman who represents only one-sixth of a district can theoretically give each constituent six times as much representation in these respects as the Assemblyman who represents a full district. This disparity of representation persists even if the state is right in arguing that the Assemblyman with only one-sixth of a vote will carry only one-sixth as much political weight when he engages in these activities.

Plan A was valid, Waterman pointed out, because it created substantially equally populated districts:

Under Plan A, the ratio of citizen populations between the largest and smallest districts in New York is 1.15:1 in the Senate and 1.21:1 in the Assembly, while the minimum percentage of citizens represented by a majority of the New York Legislature is 49.4% for the Senate and 49.3% for the Assembly. These minor deviations from perfect equality are clearly permissible under the federal Constitution.

"Of course," Judge Waterman noted, "the ultimate fitness of the scheme for their needs and purposes is for the people of the State of New York, themselves, to decide, and not for this Court to mandate."

PART II

While the Federal District Court was holding hearings on the validity, under the Fourteenth Amendment, of New York's four apportionment acts, another challenge to the Republican redistricting formulas was taking place in the New York State Supreme Court. On January 20, Jerome T. Orans, a Manhattan lawyer, obtained an order requiring Governor Rockefeller and other state officials to show cause why New York's new apportionment acts should not be declared in violation of the state constitution.

In the course of the lengthy hearings before Justice Levy that took place throughout the month of February, debate centered about the question of whether the United States Supreme Court, in its June decision in *WMCA* v. *Lomenzo,* had meant to invalidate all the provisions in the New York State Constitution that related to apportionment, or only those provisions that were clearly inconsistent with the Court's one-man, one-vote mandate.

Orrin Judd, special counsel for State Attorney General Louis Lefkowitz, argued that the effect of the Supreme Court's decision was to leave
a gap in the apportionment provisions of New York State's Constitution—
a gap that the legislature was free to fill in any way consistent with the requirements of the federal Constitution.

In marked contrast, Jerome Orans and the Village Independent Democrats, a reform club led by Edward I. Koch and Mrs. Carol Greitzer, maintained that state constitutional provisions setting a limit of 150 seats on the
size of the Assembly and requiring that town and country lines be observed
and districts be compact and contiguous still remain in full force.

Justice Levy, on March 15, handed down his ruling: He held all four
Republican reapportionment acts—Plans A, B, C and D—invalid under
the New York State Constitution. In a meticulously reasoned opinion, Levy
considered the constitutional validity of: (1) reapportionment at a special
session of the legislature; (2) the legislative increase of the number of Assemblymen; (3) the 1964 reapportionment and redistricting of the state
Senate; (4) gerrymandering under the requirement of compact and contiguous districts; (5) division of county and town lines.

Levy found no constitutional flaw in passage of an apportionment plan
at a special session, but ruled the acts invalid on grounds that they violated
the state constitutional provision limiting the number of Assemblymen to
150. Plan A, the only act left standing by the Federal District Court, had
provided for an Assembly of 165.

Reaction to the merits of Justice Levy's opinion was generally quite
favorable. R. Peter Straus announced jubilantly:

I'm absolutely delighted that the progress toward fair apportionment of the state is proceeding uninterrupted. The State Court has finished
the housecleaning chore which the United States Supreme Court and the
District Court began. The cobwebs of malapportionment have been wiped
out.
Now the legislature and the District Court are free to furnish the
state with a modern, sensible apportionment and with clean, unpolitical
districts.

In an editorial entitled "New Start on Reapportionment," *The New
York Times* commented:

The last of the cynical and politically oriented reapportionment
measures passed by the lame-duck Republican legislature in December
has now been swept from the statute books by court decision.
Three of the four bills enacted were declared in violation of the
federal Constitution by the special Federal Court having jurisdiction
over reapportionment in this state. The fourth has now been declared in

violation of the state constitution by Supreme Court Justice Matthew M. Levy. His decision will undoubtedly be taken to the Court of Appeals.

New York State is now under a mandate from the Federal Court to enact a valid reapportionment law by April 1. It seems quite obvious now that this deadline cannot be met. While the Democrats controlling the legislature have announced that they intend to enact a reapportionment plan of their own, they have not yet even begun the complicated legislative processes of introducing and printing the necessary bills, holding public hearings and presenting the measures for debate in both houses. This procedure should not be carried out in crisis atmosphere.

By far the best course would be to create an independent bipartisan commission to take the drawing of district lines as far as possible out of the hands of the politicians and to place it in those of qualified experts. Perhaps that is too much to hope for, but the restraining influence of Governor Rockefeller's veto may yet keep the Democrats from the excesses that marred the Republican bills.

It is far more important that reapportionment be accomplished equitably than that it be rushed through to meet a deadline. For that reason, we welcome the announcement by radio station WMCA . . . that it will ask the Federal Court to modify the April 1 goal.

It may even turn out to be necessary to cancel the special election of a new legislature, next November, which had been ordered by the Federal Court, because even after the new district lines are drawn the permanent personal registration cards will have to be redistributed, a time-consuming process. This delay would be regrettable, but a lesser evil than too-hasty action.

New York is fortunate to have this second chance. The legislature must make better use of it than it did of its first opportunity.

In Albany, R. W. Apple, Jr., of *The New York Times* reported, "public comments by both Republicans and Democrats . . . were guarded." Governor Rockefeller announced that the state would appeal Levy's ruling, but failed to predict whether the November election could be held, saying, "this is a very difficult, delicate, complicated situation. The whole thing depends on the courts."

Rockefeller's great concern with the fate of New York's apportionment act before the courts was amply and quickly demonstrated: On March 16, the day after Justice Levy's decision was handed down, it was announced that the state had engaged former Governor Thomas E. Dewey, the Republican presidential candidate in both 1944 and 1948 (he was defeated by Presidents Roosevelt and Truman, respectively), to argue its legislative apportionment litigation before the United States Supreme Court.

"Democrats Rage Over Dewey Job," reported Sydney H. Schanberg in the March 18 *New York Times*:

Democratic legislators exploded in heated indignation today [March 17th] over the state's hiring of former Republican Gov. Thomas E. Dewey. . . .

Democrats in the Senate shouted "fraud" and "shame" and shook accusing fingers at the Republicans.

"It's not only fraud, it's criminal," cried Majority Leader Joseph Zaretzki, "using public money for private purposes for the preservation and protection of the Republican party."

Time and again during the Senate clash, which raged for nearly an hour, the Democrats asked why the Republican administration had hired Mr. Dewey instead of relying on the State Attorney General, Louis J. Lefkowitz.

On March 25, the three-judge Federal District Court extended the deadline for reapportioning the state legislature from April 1 to May 5, 1965. Commenting on this extension in an editorial entitled, "Democratic Opportunity," *The New York Times* observed:

Postponement of the deadline for legislative reapportionment of New York State . . . gives the Democrats now in control of the legislature a splendid opportunity to redeem themselves. By producing a fair and equitable plan, free from the gerrymandering that marred the Republican redistricting efforts, the Democrats would go a long way toward erasing from public memory the disgraceful partisan squabble that kept them from the state's urgent business during the early weeks of the session.[2]

.   .   .

There is a clear, obvious need for legislation to fill the void [left by the invalidation by Justice Levy of all four apportionment acts]. The Democratic party has pledged itself to support the creation of an independent bipartisan commission to draw new district lines that would be compact and contiguous and not based on party enrollment. It should go forward speedily to keep this promise before the expiration of the new deadline.

"STATE REDISTRICTING LAW KILLED BY APPEALS COURT" read the headlines of the Thursday, April 15, *New York Times*. The previous day, by a 6–1 vote, New York's highest court had upheld Justice Levy's decision in *In the Matter of Orans*. Speaking for the majority, Chief Judge Charles S. Desmond stated:

We hold to be in full effect the flat, positive and unmistakable command of the state constitution that there be 150 members of the state Assembly. Since each of the four plans violates that command, each plan and all five statutes are invalid.

Judge Francis Bergen, concurring, agreed that the Assembly could not be enlarged beyond 150 members by legislative enactment. "But," he continued, "the limitation of the New York Constitution on legislative power to reapportion districts goes well beyond a mere numerical change in the Assembly districts." It must be remembered, he said, that:

The legislature owes its existence to the constitution. All of its powers, and the limitation on its powers, spring from it. No residual power to make structural changes in its own organization or in other branches of the government set up by the constitution is vested in the legislature. These basic structures may be altered only by the approval of the people.

The fact that the federal government has now declared that the New York Constitution is invalid as in conflict with the United States Constitution in the way it apportions the legislature does not create a new kind of ultra-constitutional power to establish a different basic pattern of representation. The people of New York retain the sole power to do this, and it has not been vested by them in the legislature even to meet an emergency created by the federal decisions.

.   .   .

To say that New York, one of the states which formed the federal government itself, is to derive a power over the reconstruction of its own government from the intimations of the judicial branch of the federal government as to what powers its legislature, ought to have is both revolutionary doctrine and a constitutional anachronism.

Judge John Van Voorhis, in a sharp dissent, argued that the 150-member provision was an integral part of the apportionment formula that the United States Supreme Court had struck down:

It would be playing fast and loose with the facts to assume that the number of 150 was arrived at independently of the formula in order to fix the numerical membership of the Assembly without regard to how they were to be distributed between upstate and downstate or among the more populous and less populous counties.

By its decision, the Court of Appeals left New York State without a valid plan for apportionment. Referring to this problem, Chief Judge Desmond stated bluntly: "It is up to the legislature now to enact a new districting-apportionment formula." Under the mandate of the Federal District Court, the legislature had precisely twenty-two days—from April 14 to May 5—in which to draft a new act, consistent with the provisions of both the federal and state constitutions.

PART III

The first week of May saw the Democrats desperately trying to prepare and enact a new apportionment plan for New York State in time to meet the May 5 deadline set by the Federal Court. The problems party strategists faced seemed overwhelming. As stated by Sanford E. Stanton in the May 3 edition of the New York *Journal-American*:

A coalition of Republicans and upstate Democrats is braced to block any redistricting plan to come out of the Democratic-controlled Joint Legislative Commission on Reapportionment.

And even if the plan could leap that hurdle, it still would face a probable veto by Republican Governor Rockefeller, who wants reapportionment under Republican plans drafted by the lame-duck legislature last December.

The political dilemma faced by Democratic leaders failed to evoke any sympathy from R. Peter Straus. In a statement issued May 4, he explained:

WMCA's interest in the New York State apportionment case is in distributing state legislative seats according to population, in one undiluted vote for every qualified voter in the state. Period.

We hold no more of a brief for a "Partisan Democratic Apportionment" now, in May, than we did for a Republican gerrymander four months ago, in December.

In December, the new majority leaders said that this session would make a straight-forward effort to comply with the Court rulings in our case. They said they would not circumvent those rulings with a partisan "tit for tat."

My party has had four months in office—four months to deliver on its promise of a fair apportionment. Now, in May, we have begun to fret about the fulfillment of that promise.

Our counsel—and disinterested attorneys throughout the state—have made it clear that four months is more than enough time to create a new, fair apportionment.

Yet now, after four months in office, the majority leaders plead insufficient time to meet the Federal Court's deadline this week.

We doubt whether the leadership's eleventh-hour delay means anything more than eleventh-hour rearrangements of district lines to calm bad political nerves.

We question whether the Court will receive better than half-a-loaf —better than a districting for one house only.

And we wonder whether the current frantic effort in Albany will yield more than token compliance with the District Court's order.

We are politically "square": four-square for a special election in November 1965. We believe that full compliance with the District Court's order for such an election is fully possible.

The following day, May 5, the New York *Daily News* reported that radio station WMCA would ask the Federal Court to appoint a special master (a court-appointed referee) to draw up a fair redistricting program in time for use in the November election. Later that day, the Democrats revealed their own districting bill for the Assembly. It shifted fourteen seats from upstate New York to the New York metropolitan region, leaving the former with fifty-six seats and the latter with ninety-four. The Democrats had not had time, however, to draft an apportionment for the Senate.

Five days later, May 10, the Federal District Court, Judges Sterry R. Waterman, Sylvester J. Ryan and Richard H. Levet presiding, conducted a hearing to consider whether the November election should still be held under Plan A that the state Court of Appeals had ruled in violation of the New York State Constitution.

Orrin Judd, representing New York State, insisted that, since the District Court had, on December 1, upheld the validity of Plan A, the November election should take place under that apportionment formula. He denied repeatedly that it would be feasible for the Court to appoint a special master to draft a new apportionment consistent with both the federal and state constitutions.

Leonard Sand accused the legislature of stalling and urged the Court to appoint a special master rather than to force the state to conduct its election under an apportionment formula that had been held to violate the state constitution. He recognized, however, that the Court did have power to order an election under Plan A. He also suggested that weighted-voting could be used on an interim basis.

Although the Judges indicated that they were not necessarily convinced of the efficacy of weighted voting, Sand's proposal did elicit from the Court favorable comment as to his role as an attorney.

Judge Ryan. I want to say, Mr. Sand, that throughout the four years [that the New York apportionment had been litigated in the District Court] you have been of great help to the Court and you have done a wonderful job as a member of the bar of this Court, in my opinion.
Judge Waterman.   I must say—
Judge Levet.   Second the motion.
Judge Waterman.   I must say that the statement you have just made is about as lawyerlike and statesmanlike a statement as you have made in four years.
Judge Ryan.   Mr. Sand has done a splendid job and so has your associate, Mr. Gross.

After hearing from Nassau County and New York City, both of which supported Sand's position, Judge Waterman announced the opinion of the Court:

All three of us are of the opinion that there is no point in any further delay with respect to holding an election to elect members of the general Assembly and Senate for the year 1965. Whether there is some purpose in taking away from the duly elected people, duly elected representatives of the people, the right which we wish they would exercise and which we have given them every opportunity to exercise with respect to the legislature which will be elected in 1966 is, of course, another question.

But as of today a majority of the Court is ordering that its previous orders be complied with forthwith, and that Plan A will form the basis for the election of members of the legislature who will hold office for one year, the year 1966, the calendar year, or whenever, and will be elected on November 2, 1965. The machinery of the election process which you gentlemen have told us about so often can therefore begin to operate.

Judge Levet dissented. In his view, the Supreme Court in deciding the Reapportionment Cases intended that only those portions of state constitutions specifically inconsistent with the federal Constitution should be invalidated. Plan A violated legitimate sections of the New York Constitution.

In an editorial entitled "Reapportionment Frolics," the New York *Post* criticized both the Court and the legislature:

The Federal Court's redistricting decision raised highly arguable questions.

As Leonard Sand, attorney for WMCA, pointed out to the Court, there were two forces at work—the GOP, doing everything possible to salvage its own gerrymander in the form of Plan A, and the Democrats, busily striving to avoid an election this fall.

Mr. Sand did not believe the Court had to confine itself to these two dubious options. The dissent of Judge Levet appears to bear him out.

Most citizens will say the Democrats brought this fiasco upon themselves. After Justice Matthew Levy's decision killing Plan A, the Democrats had ample time to turn over the job of redistricting to a non-partisan commission, as they had pledged.

Instead they came up with a gerrymander program even more grotesque than Plan A. At the same time they sought to delay the whole operation in the hope of forcing the Court to cancel the 1965 election.

Understandably this did not set well with the Court. Two of the Court's three judges ruled elections should be held even if they have to be held under Plan A and even though that plan had been ruled invalid by the state's Court of Appeals.

The legislature has until May 24 to come up with a better proposal. That could be done by enacting into statutory form Judge Levet's proposal for a one-shot election in November on the basis of existing district lines, plus the use of weighted voting.

This would be a temporary expedient. If the proposal were combined with the establishment of a non-partisan commission to prepare a plan for the 1966 elections and the calling of a constitutional convention, the package would partially wipe out the dishonorable character of the legislature's performance to date.

On May 18, the Democratic leaders of the legislature announced that they had hired former Federal Judge Simon H. Rifkind to spearhead a movement to evade a special election in November under Plan A. They also stated that they would call for a constitutional convention to revise completely the state's legislative districting laws to make them conform with the one-man, one-vote ruling of the Supreme Court. Moreover, Assembly Speaker Anthony J. Travia pledged that the legislature would immediately enact two bills: One to provide for "weighted" votes for members elected from the present legislative districts; the other to establish a non-legislative, bipartisan commission to study the districting problem and report by December 1, 1965.

The following day, the legislature did, in fact, pass a concurrent resolution.

Declaring the course of action to be taken by the legislature before the recess or adjournment of its 1965 regular session with respect to interim and long-range solutions of the problems attendant upon the reapportionment of the Senate and Assembly districts of the state and memorializing the Governor of the state to approve legislation passed at the present session submitting the questions of holding a constitutional convention to the electorate of the state at the general election in November nineteen hundred, sixty-five.

However, by May 24, when the District Court met again to hand down its formal order, the Democrats had been able to pass neither of their promised apportionment acts. Despite an eloquent appeal by Simon Rifkind on behalf of the delinquent legislature, the Court, Judge Levet dissenting, upheld its May 10 ruling: The November election would take place, as scheduled, under Plan A.

Despite the finality of the Court's holdings, the Democrats did not give up. James Desmond, writing from Albany in the May 24 New York *Daily News,* reported:

The Democrats in the legislature got together today and doggedly passed their stop-gap reapportionment bills, but the move apparently came too late.

For while the Democrats were debating the bills a three-judge federal court in New York City was ordering a special legislative election for November—the very ruling that the Democratic bills were designed to head off.

The ruling was announced on the floor, but the debate went ahead anyway because the Democrats were trying to establish a record of legislative action as the basis for an appeal to the U.S. Supreme Court from the lower court's ruling.

The bills, passed on party line votes, provide:

For appointment of a bipartisan commission of 12—six to be named by the Governor and three each by the temporary president of the Senate and the Assembly Speaker—to draw up a reapportionment scheme and report back by Dec. 1. . . .

For a system of weighted voting in the 1966 session of the legislature to give legislators elected from the existing districts—which were outlawed last year by the U.S. Supreme Court—voting power proportionate to the number of people they represent.

The bills now go to Governor Rockefeller for his signature, but their fate is in doubt, particularly the weighted voting proposal which was denounced by the New York Federal Court even before the legislature voted on it.

Three days later, May 27, the fate of the Democratic bills was determined: Governor Rockefeller vetoed both. His reasons were that reapportionment was the responsibility of the legislature, not of a so-called neutral body, and that weighted voting was unconstitutional.

Also on May 27, Associate Justice John Marshall Harlan heard arguments on whether the District Court's order should be stayed. Judge Rifkind, representing the Democratic leaders of the New York legislature urged a stay of the lower Court's order on grounds that it would "wreck havoc" with the state's political processes, and force the state and political parties to spend substantial sums preparing for the election. Orrin Judd, representing the office of the New York Attorney General and the New York Secretary of State insisted that the District Court's "unanimous determination and firm resolve that there be an election this year must be respected." At the end of an hour-and-a-half long closed session, Justice Harlan announced that, because of the great importance of the case, he would refer the matter to the entire Supreme Court.

While the Court was deciding whether or not to issue a stay order, a *New York Times* editorial berated Governor Rockefeller for vetoing the two Democratic apportionment bills.

THE GOVERNOR'S VETOES

Governor Rockefeller was wrong to veto the measure passed by the Democratic-controlled legislature for a bipartisan commission to guide the drawing of new legislative district lines. Regardless of the motives that led the Democrats to enact this measure so belatedly, it is regrettable that the Governor did not give greater consideration to the merits of the proposal.

Experience has shown that the only practicable way of eliminating the twin evils of malapportionment and gerrymandering is to take the drawing of new district lines out of the hands of the legislature and put them under control of a body less subject to immediate political pressures.

· · ·

The commission vetoed by Governor Rockefeller would have been charged with drawing up a redistricting plan by December 1, for submission to the legislature next January. This provision would have amply protected the legislature's right of final decision.

Governor Rockefeller also vetoed a companion bill put through by the Democrats, which would have provided for the use of the present legislative districts, but with weighted voting to overcome population discrepancies. The Governor's comment that this was plainly a violation of both the federal and state constitutions showed very little respect for Federal Judge Richard H. Levet, who originally advanced the suggestion in his dissent from the majority ruling.

On June 1, the Supreme Court, in a brief per curiam opinion, refused to stay the District Court's order with Justice Harlan dissenting sharply.

R. Peter Straus commented contentedly that "the high court ruling closes the books on more than seventy years of legalized malapportionment. It means a new legislative election this year. And it will mean a new balance of fair representation for cities and suburbs across the state." Republicans were generally jubilant. The Democrats viewed the decision less enthusiastically.

The New York Times, in a June 2 editorial, indicated strong dissatisfaction with the Court's decision and the performances of both the Democratic and Republican parties.

On Nov. 2 New York State voters will elect a new legislature of 65 Senators and 165 Assemblymen for one-year terms, on the basis of flamboyantly gerrymandered district lines provided in the reapportionment plan put across by the Republicans last December. This is the meaning of the United States Supreme Court's refusal yesterday to accede to the request of the Democratic leaders to delay the election.

The plight in which the Democratic party now finds itself arouses no sympathy. It must contest the election this fall on such unfavorable terms only because of the disgraceful failure of the present, Democratic-controlled, legislature to use the opportunity it has had since January to enact a more equitable reapportionment statute. It is no secret that some Democrats, at least, were gambling on the hope that the Court would cancel the election. They lost, as they deserved to lose.

But the citizens of New York are now being compelled by the federal courts to vote under a reapportionment measure that has been held to violate the state's constitution by the highest tribunal of the state, the Court of Appeals. It seems to us that this more than justifies the angry dissent by Justice John Marshall Harlan, who protested the "casual way" in which the Supreme Court refused a hearing on the application for the stay.

However, the issue of this fall's election has now been finally settled. The immediate task is for the state to prepare a reapportionment plan for 1966 and thereafter, valid under both the state and federal constitutions. Governor Rockefeller has—most unwisely—vetoed the bill for creation of a bipartisan commission to draw up a districting plan to recommend to the next legislature. Now the latter will have to start all over in January. It can learn a great deal from the mistaken predecessors to use reapportionment for gross partisan advantage. The question is: Will it?

THE LAST WORD

The Federal Court had ordered New York State to hold a special election in November, 1965, under an apportionment formula that violated the state constitution. The question, as *The New York Times* stated in a June 2 editorial, was whether the legislature would take the necessary steps to insure that by the election of November, 1966, New York would have an apportionment that met the standards set by both the federal and state constitutions. Indications were that they would.

Senate Majority Leader Joseph Zaretzki announced on June 11 that he would fight for a state-wide referendum in July so there could be a constitutional convention in the spring for the purpose of drawing new district lines. Four days later, Governor Rockefeller signed the Democratic bill into law.

The orderly manner in which the legislature had proceeded to provide for a new apportionment act contrasted sharply with the obstructionist antics of a few desperate Democratic politicians and of the judges of New York's courts. On June 21, 1965, Professor Robert B. Fleming of the University of Buffalo Law School, representing State Senator Frank J. Glinski, instituted action in the New York State Supreme Court in Albany demanding that there be no election in 1965 and that legislators remain in office until December 31, 1966. The following day, Justice John H. Pennock signed an order to show cause why the desired relief should not be granted. A hearing was set for June 28.

On June 29, a United Press International bulletin reported that Justice Russell Hunt of the State Supreme Court, after hearing oral arguments on Glinski's motion to prevent the special election, reserved decision despite the fact that all parties to the suit urged speedy disposition of the case, noting that June 29 was the first day for circulating nominating petitions for legislative office. The following Friday, July 5, Justice Hunt handed down his decision: He issued an order enjoining the secretary of state from conducting an election under Plan A.

The Appellate Division of the Supreme Court, announcing in a per curiam opinion that "we consider that we are bound, and that our decision must be controlled, by the order of the three-judge District Court [mandating a November, 1965 election]," summarily reversed the lower state court's decision. The stage was thus set for an appeal to New York's highest court, the Court of Appeals.

"STATE'S HIGHEST COURT, 4–3, BARS ELECTING A LEG-ISLATURE IN FALL AS FEDERAL COURT HAD ORDERED" blared the headline of the July 10 *New York Times.* Chief Judge Charles S. Desmond wrote the majority opinion and was joined by Associate Judges Marvin R. Dye and John F. Scileppi. Associate Judge Adrian Burke wrote a concurring opinion. A dissenting memorandum was filed by Associate Judges Stanley H. Field, John Van Voorhis, and Francis Bergan. Judge Bergan also wrote a separate dissent.

In his opinion for the Court, Chief Judge Desmond, stating that he had seen "no binding federal court order forbidding [the state courts] to deal with this problem of state government," asserted that "neither federal supremacy nor the rules against interference with federal courts by state courts have any application here." The state constitution was explicit: Elections were to be held every other year and the Assembly was to number 150. Plan A violated both of these prescriptions.

"Basically," Desmond reasoned, "the question is: Shall we obey the positive directions of our own state constitution in the absence of a controlling decision elsewhere commanding that an unconstitutional election be held? I answer 'Yes.' The injunction prayed for must be granted."

In a brief concurring opinion Judge Burke noted that the time and method of holding an election for state officials is a state question, that the United States Supreme Court had directed that the greatest possible deference should be paid to state action and that the high court "had directed that an election be held in 1965 only if there is a valid legislative apportionment." Plan A was invalid under the state constitution. "Therefore an election this year," Burke reasoned, "can only be held constitutionally by providing that the proper number of legislators be elected at large."

In their dissenting memorandum, Judges Bergan, Field, and Voorhis took sharp issue with the majority as to the question of the applicability of federal supremacy. Noting that "the decision now being handed down serves only to further confound a most unfortunate and confused situation," the three dissenting judges asserted:

> For the courts of this state now to grant injunctive relief, preventing the holding of an election in 1965, would be in direct conflict with the District Court's decision, a decision which, in view of the Supreme Court's recent denial of an application for a stay, has that tribunal's implicit approval. Such a conflict between federal and state judicial power should be avoided in the interest of the public order and the proper administration of justice.

Judge Bergen, in a separate dissent, emphasized even more emphatically that the Court of Appeals was, in effect, engaging in a direct struggle for power with the federal courts:

. . . [T]o grant a state court injunction against the enforcement of a federal court order amounts to a confrontation of power which ought to be avoided if possible, in the interest of orderly government within the federal union, entirely aside from the vagaries of the supremacy clause as applied to a situation of this kind.

The result of the decision now being made is that a court of one sovereign authority has directed the New York Secretary of State to prepare an election in 1965 and the court of another soverign authority has prohibited him from doing just that.

The legal difficulties over the exercise of the power of New York to govern itself can be resolved definitely by the Supreme Court of the United States in reviewing the decision of this court; and cannot be resolved adequately by a clash of conflicting orders between the New York Supreme Court and the United States District Court.

Martin Arnold, in a July 10 article in *The New York Times,* reported that "reaction to the State Court of Appeals ruling yesterday barring a special legislative election this fall ranged from delight to distress."

Mayor Wagner was quoted as stating that the decision "certainly eliminates the danger of an atypical, abnormal election," the results of which "would be completely nonrepresentative in a state-wide sense." In contrast, New York City Comptroller Abraham Beame, a candidate for the Democratic nomination for mayor, announced that "while I have great reservations about the Rocky-mandered Plan A, I favor an election this November, and I support any and all attempts to appeal this decision to the Supreme Court, which wisely set down the mandate of one man, one vote."

In another article, written by *Times* reporter Sidney E. Zion, Leonard Sand was said to have referred to the Court of Appeals ruling as "trivia of the highest degree." "We'll ask the Federal Court to have this set aside," Sand allegedly continued. "If the state court doesn't like the form of the Federal Court's original order I'm sure the Federal Court will issue an order that removes any ambiguities. The Federal Court has the last word." (Immediately after publication of Zion's article, Sand, claiming to be misquoted, wrote to assure Judge Desmond that he "would certainly never characterize any decision of the Court of Appeals as being 'trivial.' ")

The New York Times, in a July 10 editorial entitled, "Compounding Confusion," sharply criticized Judge Desmond's decision:

The Court of Appeals, New York State's highest judicial tribunal, ruled yesterday that the special legislative election scheduled in November could not be held because it violated the state constitution in at least two respects. By doing so it placed itself in direct opposition to the United States District Court's order that the election must be held under Republican Plan A.

Associate Judge Stanley Field did not exaggerate when he wrote in his dissenting opinion that the decision, reached by a 4-to-3 vote,

"serves only to confound the most unfortunate and confusing situation."
The minority argued that a conflict between the federal and State courts
should be avoided "in the interest of the public order and the proper
administration of justice."

.   .   .

To the layman, it would seem clear that under the supremacy clause
of Article VI of the United States Constitution the decision of the Federal
Court would be binding. But Judge Desmond explicitly stated that in his
view the supremacy clause did not apply to the case before him. . . .

Those favoring the fall election will surely go back to the Federal
Court and ask it to reaffirm its order. Meanwhile it is possible that the epi-
sode will form the basis for another appeal to Justice Harlan of the United
States Supreme Court for a stay of the election until the nation's highest
tribunal has heard and decided the case, probably long after November.
The issue which seemed settled in May is once more wide open.

On July 10, Federal District Judge Sylvester J. Ryan, acting at the
request of Attorney General Louis J. Lefkowitz, issued a temporary order
enjoining all state proceedings in conflict with the three-judge Federal Court
ruling of May 24 calling for the election of a new legislature November 2
under Plan A. A hearing was set for Tuesday, July 13.

Also on July 10, *Times* writer Sidney E. Zion reported that Judge
Waterman, in a telephone interview, when asked whether a "final and binding order" had been issued by the District Court, replied "Gee, I don't
know. We thought we were binding the litigants." After reading aloud the
District Court's order, Waterman reportedly asked, "Are there any words
you can think of that would have made that clearer?"

Two days later, the situation became even more confused as Senate
Majority Leader Joseph Zaretzki and Assembly Speaker Anthony J. Travia
sent a telegram to Justice John Marshall Harlan of the United States Supreme Court requesting that he stay the Federal Court order directing that
the November election be held.

Operating under threat of a Supreme Court injunction, Judges Levet,
Ryan, and Waterman began their hearing July 13 on the question of
whether they should enjoin all interference with the conducting of the November election.

Orrin Judd, representing New York State, assured the District Court
that "if there is chaos now, I think it is not this Court's fault; but I think
the Court, having issued the order of May 24, has the power to create order
instead of chaos." As evidence of the power of the District Court, Judd
quoted from an opinion in the Little Rock School Case,[3] *Brown* v. *Board
of Education,* wherein the Court of Appeals for the Eighth Circuit said:

We have no doubt whatever that the Federal District Court . . . had the power and the duty . . . in order to protect or effectuate its judgments, to stay the state court proceedings. A federal court should not, when prompt action is required, be compelled to indulge in useless formalities in protecting its judgments from being emasculated by state court proceedings.

Leonard Sand, after pointing out the repeated failure of the legislature, under both Republican and Democratic control, to enact an apportionment valid under both the state and federal constitutions, noted that "if there is today no ready accommodations between the provisions of the Fourteenth Amendment and the provisions of the state constitution, the responsibility for that unfortunate situation lies outside this courtroom." Sand argued that: "The basic problem in the whole area of apportionment has been the failure to recognize that we are dealing with a personal civil right guaranteed by the Fourteenth Amendment. If this were a voting case in a racial context, and if we were in some other state, there would be no hesitation at all in recognizing that federal supremacy is absolutely essential if the rights guaranteed by the Constitution are to be meaningful."

Judge Simon K. Rifkind, representing Senator Zaretzki and Assemblyman Travia, after conceding that the District Court had the power to override the state court and force a November election, argued that:

The issue this morning before your Honors is not whether this Court has the power and the determination to do what it has said it should do, the question is should it in the exercise of its wisdom, in the exercise of its discretion, in the exercise of the high function committed to its care under the Constitution, do what it has proposed to do.

I have come here this morning, may it please the Court, to champion two unpopular notions, or notions that I think are currently unpopular and in disfavor. The first of these is an almost forgotten idea of federalism. The second one is a more universal concept of moderation.

. . . Federalism is a state of mind, it is an attitude, it is a relationship, but in practice federalism means this, that when two sovereigns rule in the same territory and rule over the same people, they must so behave that they do not unnecessarily jostle each other.

The Court was visibly unimpressed by Rifkind's arguments. At the close of the hearing, Judge Waterman, addressing Orrin Judd, said, "You must have some hope at least of winning your point. Do you have a prepared order?" Utilizing Judd's offered order, the Court, following a recess of less than fifteen minutes, returned to deliver its opinion.

Judge Waterman, caustically referring to Judge Desmond's statement that he had seen no "final and binding order," stated:

We intended the order of this Court of May 24, 1965, to be exactly such an order, so directing. We believe the order did expressly state such a judgment, but to remove any question as to its purpose, intent or wording, we are entering a further order containing mandatory and injunctive provisions.

. Speaking for a unanimous court (including Judge Levet who reluctantly indicated that despite his earlier opposition, he would concur because "a shift [in the status of the election] would create endless confusion"), Judge Waterman ordered that:

Frank J. Glinski, William F. Keenan, and all parties to this action, their agents, attorneys and servants, their successors and all other persons are hereby forever restrained and enjoined from interfering with the carrying out and execution by any and all New York State officers and election officials and their successors and all other persons of the order this court of May 24, 1965 [requiring a November, 1965 election under Reapportionment Plan A].

The decision of the District Court was greeted by an almost universal sigh of relief. The election would take place, and a direct clash between the federal and state courts seemed to have been averted. *The New York Times,* however, mirrored the opinion of many when it expressed regret that the election would take place "under a highly partisan and unconstitutional" apportionment plan:

The Federal Court was quite right in not letting the Democrats get away with their obvious efforts to block the election entirely. There should be an election in November. On that point Judge Richard J. Levet, who dissented from the designation of Plan A by the majority of the Court, was in agreement with the others. He pointed out yesterday that the preparation of the election machinery was already in progress and that any change now would only cause further confusion.

But how much better off the State of New York might be today if the Court had granted the motion of counsel for radio station WMCA . . . and appointed a special master last March to prepare a non-partisan apportionment plan for use in the event the legislature failed to act. The Court indicated yesterday its intention to follow this procedure next year if necessary but meanwhile it will have imposed an unconstitutional legislature on the state.

The Democrats, however, refused to give up their fight to block the fall election. On July 14, they filed a new petition with United States Supreme Court Justice John M. Harlan seeking a stay of the latest District Court order. Their attempt proved futile. On Friday, July 17, Justice Harlan refused to bar the November election.

In a brief memorandum opinion, Harlan said:

Were [the United States Supreme Court] in session I would have referred both of these applications [for stays] to it for disposition, as was done with the earlier application for a stay of the District Court's order of May 24. I consider it, however, my duty in the circumstances to act on these applications myself, deeming that I would not be justified in asking the Chief Justice to take steps to convene the Court in special session. Given what has already transpired, I am left in no doubt as to what the decision on these applications must be.

While I have heretofore expressed my strong disagreement both with this Court's basic state reapportionment decisions and with the Court's subsequent refusal, at least so far, to give plenary consideration to any of the challenges that have been made to the particular kinds of relief granted by district courts, nevertheless I can only conclude that the denial of these applications is compelled by this Court's earlier summary denial of a stay pending appeal of the District Court's order of May 24 directing the election in question. That denial surely signified this Court's unwillingness to interfere with the District Court's direction of the election, even though the election was to be held under a plan of apportionment which violated the New York Constitution. That being so, the supremacy clause of the federal Constitution requires the state courts to give recognition to the District Court's order.

.   .   .

In conclusion, I think it pertinent to observe that these applications illustrate how important it is for this Court to act in a sensitive and not heavy-handed manner in this novel and delicate constitutional field. It is manifest from the majority opinion of the New York Court of Appeals that this present unfortunate situation would not have arisen had [the Supreme Court] explicated its reasons for refusing to stay the District Court's order of May 24.

In New York, Mayor Wagner expressed the opinion of most New Yorkers when he commented: "The last word has now been said. The problems held in abeyance pending this final action must now be confronted." Whether the legislature and the Courts would be able to come to an agreement over a valid reapportionment of New York State remained an open question. Reapportionment will continue to be an important issue in New York politics and an issue that perhaps may never be completely resolved satisfactorily either in the courts or the political arena.

Notes

[1] Author's italics.
[2] Following their victory in the November election, the Democrats assumed

control of the legislature; however, a struggle for power between the upstate
Democrats, and proponents and opponents of New York City's Mayor Wagner
prevented the selection of Senate and Assembly majority leaders until the Republican leadership joined forces with Wagner's supporters to elect Joseph
Zaretzki, and Anthony J. Travia to the two positions respectively.

[3] Following a Federal District Court order that Little Rock's Central High
School be desegregated, a citizen of the city obtained an Arkansas state court
order enjoining the school board from opening the schools.

Source Notes

Banzhaf, John F., "Weighted Voting Doesn't Work: A Mathematical Analysis,"
    Rutgers Law Review 19 (1965): 317.

———, "Multi-Member Electoral Districts—Do They Violate the 'One Man,
    One Vote' Principle?" *Yale Law Journal* 76 (1966): 1309.

Bonfield, Arthur Earl, "*Baker* v. *Carr:* New Light on the Constitutional Guar-
    antee of Republican Government," *California Law Review* 50 (1962):
    245.

———, "The Guarantee Clause of Article IV, Section 4: A Study in Con-
    stitutional Desuetude." *Minnesota Law Review* 46 (1962): 513.

Caruso, Lawrence R., "The Proper Role of the Federal Courts in the Reap-
    portionment of State Legislatures," *Mississippi Law Journal* 36 (1965):
    300.

Engle, Robert H., "Weighting Legislators' Votes to Equalize Representation,"
    Western Political Quarterly 12 (1959): 422.

Glinski v. *Lomenzo,* 16 N.Y. 2d 27, 261 N.Y.S. 2d 281, 209 N.E. 2d 277
    (1965).

Nagel, Stuart S., "Simplified Bipartisan Computer Redistricting," *Stanford
    Law Review* 17 (1965): 863.

Orans, In the Matter of, 15 N.Y. 2d 339, 258 N.Y.S. 2d 825, 206 N.E. 2d
    854 (1965).

Roeck, Ernest C., Jr., "Measuring Compactness as a Requirement of Legis-
    lative Apportionment," *Midwest Journal of Political Science* 5 (1961): 70.

Travia v. *Lomenzo,* 381 U.S. 431 (1965).

Tyler, Gus, "Court versus Legislature," *Law and Contemporary Problems* 27
    (1962): 390.

Velvel, Lawrence R., "Suggested Approaches to Constitutional Adjudication
    and Apportionment," *U.C.L.A. Law Review* 12 (1965): 1381.

Weaver, James B. and W. A. Sidney Hess, "A Procedure for Nonpartisan Dis-
    tricting: Development of Computer Techniques," *Yale Law Journal* 73
    (1963): 289.

———, "Districting by Machine," *National Civil Review* 53 (1964): 293.

The Bureaucracy   4

Daniel Ogden was a major participant in formulating proposals for the Redwood National Park, yet he is able to present a fair assessment of the proposals, strategies, and markets involved, many of which he opposed. More significantly, his study provides an opportunity for the student to view the costs and benefits associated with a particular policy in close detail. The impact of various proposals—the costs and benefits to the timber industry, local communities, the state of California, and to our environment—make this case particularly interesting from the perspective of public choice. A wide spectrum of additional topics are also given detailed scrutiny. One can observe the process by which an administration formulates specific programs, how various congressional committees are instrumental in guiding these proposals through the obstacle course facing legislation prior to its enactment into public policy, and how different interest groups exercise influence in the political system. Students might wish to examine this study carefully for examples of the competition and cooperation existing between government bureaucracies and interested clienteles and the expertise each provides.

    The making of public choices is an on-going process. The struggle for a redwood national park is not over. California has yet to cede to the federal government the three state parks comprising approximately half of the park's total acreage, even though the Nixon Administration directed the Navy Department to cede Pendleton Beach to California in April 1971. The National Park Service is still surveying the boundaries of the park, still promising a park master plan, and still trying to conciliate the timber interest. The timber companies are still cutting permanent scars in the forests around the park and still negotiating with the Nixon Administration over the price of the land they lost. The Sierra Club and other conservationists are again warning that a 58,000-acre park is too small and fragmented to be protected from the watershed-destroying logging that goes on a few hundred feet from its boundaries. A *Newsweek* magazine reporter, describing the park after touring the area, wrote that, as a result of the delays, the park is "like a partially sacked museum that still lets the vandals loiter in the courtyard."

DANIEL M. OGDEN, JR.

The Politics of Conservation:
Establishing the Redwood National Park

THE SITUATION

On October 2, 1968, President Lyndon Johnson signed into law an act establishing a redwood national park in northwestern California. The act set aside immediately, for the permanent use and enjoyment of the American people, 58,000 acres of redwood country that contain some of the most magnificent specimens of *Sequoia sempervirens* remaining on earth. Signing of this act also ended a remarkable struggle between competing interest groups, government agencies, and congressional committees.

The general public was the real victor in the redwood park act, for it gained a great natural asset to use and enjoy for generations to come. The competitive victor, however, was the Sierra Club. The Sierra Club not only overcame the opposition of the timber companies and their allies in local government and local business, but persuaded Congress to overrule Secretary of the Interior Stewart L. Udall, one of the nation's greatest champions of parks and preservation, and the Administration itself. It successfully argued that the administration proposal was too small and inadequate. Rarely has any group prevailed in such a situation.

The political struggle for the Redwood National Park passed through three distinct phases. First came a period of probing and negotiations as the key interested parties shaped their public positions. Next followed a confrontation of competing proposals in which pro-park forces divided and fought each other while anti-park forces rallied a diverse array of principally local opponents. Last came compromise and decision, the product

Daniel M. Ogden, Jr., "The Struggle for a Redwood National Park."

The content of this essay was the basis of one of a series of lectures on "the political economy of the preservation and development of outdoor recreational resources delivered by Dr. Ogden at the University of California, Berkeley, in February 1971, under the auspices of the Herman Royer Program in Political Economy. An essay based on his entire series of lectures will be published in early 1972 as part of a collection of essays by several authors, under the title *The Political Economy of Environmental Control*.

of a masterful display in the art of the possible by Senator Henry M. Jackson of Washington, Chairman of the Committee on Interior and Insular Affairs.

The Background of the Redwood Fight

Efforts to save the redwoods had been made for many years. As early as 1879 Secretary of the Interior Carl Schurz recommended withdrawal of 46,000 acres of prime coast redwoods. In 1901 the California legislature set aside Big Basin Redwoods State Park in Santa Cruz County. In 1908 Representative William Kent gave Muir Woods to the federal government, thus setting aside the first federal redwood park area. In 1918 the Save-the-Redwoods League was formed "to coordinate the efforts of the various organizations and individuals working to save the giant redwoods in their primitive condition." The league promptly identified four major target areas that were to become the four principal state redwood parks. Over the years the league raised funds, purchased land, and donated groves to the state.

In 1920 Secretary of the Interior John B. Payne, responding to a resolution by Representative Clarence Lea of Santa Rosa, California, had the Forest Service study the suitability of a redwood national park. The report recommended a 64,000-acre park on the lower Klamath River in Humboldt County and 1,800 acres on the South Fork of the Eel River. The proposal won a favorable report by the House Interior Committee and a bill to establish the park passed the House of Representatives without debate, but was never considered in the Senate.

In 1934 the National Forest Reservation Commission approved establishment of a redwood national forest. The California State Legislature enacted enabling legislation that same year and in 1935 the commission set up two redwood purchase units. The northern unit, which was to figure prominantly in the fight for the Redwood National Park, covered 263,000 acres in Del Norte and Humboldt counties. Only 14,491 acres were ever purchased—all in the northern unit.

The Physical Setting

The coast redwoods of California are native to a narrow ribbon of land that rarely extends farther inland than 30 miles and runs from extreme southwestern Oregon on the north to the Monterey peninsula on the south. Redwood trees covered some two million acres a century ago. By 1964 less than 300,000 acres of virgin stands remained, including some 50,000 acres set aside in park land.

Redwoods, the largest living plants, are also among the oldest living things on earth. Most of the large trees are over 500 years old and many are more than 1,000 years old. A few older trees have been found and a very few may even date back to the time of Christ. Their size, age, and awe-inspiring majesty give them special appeal. As the last remaining examples of the age of dinosaurs and giantism, they also offer science a valued look into the world of fifty million years ago.

By 1964, about 50,000 acres of redwoods had been saved in twenty-three scattered parks. Only one, Muir Woods National Monument near San Francisco, was part of the national park system. The rest were protected by the State of California. The bulk of the protected virgin timber was centered in four state parks.

The northernmost of these four state parks, reaching close to the Oregon border, was Jedediah Smith Redwoods State Park, displaying some of the grandest specimens of giant redwoods found along the bottom land of the Mill Creek where it enters the Smith River. Located northeast of Crescent City, California in Del Norte County, this park adjoined a large acreage of virgin timber located south and further upstream along Mill Creek, owned by the Rellim Lumber Company and slated for logging operations over a period of years.

The next unit to the south, also in Del Norte County, was Del Norte Coast Redwoods State Park, which stretched south from near Crescent City almost to the Klamath River and included several miles of unspoiled beach. Through it passed U.S. 101, the "Redwood Highway," a two-lane road that wound its way through the groves of huge trees and occasionally passed along the bluffs of the California coast.

The third major state park, also bisected by U.S. 101, lay south of the Klamath River and north of the town of Orick in Humboldt County. Named Prairie Creek Redwoods State Park, it, too, adjoined an area of substantial virgin timber to the south on other tributaries of Prairie Creek, especially Lost Man Creek, Little Lost Man Creek, May Creek, and, most importantly, Redwood Creek, where the National Geographic had found the Tall Trees.

A fourth state park that figured in some of the maneuvering but never given serious consideration as part of the Redwood National Park, was Humboldt Redwoods State Park. Lying south of Eureka and the Eel River in Humboldt County, it was the largest of the state parks but it could not be greatly expanded to preserve additional redwood groves because of earlier logging operations around it.

Timber company ownership and cutting patterns of redwood lands greatly affected the proposals and the actions of the various parties that were to enter the fight over a redwood national park. Timber company holdings north and east of Prairie Creek Redwoods State Park had been harvested systematically right up to the park boundary so that even the casual and uninformed visitor could easily follow the line of the park boundary both from the ground and especially from the air. To the south and east of Prairie Creek Redwoods State Park, three companies held virgin redwood stands. Largest holder was the Arcata Lumber Company, which owned property directly south of the park along Prairie Creek, the virgin lands in Lost Man and Little Lost Man creeks, and the largely virgin right bank of Redwood Creek, including the Tall Trees. Georgia-Pacific Lumber Company owned most of the left bank of Redwood Creek and had already logged much of the area to the west of the creek, especially in the lower stretches. The Simpson Lumber Company was also a major holder of land both in the Prairie Creek area and north of Jedediah Smith Redwoods State Park. A smaller outfit, Pacific Lumber Company, also held lands that at various times were considered for inclusion.

Thus five lumber companies owned and were logging property in the areas studied by the National Park Service. All were harvesting timber at a rate far in excess of reproduction, and all contended that the "mature" trees were "overripe" and had to be harvested to make room for new growth. New trees grow far more rapidly, especially for the first 100 years, and thus are far more productive from a timber company's point of view than an aged tree that grows very slowly.

PHASE I. PROBING AND NEGOTIATIONS

The fight that was to culminate in the Redwood National Park had its beginning in 1963. While Dr. Paul A. Zahl, senior natural scientist of the National Geographic Society, was exploring the virgin redwood forest along Redwood Creek in Humboldt County, he found a grove of trees that broke all known records. The tallest towered 367.8 feet. A short distance away another measured 367.4 feet, and a third, 364.3 feet, making them the world's first, second, and third tallest trees. Still others nearby ranked within the top ten.

The announcement of his discovery of the tall trees induced the National Geographic Society, in April 1963, to grant funds to the National Park Service to make a comprehensive study of coast redwoods and to prepare a report and recommendations for their preservation. The park service assigned to the task Chester Brown, a career park planner. Mr. Brown spent the best part of the next year studying redwoods and submitted his report in the spring of 1964.

On June 25, 1964, President Johnson reviewed the preliminary findings and asked Secretary Udall to have the study completed and to submit recommendations.

The first public step in the four-year fight for the Redwood National

Park came September 15, 1964, when the National Park Service published its "professional report" entitled, "The Redwoods—A National Opportunity for Conservation and Alternatives for Action." The park service recommended three alternative plans for a redwood national park. Plan 1, the largest, encompassed plan 2, which in turn encompassed the smallest, plan 3.

The National Park Service Report

The National Park Service proposed a substantial redwood national park of 53,600 acres based primarily upon the Redwood Creek drainage. It would encompass 10,330 acres of Prairie Creek Redwoods State Park; 21,300 acres on Redwood Creek; 14,280 acres on Lost Man and May creeks; and a 7,690-acre addition to Prairie Creek Redwoods Park. Nearly half the land, 22,580 acres, would be in virgin redwoods. The park would display the Tall Trees, Fern Canyon, and the Gold Bluffs among its other wonders. Plan 2 dropped Lost Man and May Creeks to reach 39,320 acres. Plan 3 cut the Redwood Creek acreage to 13,730, and left a park of 31,750 acres, with only 11,800 acres of virgin redwood.

Mill Creek, too, received attention, but as an addition to the state park system. All three plans urged federal grants-in-aid to buy 8,840 acres in Mill Creek adjacent to Jedediah Smith Redwoods State Park.

Park Service Plan 1 proposed acquiring major chunks of land from the three largest redwood timber companies; 18,395 arces from Arcata; 12,789 from Georgia Pacific; and 7,868 from Simpson. Whatever its professional merit, it was sure to unite the timber companies against the park.

The Fight over Highway Location

Meanwhile, the State Highway Department had noted the heavy increase in traffic on U.S. 101. Aware of its importance as a commercial highway to serve the lumber industry of northwestern California, the department proposed to replace the old two-lane highway with a modern four-lane interstate road. Routing of the new superhighway soon became highly controversial. The highway department proposed to ram the new expressway straight through Prairie Creek Redwoods State Park, or, alternatively, along the Gold Bluffs just west of the park above the beach.

Park supporters, particularly the Sierra Club and the Save-the-Redwoods League, immediately raised a loud outcry. They especially focused attention on Fern Canyon, which cut through the Gold Bluffs to the beach. An exquisite natural phenomenon,[1] it would be paved over by the highway proposal. Moreover, the Gold Bluffs beach was relatively unspoiled and was the home of the Roosevelt elk, which still roamed its reaches.

In 1965, as the controversy boiled, the Save-the-Redwoods League and the State of California jointly purchased the bulk of the Gold Bluffs area adjacent to Prairie Creek Redwoods State Park, including Fern Canyon, and added the area to the state park. This effectively killed the bluffs route as a highway, and after Governor Edmund G. (Pat) Brown intervened, the California Highway Commission in November of that year rejected all three routes proposed through Prairie Creek Redwoods State Park and directed a study to find a route east of the park boundaries.

Early Alternative Proposals

Three alternatives to the park service plan were soon offered: the state plan for redwood parks proposed by the California state park system, the Dana-Pomeroy plan published by the American Forestry Association, and the Redwood Park and Recreation Plan promoted by the Redwood Park and Recreation Committee, a twelve-man group of redwood lumber company executives and their supporters.

In February 1965, in a preliminary state plan for redwood parks, the state proposed the addition of substantial acreage of privately owned redwood lands to the existing state park system. Although the proposal had merit in state park terms it did not provide a basis for a redwood national park and never really affected the subsequent maneuvering over the national legislation.

In its May 1965 issue, *American Forests*[2] carried the American Forestry Association's plan, drafted by Samuel T. Dana, Dean Emeritus of the School of Natural Resources at the University of Michigan, and Kenneth Pomeroy, Chief Forester of the American Forestry Association. Dana and Pomeroy held that enough virgin stands of redwoods had been set aside and proposed that the Humboldt Redwoods State Park be converted to the Redwood National Park.

In their summary they consciously set forth the line the timber companies would use throughout the fight:

> Effectuation of the largest of the National Park Service's suggested plans would lead to substantial unemployment in the lumbering, wood products, and service industries, would disrupt plans of several of the larger timber owners for placing their lands under sustained yield management, would reduce the tax base of the counties and school districts and would permanently remove the lands purchased from the production of timber for commercial utilization.[3]

The American Forestry Association, having commissioned the Dana-Pomeroy study in mid-October 1964, adopted it on February 26, 1965, and accompanied its formal publication with a supportive editorial.[4] The association also urged specific additions to the state parks from lands the industry was willing to sell. The proposal was immediately dismissed in the Department of the Interior and never received serious consideration during the political maneuvering that followed.

The Redwood Park and Recreation Committee presented its plan at the American Forestry Association's Redwood Park Conference in San Francisco April 5, 1965, endorsed the Dana-Pomeroy plan and offered to sell to the State a number of scattered inholdings and small groves adjacent to existing state parks. In addition they offered to open to public recreation most of the industry-owned redwood lands, except, of course, those involved directly in logging operations.

The industry plan would have added less than 10,000 acres to the existing state park system, of which only 3,016 acres would have been "old growth" timber. Most was cutover land. However, several key tracts were offered, the most important among them being the 2,125-acre Gold Bluffs and Fern Canyon, which the state and the Save-the-Redwoods League immediately purchased. The other really significant suggestions were the Tall Tree site of 137 acres; the 809-acre Simpson Grove, lying between Jedediah Smith Redwoods State Park and the Smith River; a 1,647-acre extension of the Avenue of the Giants including 814 acres of virgin redwoods stretching northward on either side of the redwood highway along the Eel River.[5] Although the industry plan did not figure prominently in the serious bargaining over a redwood national park, it nevertheless identified appropriate acquisitions for the state park system over which there was substantial agreement and opened the way for creative additions within the budget available to the State.

PHASE II. CONFRONTATION OF COMPETING PROPOSALS

The Administration Proposal

The Administration proposal really began its life on February 8, 1965, when President Lyndon B. Johnson, in his Message on Natural Beauty of Our Country said, "In addition, I have requested the Secretary of the Interior, working with interested groups, to conduct a study of the desirability of establishing a redwood national park in California." In the year that followed, before S. 2962 was introduced February 23, 1966, Secretary Udall inaugurated a series of special studies and negotiated with conservation groups, federal and state agencies, the timber industry and key individual political leaders, especially Governor Edmund Brown and Senator Thomas Kuchel of California.

Positions hardened quickly. The five affected timber companies, meeting with George Hartzog, Director of the National Park Service, in his office on July 1, 1965, made clear their opposition to any redwood national park.

The Sierra Club, on the other hand, early made clear its unqualified support for the largest national park possible, and especially one that would save the bulk of the virgin timber along Redwood Creek.

The Save-the-Redwoods League centered its concern on saving the superlative groves in Jedediah Smith Redwoods State Park, which they felt were threatened by logging in the upper Mill Creek watershed. They felt that Redwood Creek, despite its large area, could not be protected, for the watershed was very large and most of its upper reaches was not redwood country. Moreover, Redwood Creek did not affect nearby Prairie Creek Redwoods State Park.

As events unfolded, the Bureau of the Budget determined the contents of the Administration's final proposal. Its determined eye on the federal dollar led it to place a $60 million limitation on land acquisition for the national park.

Such a limit foreclosed serious Administration attention to Redwood Creek, where a much larger sum of money would be necessary, and turned park officials toward Mill Creek, where the entire watershed could be acquired within the dollar limit the Bureau of the Budget had set to save an additional 8,540 acres of virgin timber and protect Jedediah Smith's precious groves. By buying the land between Jedediah Smith Redwoods State Park and Del Norte Coast Redwoods State Park, and including both parks, the national park could encompass 43,392 acres; nearly half—19,100 acres —would be virgin redwoods. The government would have to buy 24,960 acres of private land, of which 18,240 acres were held by the Rellim (or Miller) Redwood Company.

On June 19, 1965, representatives of Secretary Udall, the National Park Service, and the Bureau of Outdoor Recreation met with Phillip S. (Sam) Hughes, then Assistant Director of the Bureau of the Budget, and approved a preliminary plan. Fundamentally it was derived from the grant-in-aid proposal of the original National Park Service professional report.

Laurance Rockefeller, apprised of the situation and the probability of securing administration support for such a park, wrote the President on July 20, 1965, suggesting the Mill Creek area.

Ecological integrity was the central concept of the Administration proposal. Protection of redwoods along the bottomlands of a watershed was to very little purpose, the ecological argument held, if the uplands of the watershed were to be denuded by clear-cutting and the land permitted to erode. To preserve redwoods, man must preserve intact the entire physical environment in which they prosper. Preservation of key groves requires preservation of their entire watershed. As proof of the applicability of the principle, its advocates cited the Bull Creek experience in Humboldt Redwoods State Park. There the Save-the-Redwoods League and John D. Rockefeller had purchased only the high quality groves along the bottom lands and had left the steep wooded hillsides to the loggers. Clear cut, then burned, the hillsides eroded swiftly, filling Bull Creek with gravel and debris. Heavy rains in 1955 destroyed 300 big trees along Bull Creek.[6] Heavy rains in 1965 swept more than 10 feet of gravel and mud through the park picnic areas, forcing their complete replacement, and threatening the entire grove.

As negotiations proceeded without public announcements about alternative plans, the split in the pro-park forces became clear and pronounced. Newton Drewry, former Director of the National Park Service and a leader in the Save-the-Redwoods League, backed the Mill Creek proposal as the most that park advocates could hope to get.

The Sierra Club, led by Dr. Edgar Wayburn, David Brower, and Michael McCloskey, stood firm for a large park in Redwood Creek. They contended that it was too early to take fall-back positions and that the only proper attack was to ask for all that anyone could hope to get.

The Advisory Board on National Parks, Historic Sites, Buildings and Monuments, in a prophetic meeting on October 7, 1965, recommended a redwood national park designed to unite pro-park forces. It proposed a two-unit park, composed of a northern unit comprising the Mill Creek watershed with the two state parks and a southern unit consisting of Prairie Creek Redwoods State Park, the Gold Bluffs, Lost Man Creek drainage, and the lower portions of the Redwood Creek drainage, including the Tall Trees. The two units would be joined by a scenic corridor. The cost would have far exceeded the Budget Bureau's ceiling.

By October 14 Secretary Udall was ready to talk to Senator Thomas Kuchel of California and Representative Don Clausen from Crescent City about the proposal. A meeting in his office with Senator Kuchel; Representative Clausen's administrative assistant; George Hartzog, Director of the National Park Service; Edward C. Crafts, Director of the Bureau of Outdoor Recreation; and Elmer Staats, Associate Director of the Bureau of the Budget, reached substantial agreement on the essential shape of the Administration proposal, but pointed up the great difficulties left in trying to reach a concensus among the affected groups.

At this point, the Sierra Club decided the time had come to set publicly the outer demands for a large national park. On October 20, 1965, Representative Jeffrey Cohelan, Democrat of Berkeley, introduced H.R. 11705. It called for a major redwood national park of 97,000 acres primarily in the Redwood Creek drainage through the Emerald Mile, but including adjoining Lost Man, Little Lost Man, and Skunk Cabbage creeks and Prairie Creek Redwoods State Park, which by that time included the Gold Bluffs and Fern Canyon. Thus the Tall Trees would fall well within the Park boundaries. Some 42,000 acres of virgin timber would be saved.

The Sierra Club estimated the cost of its proposal at $120 million, twice Budget's figure. Opponents guessed $200 million and higher.

Throughout the fight for a redwood national park, the Sierra Club never really abandoned this plan, and the major portion of it became the heart of the park Congress finally established.

The club promptly followed up with a nationwide publicity campaign to build support for a large national park on Redwood Creek. A mighty assist came their way when the Arcata Lumber Company clear-cut its property south of Prairie Creek Redwoods State Park within sight of the Redwood Highway. Alert Sierra Clubbers took photographs of the desolate scene and cried that a similar fate awaited the magnificent groves nearby. Ads in major newspapers, pamphlets, talks, and a flood of cards, letters, and telegrams to members of Congress became their major weapons.

The Club's pressure advantage was enormous. Support for the park welled up from active conservationists throughout the nation. Opposition was centered entirely in one Congressional district in California, and it was so heavily weighted toward suburban San Francisco that no anti-park Congressman could survive. The Sierra Club thus demonstrated a basic political fact of life for conservationists: opposition to particular preservation proposals is usually local but support is national. Therefore, if decision-making can be placed at the national level, preservation can usually win.

Udall, meanwhile, chained to a $60-million park, maneuvered to minimize opposition. First he sent Director Crafts, a professional forester who had served 29 years with the forest service and had risen to Assistant Chief before moving to Interior to head the Bureau of Outdoor Recreation, to inspect the proposed park area. After a two-day trip, November 17 to 18, 1965, Director Crafts returned convinced that the Mill Creek area was really the best site for a park and contained the best specimens of giant redwoods. He never relinquished that belief, contending throughout the fight that Redwood Creek, save for the Tall Trees area, contained an almost uniform stand of 500-year-old trees, obviously dating from a major fire that had swept the area about the time Columbus discovered America. The Mill Creek area contained many larger and older trees.

On November 22 Udall met with officials of the State of California, representatives of Humboldt and Del Norte counties, members of the California Congressional delegation, conservation organizations, representatives of the redwood timber companies, and other landowners. The conferees reviewed all the current plans and expressed their views on each. A follow-up meeting the next day included Bureau of the Budget representatives, Irv Sprague for Governor Brown, timber industry representatives, and spokesmen for the National Park Service and the Bureau of Outdoor Recreation.

More talks on November 26 convinced the Secretary that the department lacked essential information about the economic impact of the park on the immediate region, and about the value and location of the superlative stands of redwood trees. He therefore asked for more definitive land, timber, and economic studies, especially encompassing Del Norte County. Because economic information was available on Humboldt County, and administration attention now was centering on Mill Creek in Del Norte County, the economic studies were to center on Del Norte and the impact of a park in Mill Creek.

Meetings immediately followed at the regional offices of the National Park Service and the Bureau of Outdoor Recreation in San Francisco. The new Chief of the Research Division of the Bureau of Outdoor Recreation, Dr. R. Burnell Held, was an economist acquired from Resources for the Future. He flew to San Francisco on his first day at work to spur negotiations with the Arthur D. Little Company for an economic study of Del Norte County. The National Park Service also employed the firm of Hammond, Jensen, and Wallin to conduct a land and timber study of the entire area in both counties.

As bill drafting on the Administration proposal proceeded, many clauses were added to quiet opponents. To meet objections by Del Norte County and its local school districts that the purchase of so much land would severely affect their tax base, "economic adjustment payments" were offered for a five-year period to help county and local governments offset tax losses while new business was developing. Payments were to equal three-fifths of one percent of the value of all properties acquired by the United States pursuant to the act—a figure designed to provide slightly more revenue than the local governments were then realizing from the lands.

At this point the state stepped into the negotiations to insist that under the state equalization laws, the State of California would make up much of the loss of tax revenues and that therefore the "economic adjustment payments" to school districts should be divided between them and the state so the school districts would not be paid twice.

Local businessmen and the employees of the lumber companies worried more about jobs, payrolls, and the amount of business that would be left in Del Norte County. The National Park Service therefore proposed a substantial development program that would create 71 permanent jobs within the first five years and spend more than $22 million in construction and operation of the park.

Initial calculations by Dr. Held demonstrated that the park would generate more jobs than the total elimination of the Rellim Company would cost. Rellim employed 207 people and generated direct jobs for 28 more. The park would create 210 jobs the first year, reach a peak of 432 the third, and level off at 330 the fifth, making an average *gain* of 90 jobs. Only in the first year would labor and business suffer a loss of about 25 jobs. Moreover his calculation assumed Rellim would shut down at once rather than process logs already on hand—a most unlikely event.

Calculations of the new tourist trade, and the multiplier effect of the added jobs, added up to a strong picture of permanent economic gain for the county.

Local businessmen were unimpressed by the analysis. They argued that lumbering was a year-round business, while tourism would be confined largely to the summer. They doubted that tourist figures would climb as rapidly as the park service estimated—despite the service's well-established habit of being excessively conservative in projecting park use.

To offset the Administration's work, the lumber industry employed Dewayne Kraeger, a Seattle economist, to make a separate study. Kraeger's report predictably showed that the timber industry's growth would bring prosperity to Del Norte; the park would ruin it.

Meanwhile, another study, by Arthur D. Little, was completed in March 1966 after the bill went in. This study found that in its first five years the park would not generate as much business nor as many jobs as the timber industry did, but thereafter it would generate more, at an ever-accelerating pace, while the timber industry would inevitably decline.

The central economic fact that the timber industry sought to hide and Administration forces sought to emphasize that the industry was then cutting timber at a rate that far exceeded the land's ability to sustain it. Once the old timber was harvested, the rate of growth of new timber would not sustain the existing industry. The industry could keep job levels at their 1964 rate only by converting to pulp and intensive wood utilization at the investment of large sums in plant and equipment. But permanent growth beyond 1964 levels was impossible. The resource simply was not there. In the long run, then, dependence on the lumber industry meant permanent operation at or below 1964 economic levels for the region. The Little report made this basic fact clear and, despite protracted arguments and counter-arguments, proved persuasive to most outside observers.

To meet the legitimate objections of organized labor, which pointed out that its skilled workmen would be displaced, as well as the concerns of local businessmen, the supporting statement accompanying the bill cited seven major federal programs that "might be used to assist Del Norte County and its citizens to adjust to changes that would be brought about by the establishment of a Redwood National Park." Among the suggestions were technical assistance, business loans, and grants for development facilities by the Economic Development Administration of the Department of Commerce; loans by the Small Business Administration; training grants from the Department of Labor and vocational education training from Health, Education, and Welfare; and public facility loans from the Department of Housing and Urban Development. Help from other programs, including the Community Action Program of the Office of Economic Opportunity, and the Farmers' Home Administration of Agriculture, also was suggested. None of these constituted special effort and proved unimpressive to labor, local businessmen, and civic leaders.

Hammond, Jensen, and Wallin reports, provided in April and July 1966, and followed by a more definitive analysis in March 1967, provided essential knowledge about the classes of trees, their location within the various park proposals, and ownership, but did not quell the controversy. It showed that superlative stands of giant redwood existed both in the Administration's proposed park and in the Sierra Club area.

Udall meanwhile was trying to find a basis for persuading the State of California to donate Jedediah Smith and Del Norte Coast parks as part of the Redwood National Park. Ample precedent existed for such state action. Virginia had purchased much of the land for Shenandoah National Park and given it to the federal government. North Carolina had offered Cape Lookout, which soon was to become a national seashore. On the other hand, recent park and recreation acquisition had come primarily from federal funds. Indeed, the establishment of the Land and Water Conservation Fund in September 1964 provided funds to accomplish just such acquisition.

California's initial reaction was to demand compensation for the parks, so it could invest the money in park land near its burgeoning cities to the south. Some state spokesmen even suggested that there might be legal questions about the ability of the legislature to authorize such donations, an issue that ultimately proved ill founded.

Secretary Udall knew he could not hope to buy the state parks with their enormously valuable stands of virgin timber. He therefore proposed a swap of federal lands for state lands in which he would make recreation lands nearer the centers of population available to California in return for the two state redwood parks. Moreover, he specifically offered to California the 31,000 acre King Range area, which included some seashore west of Humboldt Redwoods State Park, and Muir Woods National Monument just out of San Francisco. Both were to be used exclusively for park and recreation purposes, and the title would revert to the United States were they ever put to any other use.

By the time the bill was introduced, Governor Brown had agreed to use his good offices to try to obtain donation of the state parks, but never was able, of course, to promise that the state would donate them. Park managers therefore offered, as an alternative, the development of cooperative management agreements between state and federal park service personnel to ensure coordinated management of the parks.

Udall also sought to help the state acquire added lands for its other redwood parks by using a special part of the grant funds from the new Land and Water Conservation Fund.

The bill contained one other key bit of strategy—an attempt to split the solid front of the timber companies. By centering on the Mill Creek watershed, the administration proposal avoided the property of the three largest companies, Georgia-Pacific, Arcata, and Simpson, as well as the smallest, Pacific. It would, however, virtually wipe out Rellim.

Rellim was a branch operation of the Miller Lumber Company. It centers in Oregon and produces mainly pine and fir products. Park supporters calculated that liquidation of the California redwood holdings would not threaten the principal Miller operation and would reduce competition within the redwood industry. They therefore reasoned that Miller's competitors would stand with him until defeat was certain, then enjoy the benefits of dividing his redwood market.

Thus the bill tried to meet as many objections as it could by providing something for local government, something for the state, something for business and labor, and even something for most of the redwood timber companies. And for the Miller Company's 71-year-old president and principal owner, it even offered $40 million in cash for his California holdings.

To make the bill's introduction as auspicious as possible, Administration forces held up until the day the President sent Congress his Message Transmitting Programs for Controlling Pollution and Preserving Our Natural and Historical Heritage.[7] In his message, President Johnson declared:

I propose the creation of a Redwood National Park in northern California.

It is possible to reclaim a river like the Potomac from the carelessness of man. But we cannot restore—once it is lost—the majesty of a forest whose trees soared upward 2,000 years ago. The Secretary of the Interior—after exhaustive consultations with preservationists, officials of the State of California, lumbermen, and others—has completed a study of the desirability of establishing a park of international significance.

I have reviewed his recommendations and am submitting to the Congress legislation to establish such a park. This will be costly. But it is my recommendation that we move swiftly to save an area of immense significance before it is too late.

On February 23, 1966, Senator Thomas Kuchel, Republican of California, introduced the Administration bill as S. 2962. Representative Don Clausen, Republican of California's First District, which includes the redwoods, introduced the Administration's bill that same day and then later introduced a modified version as H.R. 13042.

The Subcommittee on Parks and Recreation of the Senate Committee on Interior and Insular Affairs, led by its chairman, Henry M. Jackson of Washington, and its ranking Republican member, Senator Kuchel of California, moved first. It scheduled field hearings in Crescent City, California for June 17 and 18, 1966, then added hearings in Washington August 17.[8]

The Crescent City hearings immediately demonstrated that few people were really *for* the Administration bill. Most park advocates wanted a bigger park; opponents wanted none.

Senator Kuchel, leading the Administration bill's proponents systematically showed how the bill had been designed to set aside an adequate park area, protect the interests of the State of California, maintain income for the local governments, protect the labor force, maintain business levels, and minimize the impact upon the redwood lumber industry. But he proved to be the bill's only major defender.

Across the capitol, Colorado's Representative Wayne Aspinall, Chairman of the House Interior Committee, seeing the pileup of controversy, preferred to wait. With Governor Brown locked in a major duel for his job with Ronald Reagan, he knew that no decision was likely in 1966.

In California, meanwhile, the Rellim Lumber Company moved to preclude a redwood national park carved from its Mill Creek property by cutting big trees along the boundaries of Jedediah Smith State Park and by running new logging roads along key stands of timber. Its actions soon came to the attention of sharp-eyed Save-the-Redwoods Leaguers who called the cutting to Secretary Udall's attention.

On August 17, 1966, Udall sought to stop Rellim's cutting within the proposed national park. He invited to his office Harold Miller, owner of the Rellim Redwood Company, and Darrell Schroeder, company counsel, to explore ways to end the cutting and yet protect the company's business interests. Udall suggested that funds might be available from private foundations to keep the company intact pending enactment of the redwood park legislation.

The next day Mr. Miller sent Udall a letter summarizing the conversation and touching off a bitter controversy that was to involve the Senate

Interior Committee and build public support for prompt action to save the redwoods. Miller flatly refused to negotiate on his cutting, saying:

> As we understand it, based upon the conversations, all of these negotiations would be contingent upon the company picking up and moving its cutting operations. Yet, you are aware that we had, only within the hour, testified that any moving of the cutting operations as described by yourself, would force the company to close down. This is apparently a condition precedent to such negotiations and as long as it remains as a condition, in all good faith we must advise you that we see no point in taking up your time and our time with such discussions.

Secretary Udall struck back on August 19 with a stinging reply that with Miller's letter, he released to the public the following day:

> This will acknowledge receipt of your letter of August 18, 1966. You refused to conduct a good-faith negotiation to devise a solution that would simultaneously protect the economic position of your company, preserve the integrity of the proposed national park, and give the Congress time to deliberate. This is incredible.
>
> The Senate Committee hearings held in Crescent City last month and in Washington this week make it clear there is overwhelming sentiment in Congress and the country for a redwoods national park. It is also plain from the statement which I made publicly at the hearing last Wednesday—and the assurances which I gave you later at my office—that we can obtain Foundation commitments which will enable us to pay your company losses it might sustain by moving your cutting operation outside the Park area.
>
> Your unwillingness to even seriously discuss such a generous solution can only mean that you and your associates have elected to pursue an outrageous public-be-damned, conservation-be-damned approach to this whole issue.
>
> Your reply makes it crystal clear that you and your company are determined to defeat by any means available the national park plan transmitted to the Congress by President Johnson last February. I can only conclude, therefore, that the location of your logging operations along the state park boundary and in other key spots is, in reality, a spite cutting action designed to destroy the great trees whose preservation is the main purpose of a park in the Mill Creek watershed.

Secretary Udall and Senator Kuchel of California turned to President Johnson for aid. On September 1, the President asked Congress for an emergency one-year prohibition on cutting of trees in the proposed park area.

At this point, Senator Jackson asserted the leadership he finally had to display to bring about enactment of the Redwood National Park legislation. Supported by Senator Kuchel, he personally negotiated a moratorium on cutting with Miller and Simpson, and other affected companies.

On September 8 he received, from Miller, Simpson, and the Georgia-Pacific companies, written assurances that they would defer logging operations. The Miller Company indicated it had planned to move to higher ground during the winter anyway and added, "However, out of deference to the President of the United States, and to you as Chairman of the Interior and Insular Affairs Committee of the Senate, and to Congressman Wayne Aspinall as Chairman of the House Committee on Interior and Insular Affairs, we will immediately cease cutting down trees in the area near the alleged park-type redwoods on the flats which are adjacent to the Jedediah Smith State Park." There would be no cost to the government.

That same day, at a special press conference, Senator Jackson announced that both Miller and Simpson had agreed to refrain from cutting old growth redwoods in the proposed park area. Although the carefully worded statements by the companies left some park proponents less than satisfied, Secretary Udall promptly issued a statement of congratulations.

A Changed Administration in Sacramento

Meanwhile the Brown-Reagan campaign was raising doubts about the future attitude of the State of California on the national park issue. Reagan, queried by a reporter about his attitude on the redwood park, was reported to have commented, "When you've seen one, you've seen 'em all." Widely circulated, this remark led one opposition cartoonist to depict the Republican candidate saying, "When you've seen one redwood, you've seen all we've got!"

Finding this publicity highly impolitic, Reagan then took the first of several positions on the redwood park that ultimately ended in his completely reversing his position. On October 19, in the height of the campaign, he wrote the National Park Service stating that he favored the lumber-industry-backed "Redwood Park and Recreation Plan." Then, on November 8, election day, using stationery labeled "Ronald Reagan, Governor-Elect, State of California" he wrote Robert Lunty, Acting Chief of the Office of Resource Planning of the National Park Service in San Francisco, that he preferred the modified proposal then being sponsored by Congressman Don Clausen.

Reagan's election thus brought joy to the ranks of park opponents; concern to park supporters. The opening days of the Reagan administration compounded these feelings. Early in January 1967 the new governor asked for a ninety-day delay in action on the proposal until his administration could study the situation and arrive at a position. His wishes were honored.

To head the Resources Agency of California, the new governor picked

Norman B. Livermore. A member of a noted California lumbering family, Mr. Livermore had also been a leader in the Sierra Club. He promptly became the chief California negotiator with the Department of the Interior over the redwood park proposal.

Negotiations soon revealed that Governor Reagan would use the state redwood parks to bargain with the federal government. Several pieces of federal property especially interested him. Of prime importance was a mile and a half of especially desirable surfing beach in the northwest corner of Camp Pendleton. He also showed interest in several parcels of land under the administration of the Bureau of Land Management that were located near urban centers in southern California. Secretary Udall and former Governor Brown had earlier called for a study of these lands and a team representing the Bureau of Land Management, the Bureau of Outdoor Recreation, and The Resources Agency of California had reported its findings in December 1966.[9]

The Forest Service Land Trade Issue

Most controversial of all, however, was Reagan's proposal that if the park were authorized the remnants of the northern redwood purchase unit of the Forest Service be traded to the Miller Company as partial compensation for its holdings.

Concern that such a trade might be part of a redwood national park proposal had arisen in the Forest Service at the very beginning of the controversy. On September 14, 1964, Secretary of Agriculture Orville Freeman had written Secretary Udall reporting "a persistent rumor that plans are afoot to trade National Forest lands for National Park purposes in the creation of the proposed Redwood National Park" and asking for either assurance that Interior had no such intentions or that a mutual understanding on such a proposal be worked out. Udall had responded on September 28, "I can assure you that this idea is not being considered or advocated here as part of the over-all plan."

At stake was a basic principle of federal land management: that lands needed in one federal program should not be used to provide lands for another federal program. Director Edward C. Crafts of the Bureau of Outdoor Recreation summarized the problem succinctly in a memorandum to Secretary Udall:

The danger lies in setting a precedent that would invite the timber industry to dismember the national forests by using them for payment in kind whenever the government takes private timberland for highways, reservoirs, parks, or any other public purpose.

Yet the issue kept bobbing up. On July 4, 1966, *The New York Times* had run a Sunday feature article on the millions of dollars the United States was collecting by harvesting redwood trees from its redwood purchase unit in California. The article reported the proposal to trade the unit (which was being commercially harvested anyway) for land suitable for a park and revealed the Forest Service attitude. Udall followed up by suggesting personally to Freeman that the redwood tract be protected from cutting as a natural area, then on September 19 sent the article to Freeman with a letter. Apparently discounting the political liability that continued cutting created, the Forest Service prepared a reply for Freeman the following January that rejected the Udall suggestion with the statement that the land on the northern redwood purchase unit was "ordinary redwood timberland. It is not unique nor outstanding." The Forest Service intended to go right on permitting commercial harvesting of the trees.

Following the state proposal, the Forest Service, through its Chief, Edward P. Cliff, made a similar, detailed statement on March 24, 1967, to Phillip S. Hughes, Deputy Director of the Bureau of the Budget, opposing the payment-in-kind principle. In the statement, Cliff considered, but rejected the establishment of a "cooperative sustained-yield unit" in the purchase unit, which would provide logs for the Miller Company because the existing cut was already being fully used by small commercial loggers and mills in the area.

Director Crafts, in a memorandum to Secretary Udall that same day, repeated the possibility that Interior, through the Bureau of Land Management, would join in such a "cooperative sustained-yield unit" to meet Miller's needs but pointed out the key issue was Miller's tax situation: "A sustained-yield unit approach would not appeal to Miller because he would be paid for his land and would have to buy back timber at government-controlled prices. This would not give Miller the tax advantage he would gain under a swap of government land and timber for his land and timber." Moreover, Crafts pointed out, nothing could be accomplished unless Miller were willing to negotiate, for he could always force condemnation and probably get a court award exceeding the purchase price ceiling Congress would set.

The Forest Service had thus painted itself into a political corner. It had admitted that the northern redwood purchase unit was an isolated tract, apart from other national forests, that it had no value for recreation purposes or as a "natural area," that it was being used primarily to produce commercial timber, and that the Service intended to continue to use it primarily to produce commercial timber. Members of Congress were going to be hard pressed to reject the exchange proposal if ever it were seriously presented to them.

Reagan had thus been offered the political vehicle to enable him to change sides. He could now win timber industry forgiveness and regain support from conservation interests by insisting upon barter of the purchase unit as the price for his support for a national park.

Hard bargaining then ensued between Reagan and his representatives, led by Norman Livermore, and Udall and his men, led by Ed Crafts. Key intermediary in the negotiations became Laurance S. Rockefeller, brother of the governor of New York, a leading conservationist but also a leading Republican. Long a champion of park causes, Mr. Rockefeller proved to be an able and effective broker.

On April 3, 1967, Mr. Rockefeller met with representatives of the state in Sacramento. He came armed with a variety of memoranda covering the future of Point Reyes National Seashore, a national park road from Orick through Jedediah Smith State Park and traversing the proposed national park; a statement from Defense on the availability of the beach at Camp Pendleton; a statement from Budget that if the Mill Creek unit were established the Administration would not seek to enlarge the park in the Redwood Creek area; and a memorandum exploring the possibility of an Interior-sponsored cooperative sustained yield unit to serve Miller property in Oregon.

Meanwhile the contending forces were laying their proposals substantially unchanged before the new 90th Congress. On January 18, 1967, Senator Lee Metcalf, for himself and nineteen other Senators, introduced the Sierra Club proposal. The all-liberal Democratic sponsors included Majority Leader Mansfield and Robert and Edward Kennedy. Representative John Saylor of Pennsylvania, ranking Republican on the House Interior Committee, sponsored an identical bill in the House as H.R. 1311.

The Administration also re-entered the fray. On January 30, 1967, in his Message to the Congress on Protecting our Natural Heritage, President Johnson again called for a redwood national park. On March 11 the Administration submitted its proposal, which Senator Kuchel promptly introduced as S. 1370 with the co-sponsorship of such influential Senators as Edward Kennedy of Massachusetts and Scott of Pennsylvania. In the House, chairman Aspinall introduced it, by request, as H.R. 11070.

Congressman Don Clausen, caught between park opponents in the sparsely settled northern end of his district and park supporters in the populous southern end, sought a positive alternative to what he viewed as the all-or-nothing positions of the major contestants. On March 23, 1967, he introduced H.R. 7742, to establish a national redwood park and seashore.

Although he proposed a park of 53,000 acres, the bulk of the area would be acquired by incorporating five existing state parks and extending park boundaries one mile to sea. Only 1,500 additional acres of virgin redwoods would have been saved,[10] and the bill denied condemnation power to acquire the land. A King's Range national recreation area and land exchange features rounded out the package. Senator George Murphy of California introduced a companion bill, S. 1526. The positive contribution of the Clausen bill, which ultimately became part of the Redwood National Park, was the protection of nearly 40 miles of California beach.

Park advocates immediately dismissed the bill because it did not address itself to saving redwoods. Park opponents did not really view it as a viable alternative to the Administration proposal. As a result, the Clausen bill received very little serious consideration.

Senator Alan Bible, Chairman of the Subcommittee on Parks and Recreation, promptly called hearings for April 17 to 19. Essentially the contending parties merely reiterated their stands. The only significant new position was that of Governor Reagan, presented on his behalf by his executive secretary, Philip M. Battaglia.

Governor Reagan flatly supported creation of a redwood national park, but conditioned his support upon the Administration's acceptance of eight principles designed to offer something to each of the conflicting parties:

1. The park must not deprive the residents of the area of their jobs.
2. The State of California must receive full, fair, and equal value from the Federal Government and its agencies for any State land incorporated into the national park.
3. Private interests which give up land and timber should receive fair exchange in fee title to a like kind of property.
4. Consideration should be given to the inclusion of seashore areas.
5. Other means available to maintain and encourage the economy of this area should be used.
6. Full in-lieu taxes (should be paid) on a permanent basis so that local government units . . . will not experience further hardship.
7. Harassment of the lumber industry must stop.
8. The interests and goals of the various conservation groups must be given prime consideration.[11]

The House Interior Committee promptly followed suit with hearings in Washington from June 27 to 29 and on July 12 and 19.

PHASE III. COMPROMISE AND DECISION

Having heard enough, Senator Henry M. Jackson of Washington began the search for an acceptable compromise that would unite pro-park forces and minimize opposition. He and Senator Thomas Kuchel of California, ranking Republican on the Interior Committee "came to the conclusion that a new measure was required, combining what we considered to be the best features of the bills before the Senate, and taking into account the financial limitations facing us and the impact on the affected area."[12] Accordingly they asked the committee staff, led by Jerry Verkler, to draft a new bill that would achieve those ends.

Freed from having to choose between the competing plans and to work within Budget's dollar limits, the staff moved to a compromise that combined the most attractive features of both contending proposals and threw in the constructive elements of Congressman Clausen's bill as well. The upshot was a committee bill, S. 2515, that Senators Jackson, Kuchel, and Alan Bible introduced on October 10, 1967.

The Senate Report

On October 12, 1967, the Senate Committee on Interior and Insular Affairs recommended S. 2515. It proposed a $100 million national park of 64,000 acres, 21,000 acres larger than the Administration proposal, and 33,000 acres smaller than the Sierra Club plan.

For the Administration's forces, the committee offered a north unit consisting of "Jedediah Smith Redwood State Park, Del Norte Coast Redwood State Park, land along the Smith River north of the Jedediah Smith Park suitable for development for camping and intensive use, a coastal strip extending from Del Norte Coast Redwood Park southward to the mouth of the Klamath River, a wide corridor between the two state parks, a large and superlative area of old growth redwoods in the Mill Creek Basin south of the Jedediah Smith Park, and an area on Bald Hill at the eastern extremity of the Mill Creek Basin suitable for camping and intensive use."[13] The total area, 28,540 acres, would add some 3,000 acres of primeval redwoods to public ownership. The Administration proposal for that area would have saved 7,780 acres of privately owned giant trees.

For the Sierra Club forces, and the committee offered a south unit, based essentially upon Redwood Creek and its tributaries. It included Prairie Creek Redwoods State Park, "a coastal trip from the vicinity of the mouth of the Klamath River south" to the park, the Prairie Creek watershed south of the park and west of U.S. Highway 101, "the entire Skunk Cabbage Creek drainage, a major portion of the Lost Man Creek drainage, the entire Little Lost Man Creek drainage, approximately 3 miles of the lower Redwood Creek drainage, and a narrow corridor south along Redwood Creek to include alluvial flats containing extraordinary examples of the tallest redwoods."[14]

The south unit, totaling 37,844 acres, would save 10,013 acres of old-growth redwood outside state parks. The Sierra Club's plan would have saved about 30,000 acres,

The committee also dropped most of the Administration's proposals to placate the various special interests in the region. Gone were the economic adjustment payments, which the committee dismissed as a form of in-lieu tax payment that would not be "in the national interest." Gone also were the provisions to give Muir Woods National Monument and the King Range area to the state, for Governor Reagan had indicated no interest in either.

Instead, the committee sought to strengthen the hands of park advocates. Added was the highly controversial provision authorizing exchange of the northern redwood purchase unit for privately owned lands within the park. Added also was a specific provision establishing the park, whether the state donated the state parks or not, and providing for cooperative management if it did not. Rejected was the concept that the federal government would compensate a state for lands, already in a state park, that would become part of a national park. Federal release of surplus lands for state park purposes were to be left as a separate issue to be settled parcel by parcel on the merits of each proposal.

The question of whether there would be a redwood national park was now settled. There would be. The redwood lumber industry simply could not muster a single sympathetic vote in either House of Congress to oppose this new park proposal outright.

Two interrelated issues remained: how big would the park be and whether Congress would authorize exchange of the northern redwood purchase unit to buy park land. The exchange issue became the principal fight on the Senate floor. The size issue became the principal fight on the House floor and the central issue in the conference between the two houses.

Anticipating that the Senate would take up the Interior Committee's redwood park bill on October 31, 1967, leaders of the Committee on Agriculture and Forestry announced in advance that they would move to strike the provision that authorized use of the northern redwood purchase unit for trading purposes.[15] Immediately upon the bill's call-up, Senator Allen Ellender of Louisiana, Chairman of the Agriculture and Forestry committee, sent his motion to the desk.[16] Debate thereafter in the Senate, both that day and the next, centered almost entirely upon whether national forest land should be traded to buy national park land.

Ellender's argument was simple: the Week's Act, the authority under which the land had been acquired, explicitly prohibited such trading. He quoted section 11: "the lands acquired under this Act shall be permanently reserved, held, and administered as national forest lands."

Moreover, he argued Secretary Udall in a letter to Senator Clinton

Anderson of New Mexico, dated July 13, 1967, had explicitly rejected use of national forest lands for trading purposes. Udall had said:

> The position of the Administration is firm against the transfer of National Forest lands to the State of California or to private lumber interests as part of the Redwood National Park transactions. We feel this general principle must be upheld always.
> It has been the long-standing position of the Government, and I know you are in agreement with this, that the National Forests should be maintained intact by the Federal government in the public interest, payment should be in cash and not in kind. I agree with this principle and you need have no concern on this point insofar as the Administration is concerned.[17]

The Interior and Insular Affairs Committee, argued Ellender, was overruling both the Interior and Agriculture departments as well as the President on a matter of basic principle.

Senator Jackson responded for the Interior Committee by pointing out that both the Interior and Agriculture departments have wide authority to exchange public land for private land to consolidate or "block-up" holdings to improve administrative management. "If the 14,500 acres were now in the hands of the Interior Department for administration," he declared, "there would not even be debate. I think Senators should understand that this is an ancient fight between the Department of Agriculture and the Department of the Interior which goes back to 1908."

To prove his point, Jackson then produced a letter from Secretary Udall, dated October 31, 1967, in which Udall voiced the first major break in Administration ranks on the purchase unit issue:

> If the Congress considers the land exchange provision to be absolutely essential to enactment of the legislation, the Administration is presented with a new policy issue which must be resolved. As yet, for obvious reasons, the Administration has taken no stand one way or the other on this specific question. If the creation of the Redwoods Park hinges on this kind of compromise, I can only express my own personal view that such a compromise would be acceptable only if everyone concerned pledged firm adherence in the future to the existing policy of protecting the Federally owned lands in our National Forests against land exchange.[18]

The outcome was now no longer in doubt. Every Senator knew that if pro-park forces were to unite behind any bill, a larger park than the Administration had proposed was essential. Jackson had added authority to exchange the northern redwood purchase unit in order to acquire a much larger park without enormously inflating the purchase price. Jackson thus had proposed a winner and Udall had now indicated he was prepared to make every effort to swing the Administration behind Jackson's bill. The roll-call vote on November 1 was 30 for the Anderson-Ellender amendment, 51 against.

Final passage of the bill followed immediately 77 to 6, demonstrating the overwhelming support the park proposal had gained.

The Senate's action put the Bureau of the Budget squarely on the spot. Secretary Udall and the National Park Service, well aware that the Senate bill was a much better proposal than the one they had managed to sell the Bureau of the Budget, promptly began lobbying quietly within the Administration to swing the President behind S. 2515. Only the Forest Service raised objections—and only to the provision permitting exchange of the northern redwood purchase unit.

The House Report

The focus of attention now passed to the House Interior Committee. With steam building up to create a redwood national park before President Johnson left office, Congressman Wayne Aspinall, House Interior Committee chairman, stalled action on the redwood park bill until after enactment of a crucial amendment to the Land and Water Conservation Fund. Created in 1964 the fund's $110 million per year had proved unable to provide state outdoor recreation grants and also sufficient money to buy land for new national parks, seashores, and recreation areas. An original champion of the fund, Aspinall had been leading a fight to extend it to $200 million a year using revenues from oil leases on the outer continental shelf.

Aspinall nevertheless had to show some action on the redwood park bill, so on April 16, 1968 he held field hearings in Crescent City and on April 18 in Eureka, California.

At the hearings, the State of California made a significant further concession. Speaking through Norman Livermore and William Penn Mott, Director of State Parks and Recreation, Governor Reagan agreed to inclusion of all three northern redwood state parks within the boundaries of the Redwood National Park and offered either to enter into cooperative management agreements with the park service "or to recommend to the State Legislature the donation of these three State Parks to the Federal government for incorporation into a redwood national park."[19]

Seeing the possibility of a significant breakthrough for the exchange principle, the redwood timber companies also indicated increased willingness to negotiate for sale of company holdings within the proposed park area.[20]

These two events greatly strengthened Udall's hand inside the Administration. Budget, led by Deputy Director Phillip S. Hughes, a long-time red-wood park advocate agreed to back the Senate-passed bill with the provision that three letters go simultaneously on May 17 to Chairman Aspinall, one from Secretary Orville Freeman of Agriculture endorsing the Senate bill but objecting strenuosuly to the exchange provision and one from Hughes concurring with the report by the Department of the Interior. Udall's letter carefully refrained from taking a position on the exchange question and Hughes' letter carefully endorsed only Udall's report! Thus the Administration's position was painfully clear: it did not want to go on record in approval of the exchange provision because of the bad precedent it would set. On the other hand, the saving in cash outlay that the exchange could accomplish was so enormous that Budget would not protest inclusion of the exchange provision in the act. By this device Budget could "hold the line" on expenditures while meeting the Sierra Club half way by supporting the Senate-passed bill.

The move was not lost on the Sierra Club. It promptly joined in strong support of the Senate bill thus uniting pro-park forces for the most difficult hurdle—the House Interior Committee.

More House hearings followed in Washington from May 20 to 22, centered primarily on the controversial provision to use the northern redwood purchase unit for exchange purposes.

With the Land and Water Conservation Fund amendment enacted to ensuré funds with which to purchase the park, Aspinall moved promptly to propose a countercompromise to the Senate-passed bill. On July 3, 1968, his Committee recommended an emasculated version of the Sierra Club proposal in the form of an amendment to S. 2515. The park would contain but 28,400 acres, and would save only 5,160 acres of additional old growth trees, largely on Redwood Creek. Essentially it consisted of Del Norte Coast Redwoods State Park, Prairie Creek Redwoods State Park, and a strip of coastal land connecting the two, a Redwood Creek Corridor, including the Tall Trees and the Sierra Club's "Emerald Mile"; and uplands adjacent to the Emerald Mile. Twenty-four miles of coastline would be protected. Cost was estimated at $56,750,000—just under the Bureau of the Budget ceiling. An added $10 million was authorized for park development.

Even more significantly, the Committee deleted the controversial provision permitting exchange of the northern redwood purchase unit. As a special concession to the concept of protecting entire watersheds, the Committee added authority for the Secretary of the Interior to negotiate agreements with the land owners to follow practices in logging that would "protect the trees, soil and streams within the park."[21]

The final issue was now clear-cut: A small park and no exchange provision versus a large park and exchange.

Unhappiness with Aspinall's bill was immediate, vocal, and widespread. Ten members of the Committee entered supplemental views calling the proposal inadequate.[22] Newspapers from the *San Francisco Chronicle* to *The New York Times* denounced the proposal. Supporters of the park called for early debate and amendment on the floor to produce a park "worthy of the name."

At this point Aspinall engaged in a parliamentary maneuver he defended as necessary. The move, however, won him further condemnation from park supporters from both sides of the aisle. Reporting that the Rules Committee had informed him it was too late to obtain a special rule to consider the bill during the session of Congress, Aspinall arranged to move consideration of the bill under suspension of the rules on July 15, 1968.[23] This move made the bill unamendable. Outraged, park supporters obtained the signatures of 73 congressmen on a petition denouncing the maneuver and demanding an opportunity to propose expansion on the floor.[24] Congressman Phillip Barton of San Francisco, sponsor of a large park bill, declared that he had checked with several members of the Rules Committee and that a Rule could have been secured. He concluded, "We must now accept the outrageously inadequate proposal for a redwood national park . . . or it will again be too late."[25]

John Saylor, ranking Republican on the Interior Committee, a sponsor of the Sierra Club bill and sure to be a member of the Conference Committee that would inevitably be appointed, denounced Aspinall's maneuver on the floor of the House and candidly declared, "The final bill will be written when we go to Conference. . . . I pledge to the Members my efforts for a larger Redwood National Park."[26] He then proceeded to discuss the *Senate* version of the bill and to vote with Barton and 13 others in protest *against* the final passage of the House version.

Most members, however, realized that the tactical situation now demanded prompt passage of any version of S. 2515. Given the attitude of most prospective conferees, the House version obviously would not prevail. The roll-call vote was 389 yeas, 15 nays, reflecting the political mileage that a pro-park vote meant back home for virtually all members and the difficulty most faced in explaining a "no" vote as a protest against the bill's shortcomings.[27]

Compromise in Conference

Jackson and Aspinall then led a ten-man Conference Committee to decision. On September 11, 1968, the Conferees reported agreement on a redwood national park bill that closely resembled the Senate version.

The park would contain 58,000 acres, including approximately 32,500 acres of virgin redwood, and would cost $92 million. All three state parks were within the boundaries, accounting for 27,468 of the acres and the bulk of the giant trees. Added to the Senate version was the "Emerald Mile" on Redwood Creek above the Tall Trees. Out was the Skunk Cabbage drainage. The park was established without requiring donation of the state parks, and provision was made for cooperative management agreements as an alternative. No ceiling was placed on park development, but the park service would be expected to lay its plans before Congress before implementing them.

The northern redwood purchase unit, except for the 935-acre Yurok Experimental Forest, would be available for trading. Thus the choice was made: a large park with exchange rather than a small park without exchange.

Most important of all, however, was a brand new provision the Solicitor of the Department of the Interior had earlier recommended to the House Committee but which the Committee had turned down: an immediate "legislative taking" of the property:

"Sec. 3 (b) (1) Effective on the date of enactment of this Act, there is hereby vested in the United States all right, title, and interest in, and the right to immediate possession of, all real property within the park boundaries." State parks and existing private residences were exempted. Thus did the conferees end price speculation during negotiations with the owners, the possibility of spite cutting, and the possibility that large sections might never be acquired for want of appropriated funds. The cost of the park became an immediate debt of the United States. The only issue left was the amount owed.

The House accepted the Conference report promptly on September 12, passing the act with but one dissenting vote.[28] The Senate followed September 19 by voice vote.

On October 2, 1968, the Redwood National Park Act became Public Law 90–545. At a special White House ceremony that afternoon, President Lyndon B. Johnson signed the "conservation grand-slam"—four key outdoor recreation laws that marked the culmination of years of hard work: the Redwood Park, the North Cascades National Park, the National Trails System Act, and the Wild and Scenic Rivers Act.

Notes

[1] Melville Bell Grosvenor, "A Park to Save the Tallest Tree," *National Geographic* 130, No. 1 (July 1966): 67.

² Samuel T. Dana and Kenneth B. Pomeroy, "Redwoods and Parks," *American Forests* 71 (May, 1965): 3–32.

³ *Ibid.,* p.˙ 32.

⁴ *Ibid.,* p. 36 and p. 37.

⁵ Redwood Park and Recreation Committee, *The Redwood Park and Recreation Plan* (Eureka, California: 1965).

⁶ Melville B. Grosvenor, "A Park to Save the Tallest Tree," p. 63.

⁷ U.S. Congress, House, *Preserving Our Natural Heritage,* Document 387, 89th Cong., 2d sess., 1966, p. 8.

⁸ U.S. Congress, Senate, *Redwood National Park,* Hearings before the Subcommittee on Parks and Recreation of the Committee on Interior and Insular Affairs, U.S. Senate, 89th Cong., 2d sess., 1966.

⁹ Bureau of Land Management, Bureau of Outdoor Recreation, The Resources Agency of California, *Possible Use of Certain Federal Public Domain Lands for California State Park System Purposes* (December, 1966). (Mimeographed.)

¹⁰ See U.S. Congress, House, *Authorizing the Establishment of the Redwood National Park in the State of California, and for Other Purposes,* 1968, H. Rept. 1630, p. 5.

¹¹ U.S. Congress, Senate, *Redwood National Park,* Hearings before the Subcommittee on Parks and Recreation, Committee on Interior and Insular Affairs, 90th Cong.. 1st sess., 1967, pp. 64–65.

¹² U.S. Congress, *Congressional Record,* 90th Cong., 2nd sess., 1968, S11042.

¹³ U.S. Congress, Senate, 90th Cong., 1st sess., 1967, S. Rept. 641, p. 4.

¹⁴ *Ibid.*

¹⁵ U.S. Congress, *Congressional Record,* Vol. 113, Part 23, p. 30326.

¹⁶ *Ibid.,* p. 30650.

¹⁷ *Ibid.,* p. 30746.

¹⁸ *Ibid.,* p. 30750.

¹⁹ U.S. Congress, House, *Authorizing the Establishment of the Redwood National Park in the State of California, and for Other Purposes,* 90th Cong., 2d sess., 1968, H. Rept. 1630, p. 18.

²⁰ *Ibid.*

²¹ *Ibid.,* p. 6.

²² U.S. Congress, *Congressional Record,* Vol. 114, Part 16, pp. 21399–21400.

²³ *Ibid.,* p. 21388.

²⁴ *Ibid.,* p. 21407.

²⁵ *Ibid.,* p. 21397.

²⁶ *Ibid.*

²⁷ *Ibid.,* pp. 21413–21414.

²⁸ *Ibid.,* Part 20, p. 26588.

Local Government   5

This study describes the strategies of various groups in their support for or opposition to the plan to integrate the New York public schools. The school board had adopted the Princeton Plan, pairing contiguous predominately white and predominately minority-group schools as a means of integration. Since an integration plan was definitely to be adopted, the groups favoring integration were faced with the situation of making it the most favorable to them; they had the ear of the administration and were thus able to adopt strategies suited to bargaining and compromise. Those groups opposing integration found themselves in a position that dictated a different set of strategies; since they had lost in the exchanges within the market they had to resort to boycotts and mass protest movements. The respective roles of these competing groups is, of course, usually reversed.

BERT E. SWANSON

The Politics of School Integration:
Two Strategies for Power

. . . The behavioral patterns reported here provide the raw materials of
the politics of education. The first section describes how the pro-integration
forces developed a dialogue with the superintendent and their efforts to bargain and negotiate for liberal policy as well as for better implementation of
plans already adopted. The section illustrates the efforts of conservatives
who, feeling powerless to secure any modification of integration plans,
developed the strategy of securing citizen support for their position in the
form of a mass movement at the local school level.

A LEADERSHIP DIALOGUE

A dialogue between then Superintendent Calvin Gross and the pro-integration forces was established following the announcement of the 1964–1965
plans. The meetings were a form of bargaining or negotiating. There were no
written agreements and no mechanisms to adjudicate in cases of alleged
breach of faith or good will. Yet Dr. Gross seriously considered the views
and imaginative ideas of liberal leaders and modified many parts of his plan
in the course of meeting with them, suggesting that the analogy to collective
bargaining sessions was not without empirical justification. At the outset
Dr. Gross established ground rules according to which the meetings would
range over a number of specific issues. Through mutual exploration of these
specific issues he and the liberal leaders would formulate general policy, and
in fact they would proceed as if there were no existing board or school
policy.

These meetings, at least the early sessions, facilitated a closing of ranks
and effected a working consensus within the white liberal-civil rights camp
for the first time in the history of school integration controversies in New
York City. Many participants observed that the meetings were revolutionary

Bert E. Swanson, *The Struggle for Equality* (New York: Hobbs, Dorman
and Company, Inc., 1966), pp. 79–99.

departures from the past Board and Superintendent practice. Issues that never before had been subject to negotiation were discussed rationally between Dr. Gross and a widely representative liberal group that was united for the first time. Unfortunately for the liberal group, its consensus, so effectively engineered by David Livingston [of the Conference on Quality Integrated Education], was short-lived and some groups constantly threatened to withdraw or at least disagree strongly with the majority of view.

Livingston and [the Rev. Donald] Harrington [of the Community Church of New York] were skillful negotiators, sophisticated in analyzing the social forces that had to be mobilized to assure success. From the start they tried to enlarge their constituency to include the more moderate groups. They contacted Fred McLaughlin of the Public Education Association (PEA) and attempted to enlist the support of Harold Siegel of the United Parents Association and the Citizens' Committee for Children. A five-hour meeting that took place in late spring included Livingston, Harrington, McLaughlin, and Harold Shiff of the ADL [Anti-Defamation League], but to no avail. The PEA has many ties with such moderate conservative groups as the City Club, the state bar association, influential business and labor leaders, the Mayor, the Democratic party, and others. PEA has been progressive in its activities for school integration over the years. They sponsored one of the first studies in 1955 on the quality of schools in ghetto areas and coined the term de facto segregation. However, PEA could not endorse a conference that included organizations too militant for its own views. Nor did UPA join the Conference. They were even more restricted by constituent groups that were neighborhood-based and more conservative than PEA on the subject of integration.

A brief chronology of the meetings between Dr. Gross and the civil rights groups during that summer will suggest the range of issues on which the latter were attempting to exert their influence. At the first meeting in June the liberal leaders told Dr. Gross of their regret (1) that he had so watered down the Allen plan [a report authored by New York State Education Commissioner James Allen] in his own report to the Board and (2) that the first frank discussion between him and the liberal spokesmen about plans for the fall occurred only after he had released them to the press. Apparently this was to avoid his seeming the captive of any group. Despite these disagreements, four six-hour meetings took place in early June. Information about these meetings was withheld from the press in order to create a climate that would encourage free exchange.

Dr. Gross's initial position, from which he retreated in the course of the first few meetings, was that he had a choice between improving radically the quality of education in the Negro ghetto and moving immediately to take Negro children from their neighborhood by means of pairing and mass transportation. One upshot of the meetings was that Gross was encouraged to redefine the situation so that both goals (moving children around and upgrading the ghetto schools) would be worthwhile.

A few very specific issues, all related to the Allen Report, were the focus of discussion throughout the summer. The first question was how to handle the many sixth-grade children who were moving from segregated Harlem schools into junior highs. The civil rights groups suggested that sixth graders from ghetto schools be distributed to underutilized, white junior high schools. This would help rid the system of the substantial amount of segregation at the junior high level. Dr. Gross considered this a good idea, but it took several days to gain acceptance. Finally, he agreed on a compromise plan that, while it may have alienated some of the militant integrationists, did not break up the meeting. He agreed to offer parents of sixth-grade children a choice of transferring to underutilized white junior high schools or remaining in segregated ones. There was much discussion about the method, which finally was established on a permissive rather than a consignment basis.

A second issue, more general in nature, bore on the relation between Dr. Gross's plan and the Allen Report. Gross said that he accepted the Allen Report in ·its entirety, although with some reservations because of its extremely general nature. He claimed that his plan was consciously formulated as a first step to implement the Allen Report, whose provisions he felt could be put into effect only over a long time period. Civil rights leaders pointed out that the press version had led most interested parties to conclude that his plan was either in direct opposition to Allen's or at the very least represented a serious dilution. In fact, some white liberal groups had opposed the Allen Report and embraced that of Gross, who stated emphatically that the Allen Report was the single most effective measure in getting the Board to take action. This implied criticism of the Board may have facilitated the negotiations, for it became apparent to some that Gross was now exerting stronger leadership.

The one serious reservation held by Gross about the Allen Report was the 4–4–4 plan, the basis for the whole structural reorganization. There is little empirical evidence that this plan is better educationally than others. Clearly the 4–4–4 plan would improve the educational quality in ghetto areas without hurting it elsewhere. The principal result would be to empty two grades from grammar schools so that nursery school classes of ages three–five could be started on a saturation basis. The burden of proof rests not with the proponents of the plan but with the skeptics.

It seemed to civil rights leaders that Dr. Gross had changed his conceptions of his role since first coming to the city. Apparently while he was still learning his new position he defined the role in somewhat narrow, technical terms, as do many educational administrators. He proceeded in the usual manner of educators to consider that school and political matters must be kept separate. The two boycotts seemed to change this opinion, and as the spring wore on and he was pressed by civil rights leaders, Parents and Tax-payers Coordinating Council (PAT), factions within his own board, and his school supervisors, he began to consider his situation in political terms. He saw that his position in the city was insecure and that in the long run the civil rights groups might become his staunchest allies. Since he had been estranged from the Board, he needed supporters desperately and welcomed opportunities to build up a relationship with what he believed to be a responsible segment of the community who shared many of his views, despite some militant members.

Within the civil rights–white liberal camp concensus was unstable. Some members suspected Dr. Gross's intentions or doubted his ability to keep promises. Others, however, were interested in continuing to meet and negotiate. The degree of consensus ranged from a fairly general agreement on long-range goals and a willingness to work together at the early stages (June and July) to periodic threats of withdrawal on the part of some groups (Parents' Workshop, Harlem Parents, and CORE) when it became evident that Gross's own supervisory staff was not implementing his integration plans. About September 10, a few days before school was to open, there seemed to be broad public consensus on the minimum program put forth by Dr. Gross. There were rumblings of discontent, for example, one civil rights leader's initial unwillingness to sign a statement endorsing Dr. Gross's plan. However, when PAT announced its boycott intentions, cohesion once more prevailed in the liberal camp. Each time the opposition dramatized its case, civil rights and moderate groups became reconciled.

When the meetings with Dr. Gross began, there were a number of points of agreement among the negotiators. All favored the Allen Report and opposed Gross's proposals. All were in favor of continuing discussions with him to see how far they could carry the dialogue. They were pleased with the extent to which they saw his position change as a result of their meetings. Furthermore, many Board policies that most civil rights leaders had originally interpreted as conscious acts against integration turned out on closer examination to be simple bureaucratic oversight. One civil rights leader remarked that he had never seen a bureaucracy quite so riddled with compulsive rule followers who were so enmeshed in procedure that they had lost all perspective of the outside world.

As the meetings proceeded during the summer a number of agreements were hammered out on specific matters. (1) Dr. Gross promised that the city would not build any new schools in segregated areas, especially in Negro ghettos. (2) By 1965 the segregated junior high schools would be eliminated and a good beginning would be made in building middle schools on an integrated basis, as part of Commissioner Allen's educational parks concept. Dr. Gross promised that some of these middle schools would be started in 1965. (3) He promised always to discuss from their very inception any plans for integration with civil rights groups rather than calling them in after decisions and plans had been made simply to inform them of faits accomplis.

Yet there were also areas of strong disagreement between Dr. Gross and these groups. Civil rights leaders were especially upset about the permissive character of the assignment plan for sixth graders to move into underutilized white junior high schools. The more militant wing was extremely displeased, having become disenchanted with open enrollment over the years. Open enrollment frequently has been used a a defensive maneuver by white leaders to dampen integration efforts. In Manhattan, however, up to 50 percent of the Negro parents given this option chose it, although in other areas the percentage was much lower.

At one point in late June or early July, after the negotiations had proceeded quite far, civil rights groups learned that some supervisory personnel —associate and assistant superintendents and principals—were not following Dr. Gross's recommendations at all. In fact, they were persuading parents in Negro areas not to send their children from their neighborhood schools into some new white areas in the Bronx where they had never been before. In a sense, these people were vetoing plans and policies that had already been agreed on at the bargaining table. This conflict was taken up with Dr. Gross at the next meeting. It became clear that the supervisors were reinterpreting Gross's general policy directives to fit their own needs and interests. Two techniques were particularly noticeable: (1) teachers and principals encouraged the Negro parents to maintain the status quo, and (2) high-level supervisors would impose procedures upon teachers that lowered their morale and willingness to accept change.

One critical incident has much broader implications for understanding how the educational bureaucracy has thwarted integration efforts. In one junior high in the Bronx, where the Allen concept of middle schools was being put into effect, ninth graders were being moved into high schools and sixth graders into the junior high or emerging middle schools. The vacancies in the grammar schools created by the exodus of the sixth and later the fifth graders were filled with nursery school children from depressed areas who were to be served on a saturation plan basis. Apparently there was such resentment among teachers in one school that a United Federation of Teachers (UFT) local representative protested to UFT headquarters about teaching conditions. Principals imposed burdens on teachers in the school that could have been avoided: (1) The same teachers were being compelled to teach both English and social studies, despite city and state rules that prevent such activity, designated as teaching out of license. Both subjects were placed in the same block of class time. (2) Though the UFT had bargained for a yearly decrease of one class period a week, one high level superior is reported to have told teachers, "You can't have two experiments at the same time, so you won't get any reduction of one period this year." (3) Since the need for shop teachers inevitably decreased with the exodus of ninth graders, and the new sixth grade was judged not quite ready, some teachers had to look for new situations. Several were kept waiting for a week or more instead of being helped to relocate. (4) Many new clerical burdens were imposed on the teachers. Since the number of graduating and entering classes was doubled (ninth and eighth graders would exit while sixth and seventh would enter), the volume of various health records, reading, IQ, and other scores increased. The upshot was that teachers picketed the school and were supported by some parents.

There are some explanations for this resistance to the middle school plans. First, supervisors and teachers generally have resisted major reorganization. Second, junior high school principals long had been lobbying to have their salaries made equivalent to those of high school principals, arguing that they had equal responsibilities and training.

Now that the middle schools would include fifth and sixth grades, these demands were less justified. Apparently, then, a combination of conservative and economic self-interest concerns triggered the uprising. Never before, said the head of the UFT, had supervisors and teachers acted with such unanimity. One lesson to be learned from all this is that the supervisory staff have considerable influence. Both the assistant superintendent and the principal are key figures at the local grassroots level.

Such tactics on the part of supervisors and teachers tend to reinforce the cynicism and alienation of militant civil rights leaders. The teachers claim that promises have been broken since the first attempts in the mid-1950s to integrate the schools. They have responded by making stronger demands on Dr. Gross, accompanied by threats of boycott or of withdrawal from negotiations. These threats exert pressures on those who wish to restrain such behavior and hold together a working consensus.

The next series of negotiating sessions with Dr. Gross covered school budgets. Civil rights groups recognized this as a key area of decision-making on which they would have to exercise pressure if they were to influence the speed and course of school integration. When negotiations on this subject first began, civil rights leaders claimed that over half the schools scheduled to be built from 1965 to 1971 were in ghetto or segregated areas. Dr. Gross agreed that the building program should be changed and said he was prepared to go to the Board of Education and even the Board of Estimate, if necessary. He agreed to the criterion that any future building plans should be dropped if they did not contribute to or detract from integration: He further agreed to operate as though there were no previously stated or established school or Board policy on construction.

One issue that came up quite early in the capital budget negotiations was the status of some decisions and the criteria for deciding which of them were too well advanced to reverse. More specifically, thirty-eight schools were to be built in the fiscal year 1965–1966. It was still possible to relocate twenty-three of them. The negotiators considered this to be an indication of flexibility and good will on Dr. Gross's part.

Negotiating leaders remained divided throughout August. One faction took the position that the commitments Dr. Gross had made were the best so far in New York City, and that if they were carried out they would lead to substantially more integration. This group maintained that while they should bargain aggressively, they should also bargain in good faith and try to understand the problems of the school people. Their view was that if Dr. Gross's plans and commitments were not carried out, the responsibility for failure could be attributed to him and so publicized. However, his intentions seemed good and his commitments were more radical than anything in the preceding ten years. Some people asserted that since this is an imperfect world, not a utopia, the civil rights groups should be satisfied with the changes, even if they seemed less than speedy and radical. The final public statement of a plan, formulated at the end of August and signed at an open board meeting by all civil groups, was a serious test for this bargaining group. It contained a minimum of change, even by the standards of some moderate groups, in order to keep many undecided white middle class parents committed to the city's public school system. This first group in the civil rights–white liberal camp might be labeled the pragmatists.

A second point of view expressed by ideologists was uncertainty of the integrity of Dr. Gross. They were not sure that he meant what he was promising in the meetings, and they suspected that even if he did, the white establishment (UPA, PEA, and others) would force him to renege on the agreements he had made as too radical, irresponsible, and not taking into account the quality of education.

Several members of the Board of Education were disturbed that Dr. Gross developed such a close relationship with the civil rights leaders. He was subjected to pressure from such moderate groups as PEA and UPA as well as from some Board members to dissociate himself from identification with civil rights groups. He responded by asking them to think seriously about increasing the size of these meetings to include PEA, CCC, UPA, ADA, ADL, AJC, all traditional educational and intergroup organizations in the city and many embued with the spirit of social reform. When this issue was raised at the August 24 meeting of the Conference, the only agreement with Dr. Gross's revised point of view was expressed by one representative, who remarked that many like himself had been in operation much longer than the Conference, which could not possibly represent all the traditional views. He went on to state that if Dr. Gross met only with militant groups, this would polarize the sides once more and bring integration efforts to an unfortunate halt. It was most important for Gross to increase his communications with all groups in the community.

The proposal to enlarge the negotiating body was rejected by the Conference. It was noted first that Dr. Gross himself had made the original commitment to restrict the sessions to that limited group. Second, it would be very difficult to maintain the rapport established with Gross if other groups were invited. Third, but closely related to the second point, it was difficult enough to maintain the working consensus developed in a very small group. If more groups were added, the present working arrangements might break down. The Intergroup Committee was cited as a dramatic illustration of how political effectiveness could be hampered by too many members with diverse points of view. Finally, since the Conference already represented the groups Dr. Gross had suggested, why double the representation?

A compromise proposal involved holding some larger, periodic briefings of all citywide groups with the Board as an activity apart from the closed negotiating sessions. Since the public had been so uninformed about many Board policies, this was an opportunity to correct one defect of the system while at the same time satisfying the need to include a larger representation of community groups.

The negotiations of the Conference with Dr. Gross were basic to the future course of school integration in New York City, not only in terms of the specific policies and general programs that evolved but also because of the relationships that were established and the reactions of influentials who were not included to the legitimacy of the representation of negotiating parties. The civil rights–white liberal coalition is the most effective one to be assembled in the eleven-year history of integration activity in New York City. Like most coalitions in New York City politics, however, it is tenuous. Leaders of the coalition are unwilling to predict its longevity. Some members feel that the time of greatest cohesion was in the fall of 1963, when the Board and Dr. Gross were at odds, and also shortly thereafter, when the Board announced plans for thirty pairings (January 31, 1964). Others consider this cohesion dubious in view of the deep-seated disagreements within the group over policy. Furthermore, since several leadership styles are likely to persist within the civil rights movement for some time to come, with each interpreting the needs and exigencies of the movement differently, long-term cohesion seems unlikely.

Apparently any strong indications that the white community is making major concessions and changes, even if they fall short of expectations, lead to increased cohesion. This happened just before the first Negro boycott and later after the Allen Report, although the situations were perceived differently. Whenever there is lack of cooperation by the white community, a split occurs between the militant ideologists and the pragmatists, as, for instance, at the time of the second boycott and again in July, when evidence of supervisory tactics were uncovered in the Bronx.

Civil rights leaders were under extreme pressure to produce a plan, almost any plan, regardless of its educational feasibility, to professional educators and moderates. They had to show both constituents and skeptics some quick victories and concessions if the coalition was to stay alive. Dr. Gross, on the other hand, had other publics with which to concern himself. He had somehow to avoid alienating either the establishment or the Mayor, since they were generally in agreement with liberal leaders on the goals of better racial balance and upgrading the quality of education. But the Conference had to avoid extreme criticism of the educational system and the white power structure if it was to continue to gain concessions. It is possible that the right combination of events will produce both an absence of polarization on a citywide basis, continued communication among groups holding different views, some flexible negotiation and bargaining, and orderly and fairly accelerated change. This situation suggests the need for some kind of transactional model of the requisites for change and administrative effectiveness in school integration efforts.

The PAT Boycott

The second major strategy deployed is the boycott. Three major boycotts were used in 1964. The first was organized by the Negro civil rights groups in February, the second by the dynamic Rev. Milton Galamison, the Parents' Workshop and the Harlem Parents in March, both before the period involved in this field study. The third was a counterboycott staged by the white PAT and the Brooklyn Joint Council in September. Since this last boycott occurred during the study period, it is covered here in some detail as a manifest strategy used by those who wish to be heard and to prevail in the integration controversy but who have limited access to the core.

One of the most basic concerns of both PAT and the Joint Council was to preserve a situation of free choice or voluntarism for parents as to where to send their children to school. They opposed any compulsory transfer of pupils, white or Negro. In their more polemic statements PAT spokesmen referred to the dictatorial and totalitarian methods used by Dr. Gross and the Board in attempts to integrate the schools. They argued that they did not oppose integration at all, and that in fact they had contributed their services in previous integration plans, such as open enrollment. The argument about preserving freedom and voluntary free choice for parents, and its corollary, that the government and public agencies like school boards were usurping too much power and were engaged in compulsory programs that encroached on citizen rights, were generalized into an attempt to halt what they called the main drift of American life. The counter-argument—that the Board had been making major educational decisions about zoning, curricula, and the like for years and that they should continue to do so, both as the voice of the broadest possible public interest and because of their greater educational competence—never was accepted by PAT and Joint Council followers. However, it certainly was not revolutionary for the Board to decide which schools children would attend.

It was argued that the preservation of neighborhood schools would provide people with a sense of community that they would lose under the Board's present integration plans. Indeed, it was charged that such plans as pairing would have a disintegrating effect on families and communities. Parents would be obliged to send their children to different schools and would have less time and energy to devote to Parents' Associations. It would be very difficult to have any sense of identification or involvement with a school that was far away. Furthermore, a mother would not be able to accompany each of her children to school so easily as in the past, since they would go in different directions. Older children would no longer be able to accompany younger siblings to school. Families and local neighborhoods would be broken up by such integration plans. Some of the more articulate spokesmen for this neighborhood school concept went on to point out that it had been the established doctrine for educators for several generations. Why should teachers or parents suddenly have to change their outlook on such a basic issue?

Another argument was that the quality of education for white middle-class children would decline if they were integrated with Negro children in pairings or educational park arrangements. Since there were no empirical data to substantiate this argument, the anxieties of some white parents could not be dispelled by Board representatives. As a matter of fact, UPA claimed to have data suggesting that Negro children bused in under the open enrollment plan were generally six months behind the white children in the receiving schools. This was interpreted as having the likely effect of lowering the level of the white children's instruction. Furthermore, since Negro pupils whose parents chose to send them to predominantly white schools under open enrollment were generally more advanced in IQ, reading level, and general academic achievement than their peers who remained in the ghetto schools, the quality of education would become even poorer under pairing and middle school plans.

It is essential to recognize that the arguments of PAT followers often masked even more basic needs that are difficult to express publicly. There are both public and private ideologies that must be distinguished in order to understand the dynamics of the PAT movement. One of the most basic underlying feelings is an acute sense of panic and anxiety. Some of this is simply the opposition to change that characterizes any conservative population. Earlier generations were hostile to succeeding waves of ethnic minority immigrants. Just as businessmen, anxious to preserve their property rights and managerial prerogatives, reacted to the increased demands and rights of labor, those elite groups who enjoyed a clear advantage over others had a vested interest in preserving the status quo. The social situation favored them and they intended to keep it that way.

The resistance to most recent Negro demands for rights and opportunities previously denied them seems to differ, however, in both degree and kind from previous reactions. Now the panic stems from anticipating where school integration will lead. The conservatives fear that the Board has some long-run plans and timetables that will involve mass busing of many more white children. They fear that contact with Negro children will acquaint white children with less desirable ways of life. They fear that more white children will be forcibly bused into squalid Negro neighborhoods. They fear that school integration ultimately will encourage Negro families to move into white neighborhoods, bringing with them the same lowering of property values and local deterioration that has been experienced in Brooklyn, the East Bronx, and other areas of the city. Finally, they fear that increased social contact between Negro and white children eventually will lead to intermarriage and a lowering of the quality of the white race. Underlying all these fears is an extreme sense of resentment against the system for forcing such changes on the white community without allowing for any negotiation, compromise, or democratic dialogue for the expression of community sentiment. The refusal of the Mayor or the City Council to grant a simple referendum on school integration plans, methods of recruitment to school boards, or other educational matters was cited as indicative of how the system overrode the white community.

The first organized effort of the school integration opponents was a PAT-organized protest march and demonstration on City Hall and the Board on March 13, 1964. This was in response to a successful show of strength by the Negro February and March boycotts. News reporters estimated that as many as 15,000 parents, mostly women, turned out for the occasion, despite adverse weather conditions. The leaders held meetings with Dr. Gross, Board President James Donovan, City Council President Paul R. Screvane, and Deputy Mayor Edward F. Cavanagh, Jr., but they received no satisfaction on any occasion. Obviously this was an extremely well-organized movement, one that could not be disregarded. All through the spring and early summer months responsible civil rights leaders warned the white community of the threat to its integration plans from the PAT-Joint Council group. They reiterated that there was a leadership vacuum among moderate groups in New York City, as there was in many southern communities, and that unless the responsible white groups spoke up much more vigorously for integration and provided some leadership, the opposition group (PAT-Joint Council) would flourish. The result could be to set back integration efforts for many years.

The NAACP and more militant Negro point of view defined the situation as a white problem that must be met by white, not Negro, leadership. Since PAT appealed primarily, indeed overwhelmingly, to the white community, it was the task of responsible community leaders to speak out not against boycotts per se but against PAT and what it stood for. The situation was seen, then, as a white problem and as an opportunity for whites to take a stand.

The first concerted strategy of the parents' group was to attempt to win over the Board and Dr. Gross to their point of view in private meetings with Dr. Gross and at various open meetings of the Board. Dr. Gross aroused their anger almost to fever pitch as he informed them that the integration plan was an accomplished fact and that if there were to be any changes in the plan they would take effect in September, 1965.

This action, of course, shut him off from any bargaining relationship with PAT and Joint Council leaders. His strategy for handling the latter was to mobilize as large a coalition behind his program as possible, hoping thus to minimize his opposition. Since PAT–Joint Council requests for an end to Board transfer plans, changes in school boundaries, and other measures were unacceptable even to many moderate groups, Dr. Gross had no choice but to stand by the plans he had evolved in negotiating sessions with liberal leaders. He realized that any attempt at bargaining and compromise with PAT and Joint Council leaders would be political suicide. His main hope was that the moderate groups would sway enough potential opponents of the plans so that the opposition movement itself would subside.

Gross did receive some help from the moderates. As early as June 5, Dr. Frederick C. McLaughlin, Executive Director of PEA, declared:

The plan provides a basis for moving forward. All groups should now close ranks behind the Superintendent and his staff and help, where possible, in securing resources for the implementation of the new program. Such support in no way limits future action. Continued opposition, however, endangers not only education but our whole democratic process.[1]

Both the PEA and the UPA regarded their roles as those of maintaining continued communications with opposition groups at a time when it seemed that such communications were impossible for any other citywide groups. Even though rank-and-file Negro parents were not as militant as some of their leaders, there certainly was pressure on leaders to make some progress after what were considered ten years of extremely limited success.

The repeated failures of integration opponents in their attempts to deal directly with the Board were followed by a summer of legal battles. Three influential PAT leaders were lawyers. They brought six suits against the Board of Education, attacking the constitutionality of the pairings for the fall of 1964. They lost five of the suits. Their argument was that the Board could not force children, solely on the basis of color, to attend schools outside their neighborhoods. They maintained that zoning could not be based on racial factors. Though PAT lawyers were willing to admit that de facto segregation existed and that it was undesirable, they charged that the problem must be attacked in other ways, for instance, through changes in housing patterns. The Board contended that the pairing was not planned solely for the purpose of achieving greater racial balance. It was also intended to upgrade the quality of education in both paired schools, e.g., to relieve overcrowding and make possible smaller classes and improved services. All the cases were in paired areas—one in Lincoln Towers, one in Long Island City, two in Jackson Heights, and one in Brooklyn Heights. The one PAT victory was in Jackson Heights, where Justice Henry J. Latham ruled in July that the Board could not transfer three white children from a school across the street from their homes. However, the judge said nothing to suggest the unconstitutionality of pairings as such.

Another major court defeat for pairing foes occurred just a few days before school opened. Justice Sidney A. Fine refused to permit a citywide referendum on the Board's pairing plan. The court based its rejection on the preeminence of the state in establishing educational policy and the lateness of the petition seeking the referendum. Pairing foes had been working that summer to secure the necessary 30,000 signatures to make valid their petition. For a number of reasons they had been unable to convince the court that they had the necessary signatures until it was almost too late to make a ruling for the fall. At one point in July the City Clerk had questioned the legitimacy of some signatures, implying that they were from parents not involved in the city's pairings or public school system.

Justice Fine based his ruling on the following arguments: First, a recent decision of the Court of Appeals, the state's highest tribunal, established a precedent in contending that the Board of Education has "express statutory power to select a site and to determine the school where each pupil shall attend." As a result, Justice Fine said, "the proposed local law would thus, in effect, supersede state statutes referred to by the Court of Appeals" and be illegal under Article 9 of the State Constitution, which prohibits enactment of a local law over a state law. Second, he ruled that the petition had been filed too late for the November 3 election.

One tactic attempted by Bernard Kessler, who represented PAT in most court suits, involved invoking the Civil Rights Act against Board pairings. This maneuver was tried in a suit against the PS 111–112 (Long Island City) pairing. The move was rejected. The law states that "desegregation shall not mean the assignment of students to public schools in order to overcome racial imbalance." Justice Nicholas M. Pette refused to accept this provision of the law as any basis for ruling against pairings. To accept the PAT contention that the Civil Rights Act would negate the Board's pairings would transmute that act into a segregation law when its clear import was antisegregation.

Justice Pette's summary statement probably set the precedent for future court cases. He observed that other cases on the constitutionality of pairings already had been tried and ruled in the Board's favor. The main argument in the Board's defense was that the reduction of racial imbalance was not the most important factor in its decision to pair. Rather, the pairings had contributed to an upgrading of the quality of education in each school, thereby permitting substantially reduced class sizes, additional professional services, and other educational advantages as well as offering an early opportunity for children to live and work together in a multiracial setting. Thus, the Board had been so circumspect in its final pairing plans, having decided against many others, and it was careful to provide an incentive each time, that no convincing case could be made in opposition. PAT lawyers still plan more contests, however, pursuing a different line of argument. Instead of concentrating on the constitutionality of pairings, rezoning, and new middle schools, PAT lawyers will challenge such plans on the ground that they are educationally unsound.

Having lost, then, in its attempts to negotiate either directly with the Board or through the courts, the opposition turned to Mayor Wagner and the City Council for help. At first Mayor Wagner made himself unavailable, stating that educational matters must be kept out of politics and decided by educational professionals. The opposition threatened to demonstrate at the Democratic National convention in Atlantic City, where Wagner was being considered for the Vice Presidential nomination. In fact, they exerted pressure on members of both conventions to include in their party platform a provision upholding the neighborhood school. Mayor Wagner finally met with them in September in an attempt to temper their emotions. He handled this situation as he had many others in his long service as Mayor. First, he told the group that he was powerless to interfere, because the Board of Education was a semi-autonomous agency under state jurisdiction. He sought to rely on court decisions to avoid being pushed into exerting direct influence himself. The courts, as well as the authority of the State Board of Education, the Board of Regents, and the legislature thus could help him out of his predicament. Since Wagner was playing this issue to a national as well as city-wide audience, he wanted to maintain an image of not catering to extremists. Therefore he would not yield to the PAT-Joint Council pleas. He also promised to study the situation and speak with members of the Board, but this delaying tactic was perceived as such. The PAT-Joint Council people were especially bitter about the Mayor's failure to act when Council Minority Leader Angelo J. Arculeo (Republican) of Brooklyn and four other councilmen had petitioned him on August 18 to call a special session of the Council to consider four pieces of anticompulsory integration legislation. Arculeo claimed that the New York City Charter stipulated that the Mayor was required to call such a session upon receipt of the signatures of five councilmen. "By his illegal refusal to call a special meeting," Arculeo charged, "he is depriving the people of their right to have their elected representatives heard before the Board's disastrous plan is put into effect."[2] Arculeo vowed to sue the Mayor and went so far as to call on Corporation Counsel Larkin to force Wagner to convene a special session of the City Council before the schools opened.

In early August, when it became clear to PAT-Joint Council leaders that they would not win either in the courts or through direct negotiations with Dr. Gross and the Board, they decided to stage a massive white boycott of public schools on opening day. They may have assumed that the Board could be swayed as it had been after the Negro boycotts of February and March. They may also have assumed that such a demonstration would force the Mayor to move, knowing as they did his strategy of negotiating a deal at the critical eleventh hour. At any rate, most of the public discussion and influence-weilding from August 10 through the opening of school related to the proposed boycott.

A main target of PAT attacks in preparation for the boycott was Mayor Wagner, rather than Dr. Gross and the Board. An attempt was made to single out the Mayor for blame, thus trying to force him to intervene. As Frederick Reuss, Queens PAT leader, declared:

Mayor Wagner and his political cronies, by refusing to listen to the voice of the people or to consult with representatives of the majority of the people, have made it necessary for PAT to take this step. He will either have to represent the people or step down from his high office in order that the people may be represented by a man more willing and able to understand the problems of this city.[3]

The boycott was portrayed as a democratic protest by a majority of the populace whose interest heretofore had been denied.

PAT leaders hoped to use the threatened boycott to negotiate with Dr. Gross and the Board. They offered to cancel the boycott if the Board would cancel its four pairings. They expressed willingness to abide by all other voluntary integration plans, such as open enrollment, an offer that they felt clearly demonstrated their lack of prejudice. The Board, of course, refused to engage in any negotiations to weaken its already modest plans. Therefore, PAT considered all meetings with the Mayor unsatisfactory in dealing with the real issues, and they continued with their preparations.

The Board and Dr. Gross, on the other hand, embarked on an intensive public relations program in an attempt to mobilize as much citizen consensus behind their plan as possible. Liberal critics of the Board and Dr. Gross, while pleased with such a spirited defense of the integration program, were concerned that its formulation had taken so long. Any politically sound program, they argued, should have planned for a longer term effort to gain citizen acceptance.

In anticipation of widespread support for the Board's plans from many groups, PAT-Joint Council leaders developed a counterstrategy, hoping to keep or win back white parent followers. On September 8 they suddenly limited their plan for a school boycott of what had previously been declared indefinite duration. Instead, they asked parents throughout the city to keep their children out of school for just the two opening days of the new term, September 14 and 15, except for those pupils who were involuntarily transferred and would remain out until they were again admitted to neighborhood schools.[4] In order to gain greater parent acceptance, the statement said that the withdrawal would have no adverse educational effect, for practically no school work would be begun until after the Yom Kippur holiday on September 16.

PAT-Joint Council preparations for the boycott indicated the effectiveness of their organization. Many white parents in Queens, Brooklyn, and the Bronx, who previously had not participated in such activities, willingly volunteered their help in preparing pamphlets, making phone calls, and doing other tasks to mobilize the largest possible following. Many of these women had no other interest or activities, and the boycott provided meaning in their lives. One editorialist wryly observed, "If this much personnel, time, and energy were redirected to actually improving the quality of education for all children, we would have much to look forward to for New York City's public school system."[5]

Meanwhile, Dr. Gross and selected representatives of the Board were busy presenting their plan to the community. Negro civil rights leaders did not participate directly, for they considered this as a white parents' movement that must be countered by white parents. EQUAL played a major role, attempting to hold neighborhood meetings for parents at which the Board's plans were explained, sending out notices and pleas to white parents throughout the city, attempting to influence opinion leaders in local areas, and finally appearing on television in dramatic, last-minute requests to white parents to send their children to school. They also conducted the silent vigil referred to by Mrs. [Ellen] Lurie outside the day school hastily set up in the basement of a cooperative apartment building in Jackson Heights.

In addition, all the moderate groups openly opposed the boycott. One of the most significant groups in terms of political power was the UPA, which represented 400,000 parents in Parents' Associations throughout the city. Both the CCC and PEA issued strong statements against the boycott. Most of the statements announced that these groups were against the principle of boycotting and, as so many said, "of using the children as pawns in adult struggles." There was a conspicuous absence of statements to the effect that these groups opposed this particular boycott because it represented an unwillingness to accept an even modest integration program and therefore condoned a continuation of de facto segregation.

James B. Donovan, Board President, appeared on television to defend the Board and its plans. Donovan inflamed the opposition by threatening the boycotting parents with legal sanctions. The most forceful statement of all came when Dr. Gross made a fifteen-minute television appearance shortly before the schools were to open. This was a taped telecast that was repeated many times that evening. Gross's statement was the strongest to be made by a school official. The main theme was that New Yorkers had been treated to a barrage of inflammatory statements that simply were not true and that the city needed to clear the air with the facts. He charged that many false and misleading statements had been made by PAT leaders, who said that there would be many more future pairings. Gross called their predictions silly and fantastic. He berated the PAT leaders for urging parents to break the law by using their children as pawns in a reprehensible power play. He effectively attempted to dispel the many rumors that were so rampant, appealed to law and order, and asked for cooperation with the Board's plans. Most important, he stressed the limited amount of extra busing involved in the new plan and the considerable attention given to upgrading the quality of educational services in paired schools. He spoke about his goal of better schools for all children to preserve community solidarity and upgrade the educational opportunities for children from ghetto areas.

Dr. Gross explained all the facets of the plan in great detail, underlining the fact that this was a modest beginning. He stated emphatically that the Board believed in the principles of maintaining a democratic society and implied that this was not the belief of opposition groups.

Boycott plans were too far advanced by now, however, for any last-minute pleas to have much impact. It was apparent to all moderate and liberal groups that PAT-Joint Council leaders were very well organized, had an abundance of personnel and finances, and were prepared to fight the Board's program to the end.

Despite the last-minute efforts of Mayor Wagner, who responded characteristically in such a crisis with efforts at mediation, the boycott took place during the first two days of school. Dr. Gross, Jacob Landers, the Assistant Superintendent for Integration, PEA officials, Mrs. Ellen Lurie of EQUAL, UPA leaders, and others all had urged parents in paired areas and elsewhere to send their children to school.

On the first day 275,638 pupils stayed home, a figure that was 175,000 over the normal 10 percent absence rate. One school, PS 112 in the Bensonhurst section of Brooklyn, was empty, despite the fact that it was not involved in any pairing and was quite far away from schools that were. As one parent from this school put it: "We know that eventually the Board of Education will come down to our school with its plans." Though this unusual case was not repeated anywhere else in the city, it did serve to dramatize the fear and anxiety of many white parents for the future. Certainly these fears were continually intensified by PAT and Joint Council leaders. Most surprising in the PS 112 situation was the fact that the principal was completely unaware of the effect of the impending boycott. The principal, a man who had spent twenty-six years in the school system, very much favored integration, and seemed to have the support of parents in his community, said he was stunned by the total absence record in his school.

NOTES

[1] Leonard Buder in *The New York Times,* June 6, 1964, p. 1.
[2] *New York Post,* September 10, 1964.
[3] *The New York Times,* August 11, 1964.
[4] *The New York Times,* September 8, 1964.
[5] *New York Post,* editorial, September 6, 1964.

Political Parties 6

The rise of the "New Politics" has been mentioned extensively in recent commentary on political parties. The phrase implies several different things, as the authors of this case study point out. One interpretation is that a new and vigorous coalition of youth, minority group members, poor people, and the like will become the dominate force in American party politics. Attempts to take over a political party have met with some success, witnessed by Eisenhower's nomination at the Republican Convention in 1952 and by the Goldwater nomination in the 1964 Republican Convention. It certainly must be considered a viable alternative to other forms of attempting to change the system. However, as the present case makes clear, success in using such a strategy depends upon available resources. To miscalculate the extent of those resources can have disastrous consequences. Under what conditions might a new majority coalition succeed? The student might also wish to consider the consequences when such a sizable and active segment of the political community fails.

"New Politics" is also used to denote the widespread use of mass media in modern campaigns. The new politics discussed in the case of Nelson Rockefeller raises serious questions concerning our ability to use elections in making meaningful choices. Those who feel that the image-makers will soon dominate American electoral politics might take some consolation in the fact that the major practitioners were only successful in about 50 percent of the campaigns they ran in the 1970 elections. But the moral and ethical questions of using modern merchandising techniques as a means of securing elective office remains. Hopefully, upon completion of this selection, students will have an opportunity to investigate the implications of both meanings of the "New Politics" upon the American system.

LEWIS CHESTER, GODFREY HODGSON,
and BRUCE PAGE

New Politics and Old Pols:
Two Case Studies in Insurgency

Robert Kennedy's friends and followers admired him not merely as a brilliant figure within the established tradition of American political leadership, but because they saw him as the prophet of a New Politics. None of them believed this more passionately than his young speechwriter Adam Walinsky. One winter afternoon, some six months after Kennedy's death, Walinsky sat in the living room of his house in a Washington suburb and explained what the New Politics meant to him. He talked about a new style, a new compassion and commitment, a new constituency of the young, the black, the poor, and some middle-class people. Above all, he identified the New Politics with youth. "Yes," he was asked, "but isn't the New Politics also a matter of technique?" He agreed. He mentioned, inevitably, Marshall McLuhan. And then he grinned. "Robert Kennedy always understood Guthman's Law: three minutes on the six-o'clock news is worth all the rest of the publicity you can get." (Edwin O. Guthman was Robert Kennedy's director of public information at the Justice Department and later his press assistant in the Senate; he is now national news editor of the *Los Angeles Times*.) To Walinsky and to many others of the bright young men around Kennedy, there seemed to be no contradiction between a New Politics of commitment to radical social change and something quite different: a new sophistication in the use of modern political technology.

Every year in the United States there is a new Ford, a new Chevrolet, a new Chrysler, and a New Negro. At less frequent intervals, a New Woman, a New Child Psychology, and a New South make regular appearances. At the beginning of 1968, New Politics were in the air. Politicians talked about them. Journalists wrote about them. Pundits and academicians cranked themselves up to analyze them. The only trouble was that nobody agreed on what they meant.

Some greeted the New Politics as Wordsworth greeted the French Revolution: "Bliss was it in that dawn to be alive, but to be young was very heaven!" For them, New Politics meant the politics of "ordinary people who are fed up with the superficial and hypocritical politics of the two major parties." This was not a matter of anything so base as political technique. It was a mood, a style, a cause, and a commitment. There were more practical people, too, like Robert Kennedy's friend Fred Dutton, who felt that, though there might be short-term swings to the right, in the long run the future lay with a new radical coalition. It would be free from the narrow concerns of the older blue-collar workers with their own economic interests, free from the old ethnic obsessions, concerned at last with "the quality of American life." A new constituency was coming into existence, according to this school; an alliance, as Jack Newfield put it, of "campus, ghetto, and suburb."

It was doubtful how much validity, or even logic, there was to such theories. Pessimists noticed that all too often the economic and practical interests of these three groups were opposed. Some of the spokesmen for the New Politics seemed to confuse a temporary coalition, brought together by opposition to the war and to Lyndon Johnson, with a secular shift in the sociology of politics. But the fact was that on the left—and *to* the left—of the Democratic Party, especially among some of the most influential younger journalists, there was an unshakable faith that a new day was a-coming in 1968. The essence of the New Politics, for them, was contained in the lessons learned in the peace movement and the earlier civil-rights movements: that the old rules could be circumvented by action, mobility, drama, involvement, and confrontation; by learning all the ways in which determined People could wage guerrilla war against the Machine.

But for others the New Politics meant something completely different from this. "There are two essential ingredients of the new politics," wrote a Washington reporter for the *National Observer* named James M. Perry in a careful, and on the whole pessimistic, book published in January 1968:

One is that appeals should be made directly to the voters through the mass media. The other is that the techniques used to make these appeals —polling, computers, television, direct mail—should be sophisticated and scientific.

Perry's book, entitled *The New Politics: The Expanding Technology of Political Manipulation,* described in detail the contributions made to the development of the techniques of political management by such political-management firms as Spencer-Roberts and Whitaker and Baxter in California, by Joseph Napolitan, by Fred Currier and Walter De Vries in Michigan, and by Dr. William Ronan and the Jack Tinker agency in the Rockefeller campaign of 1966.

Perry drew an alarming portrait of a Presidential candidate under the new dispensation:

The candidate's travels . . . will be scheduled by a computer. The campaign will be laid out by the critical path method. Polls will be taken over and over and analyzed and cross-analyzed. Spot commercials will be prepared weeks in advance of the election, and their impact will be almost subliminal. Researchers will read the polls and study the data from a "simulator"; the issues they develop will . . . be aimed like rifle shots at the most receptive audiences. . . . And the candidate? He will be out front, moving with a robot-like precision, being fed with data from the polls and the simulator. He will no doubt be articulate, and probably he will be handsome and vigorous. And he may or may not be qualified to be the next President of the United States.

This was presented as a would-you-believe-it warning of what some future campaign might be like. It was written in 1967. Yet, with the single exception of the simulator, every one of the techniques Perry listed was used by most of the major candidates in 1968.

In another book published in early 1968—*Robert Kennedy and the New Politics*—a Columbia professor named Penn Kimball, who is also Louis Harris's right-hand man, attempted a definition of the New Politics:

the contemporary contest for political power characterized by primary reliance on personal organizations in preference to party machinery, emphasis on consolidating voters rather than on dividing them along traditional lines of class or region, projection of political style above issues, and exploitation of the full range of modern techniques for mass communication.

There are four ideas, or criteria, contained in that definition. The first and third are closely connected and belong to what we have called "bastard feudalism." There is not the faintest reason why either should be correlated with compassion; they might be, or they might not. It is hard to see the originality of the second: national politicians in America have always tried to achieve consensus. As a matter of fact, some "new politicians," notably Kimball's particular subject of study, Robert Kennedy, have permitted themselves a good deal more dividing than, say, Johnson in 1964 or Eisenhower, to name two "old politicians." And there is one very good reason why the fourth criterion, the exploitation of mass media, should actually be negatively correlated with radicalism.

The new political technology is very expensive. It depends on computers, public-opinion surveys, film, videotape, and other expensive toys. It also depends on the services of clever, highly educated and trained people to use these techniques. Such people don't come cheap. "The professional managers are mercenaries," Perry wrote of these very people. "They are willing to go almost anywhere for a buck." Not many of those bucks are to be earned by working for the young, the poor, or the black. Walter DeVries himself points out that Joseph Napolitan is the only one—of a dozen or more political "mercenaries" with a national reputation in America—who works for Democrats. And Perry suggests the reason is that, more than money, "these new technologists seek power. I suspect they get more satisfaction—more sense of power—working with a man of ability and potential than they do working for an institutionalized organization." In general, it is naïve to suppose that techniques which can be used only by those with access to enormous financial resources will often be available for any really damaging assault on the status quo.

The objection might be made at this point that the candidates who have made the most of the new political technology are not typically conservatives—though they do include conservatives like Ronald Reagan. More typically, they present themselves as liberals or moderates: Robert Kennedy, George Romney, Nelson Rockefeller. But these examples do not contradict the proposition that the New Politics of technology are unlikely to be found in the service of a New Politics of radical dissent. For moderate liberalism *is* the doctrine of the status quo in America, and it is not to be confused with radicalism. There is only one circumstance in which the poor, the black, and indeed the young are going to find computers, polls, and scientific campaign management used on their behalf: that is when a wealthy candidate appoints himself as their champion. The user of technology should not be confused with his clients. It is one thing to say that Robert Kennedy, who could and did afford to use "the full range of modern techniques for mass communication," felt a genuine concern for the disinherited. It is quite another to say that, because of this, the blacks of Watts or Bedford-Stuyvesant or the Mexican migrant workers acquired control of computers and pollsters and advertising agencies. And in politics, it is control that counts.

There were actually two brands of New Politics on display in 1968. Each represented a challenge to the old pols and to their established order. After Robert Kennedy's death, the old pols looked firmly entrenched in both parties. Newspapers, wire services, and magazines published "delegate counts" purporting to show that it was all over: headlines announced that Richard Nixon and Hubert Humphrey had the nominations of the two parties sewed up. But, with remarkable symmetry, the same development was happening in each party: a challenge to the old pols in the name of a New Politics. The brand of New Politics with which Humphrey was challenged was something very different from what Nixon had to cope with. The pattern of preconvention politics dictates that the same issues are raised, and the same tactics used, in state after state. Rather than follow the Rockefeller and McCarthy campaigns chronologically, it seems best to let two case studies illustrate the way two kinds of New Politics worked in the two parties. The Rockefeller advertising campaign and the McCarthy campaign in Connecticut illustrate the total difference between the two kinds of New Politics very clearly.

On April 30, in Albany, just under six weeks after his withdrawal, Nelson Rockefeller had announced his "active candidacy" for the Presidency. He said he had been deeply disturbed by the "dramatic and unprecedented" events of the past week and that he could no longer stand on the sidelines. He added that he had been urged to run by "men and women in all walks of life within the Republican party."

The phrase about walks of life conjures up a charming eighteenth-century vignette, in which respectful delegations of honest cobblers and blacksmiths wait upon our hero and remind him of his duty to save the country. It wasn't quite like that. "On March 22," the day after his withdrawal speech, says Emmett Hughes, "a group sprang up like flowers out of a rock and said to George Hinman, 'You can't let this happen!' " The prime mover was John Hay Whitney, with Walter N. Thayer at his side. Whitney, the angel of *Life with Father, Gone with the Wind,* and the somewhat less successful New York *Herald Tribune,* breeder of bloodstock and former Ambassador to the Court of St. James, had been left by his father, in 1927, the largest estate ever probated up to that time. His present wealth is estimated by *Fortune* magazine at between two hundred and three hundred million dollars. Thayer might be called his man of business, his George Hinman, a lawyer who has worked shrewdly and loyally for him in various ventures for twenty years.

Between them, Whitney and Thayer managed to round up on behalf of Rockefeller a good cross section of the old-money WASP business aristocracy, not just of New York—which would have been fatal—but of the country. There was a group in Chicago and even a little group in Texas. There were Gardner Cowles, whose family owns *Look* magazine and newspapers in Minneapolis and Des Moines; Ralph Lazarus of Federated Department Stores; H. J. Heinz, II; and Henry Ford, II. One of the most active was a Yale and Oxford graduate from Indiana called J. Irwin Miller, who runs the Cummings diesel firm.

Quite independently, a short while later, Rockefeller was approached by leaders of that other great financial oligarchy, the liberal Jewish business leaders in New York. These are not Republicans by habit and inheritance, like Whitney's WASPs. Some of them are Democrats. Others would classify themselves as independents. But there is a passionate liberal tradition in this world. Many of the leading Jewish businessmen in New York had already supported Rockefeller for governor, while contributing to the Kennedy and Johnson presidential campaigns. What they said, in effect, through various intermediaries, was: "We would rather be with you than with Humphrey, but we have to be for someone who isn't Nixon. We have to know now, because if you don't go, we will have to go for Humphrey. Are you going to do it or not?"

The thing that most changed Nelson Rockefeller's mind between early March and late April, in the opinion of those in a position to know what he was thinking, was not Lyndon Johnson's withdrawal, or Martin Luther King's assassination, or the riots, or the international monetary crisis, although all of those events influenced his decision. The most important thing was that, for the first time, he felt he was being asked to run. For the first time in his life, he had widespread national support in the business world.

By the middle of April, Rockefeller was again seriously considering running. J. Irwin Miller set up a Rockefeller for President committee with a Minnesotan called Jerry Olsen to run it; this gave it a solid midwestern flavor, but in the background George Hinman was pulling the strings. As soon as he thought his man was going to go, he knew exactly what to do next. He placed a call to an advertising man who happened to be in Clearwater, on the west coast of Florida, at a Humble Oil meeting. The move, as always with Hinman, was extremely logical.

"The situation is more fluid than some have thought," Nelson Rockefeller told the politicians and the reporters in Albany on April 30. "There has not been a crystallization of thinking to the point where we are faced with a closed convention." That sort of talk was all right for the record. What candidate is going to announce that he is engaged upon a forlorn hope? ₒBut afterward, as they mixed with reporters in the executive mansion and looked at the Picasso tapestries their boss has had made ("It's the only way I can get these great paintings!"), Rockefeller's professionals did not bother to keep up pretenses. They knew that Nixon had a long lead and that they had only one persuasive argument going for them. As a matter of preference, the great majority of Republican delegates would take Nixon if they could. Rockefeller's only hope was to persuade these men that picking him would make the difference between victory and defeat. His people had to put across the idea that Rockefeller could beat a Democrat and Nixon could not.

There were two ways of selling this case. The first, the orthodox way, would be the direct method. Rockefeller and his lieutenants would have to get out and make their pitch to the politicians. But, in fact, as Hinman and Hughes and Len Hall and Alton Marshall and the rest of them knew—as Thruston Morton and Bill Miller knew best of all, because they had just come back from a last-minute reconnaissance in six states—it was not going to be easy. It was not even going to be possible unless he could produce evidence.

Therefore, Rockefeller, like McCarthy, had to appeal to the people over the heads of the politicians. But he was going to do it in a different way. The central idea of his strategy was simple, bold, and rational. It was too late to bind delegates by primary victories. And it was unlikely that he would be able to persuade enough delegates directly. Therefore, he must use the media to influence public opinion—the opinion, it should be noticed, of Democrats and independents as well as Republicans. That would be reflected in the polls, and the polls in turn could be used as a compelling argument with the delegates. But the whole venture turned on whether, at the end of the day, the polls showed, not merely that Rockefeller was more popular than Nixon, but that Rockefeller could win and Nixon could not.

These were the two sides to Rockefeller's campaign: the orthodox campaign of direct delegate persuasion, and the effort to persuade indirectly through the polls. As soon as he announced, Nelson Rockefeller set out on a furious three months during which he met and talked to delegates in forty-five states. The Republican convention was due to begin on August 5. It was not long for a national campaign. He was most effective in what his staff called dehorning sessions: he would meet a group of delegates behind closed doors and try to assure them that he had not sabotaged Dick Nixon in 1960 or Barry Goldwater in 1964, that he was not a wild socialist spender in New York, that he was, in short, a loyal Republican and a regular fellow. He tried to persuade them, not to come out for him, but to stay loose. And up to a point, with the delegations from the key industrial states, he was successful. We are not going to describe these journeyings in detail, because it was the other side of Rockefeller's campaign that was both more important for him and intrinsically more interesting. The Rockefeller media campaign in 1968 is a classic study in the New Politics of technique. It deserves to be studied in detail, because it shows how the New Politics work—what they can do, and what they can't.

There are many media. Some can be paid for. Others must be played for in ways that are also not free. Three minutes of coverage on the six-o'clock news cannot be bought, but getting it may cost more than you would pay for three minutes of network prime time. The Governor must make news: He must be seen flying to exciting meetings, making speeches, shaking hands. He must put out a stream of statements, reactions, proposals to be reported on television and in the press. This aspect of the media war was the responsibility of Leslie Slote, Rockefeller's press secretary. Slote is a gregarious and agreeable man, but he is curiously lacking in enthusiasm for talking about the little tidbits of personal detail that are the spice of a reporter's material. This may well be a necessary precaution, since Rockefeller has always felt that his private life is nobody's business, and he defines privacy more inclusively even than the Kennedys. But it did mean that Rockefeller did not have the advantage the Kennedys have always enjoyed —a stream of gushingly favorable or at least fascinated free publicity.

That was why Hinman's call to Clearwater, Florida, was so important. The man he spoke to was Tom Losee, who runs the Houston office of America's second largest group of advertising agencies, McCann-Erickson, and who has worked in Rockefeller's political campaigns since 1958. Losee is a tense man with straw-blond hair whose sharp, nervous anxiety to impress you with his speed and toughness of mind would be a caricature of the Madison Avenue style if the qualities were not in his case real. When Hinman came on the line, Losee knew immediately what he was calling him about. Quickly, he flew to New York and greeted Hinman with, "What's cooking?" Hinman, whose manner was formed in a courtlier school than Madison Avenue, said carefully, "We don't know whether the Governor is thinking of going or not, but we rather think he may." Losee was not deceived. He got on the phone to a certain Gene Case. "Boys," he said, "here we go again!"

Case is a partner and the "top creative man" at a New York advertising agency called Jack Tinker & Partners, part of the McCann-Erickson/Interpublic empire. The agency is quite small and has a specialist reputation for original, intelligent advertising whose strength is that it tries to communicate with the consumer through a kind of dialogue, rather than by bludgeoning him. The account that made Tinker famous was Alka-Seltzer, for whom Case, among others, devised a campaign that was regarded in the trade as daringly cerebral. Tinker was hired by Dr. William Ronan, then dean of the School of Public Administration and Social Services at New York University, to do the advertising for Rockefeller's backs-to-the-wall 1966 campaign for reelection. The television advertising the Tinker people did for that campaign is regarded as a model. One commercial in particular, an interview with a large-mouth bass about water pollution, is regarded as a classic by the *cognoscenti*.

Losee had worked in that campaign with Ronan and the Tinker people, and in 1968, he was able to work with exactly the same team. It included five of the Tinker partners: Case; the art director, Bob Wilvers;

Myron McDonald, head of the firm and a marketing man whose specialty is planning; Clifford Botway; and Dr. Herta M. Herzog, a lady sociologist from Vienna. Altogether, fifty people were available to work on the Rockefeller account.

They started work on May 1, in the trendily decorated Tinker offices on West Fifty-seventh Street. Losee didn't have a completely free hand: he was responsible to Emmett Hughes, in charge of media, and Alton Marshall, Rockefeller's executive officer in Albany, a burly professional whom Rockefeller trusts as much as anyone. On May 30, with in effect only the two months of June and July left, Losee and his people presented a "concept," a detailed media plan, a budget, and actual specimen ads at a meeting at 22 West Fifty-fifth Street.

Their recommendations were based on a strategy paper presented at that meeting. Typed on loose-leaf paper, it runs to twenty-nine pages. As a sample of the shrewdest and most expensive advice available from the professionals of the new politics, it deserves extended quotation.

The paper is described as representing "the consensus of Tinker thinking concerning those aspects of the situation affective, particularly of the public and, therefore, the polls and, therefore, the politicians . . . the governors, the delegates, et al." After this rather jerky, rowboat launch, the Tinker thinkers' prose sails away more smoothly: "The American crisis," they assert boldly, "is not the war in Vietnam, nor rioting in the cities, nor inflation, nor deterioration of respect among our friends, nor any specific. It is a failure of leadership." The paper goes on:

WHAT IS A LEADER?
    A leader is bold, aggressive, positive, creative. . . .
    Despite the computerized complexities of modern life, the leader in his field is still the emergent hero. And America is, has been and (God willing) always will be hungry for heroes. Her treatment of them . . . from Lincoln to Babe Ruth to Martin Luther King amounts almost to canonization, so deeply is the need felt.
    Who among us is up to this?

No prizes offered for the answer to that one. But the answer doesn't come for another seven pages, in the course of which Nelson Rockefeller and his advisers are given a brief excursus on the other candidates:

> Eugene McCarthy . . . A Pied Piper who almost bridged the generation gap until the visceral pyrotechnics of Kennedy interrupted the quiet communication . . .
> Robert Kennedy . . . A controversial figure. . . . In him, the recollection of a hero who fell in Dallas . . . shorter, more prolific progeny-wise, more enigmatic, less outgoing, but becoming

more so . . . Kennedy's problem is to establish himself as a
whole hero and not just as a sibling substitute.
Richard Nixon . . . It is difficult just now to see him as *the* leader.

Having thus glibly slain his rivals, the Tinker men feel free to turn
to their client. Without fear or favor, they press relentlessly on through
the catalogue of his virtues.

The only potential leader . . . the man with the guts to do the right
things . . . a man from a famous American family. . . . His willingness to take action, after counsel, is perhaps his greatest strength in the
current visceral contest. His vision of the world and its true momentum
if one is permitted to divine it, is contemporary, ongoing, creative.

And so, at length, to the issues. One can picture the giant brains
locked onto the world's problems, high above Fifty-seventh Street, the
pipe smoke wreathing above the domed skulls, the final triumphant
"Eureka!" and the salutes that greeted the following analysis as it fluttered
from the flagpole:

It is clear today that American society is divided between those who wish
slower change and those who wish more rapid change. This dichotomy is
more severe and more widespread than at any time in our history. . . .
It is clear from Lloyd Free's preliminary report on American public
opinion in early 1968, that certain of the Governor's positions coincide
with those sought by the majority in many cases. It is also clear that
when one cuts through the bafflegab of label rhetoric to real meanings,
other of his positions can be seen productive of the actions and conse-
quent results people really want. . . . What is really wanted is better
"big government." . . . And in the heart of its Judaeo-Christian economic ethos, the American public really knows it is not going to get
something for nothing!

Cutting, so to speak, through the bafflegab of label rhetoric, what
the Tinker thinkers seem to have been trying to tell Rockefeller was this:
that the best case he could make for himself was as a new leader, and that
in pressing this case it would do him no harm to admit that he was a liberal.
Rockefeller scarcely needed to be told this. The same idea had been expressed, much more clearly and succinctly, by Emmett Hughes in a private memorandum he wrote on May 19, summarizing points made in a conversation two days before:

I believe it is essential, in the weeks and speeches immediately ahead,
that you make *clear*—as *sharply* and *incisively* as possible—*the CHOICE
that you are presenting to the Republican Party.*
This means making clear—without any explicit dealing in person-

alities as such—that Nelson Rockefeller and Richard Nixon stand for *two profoundly different views.* . . .

1. Your entire candidacy rests on the promise of giving the Republican Party a *choice*. It thus becomes our logical and central task to make *forcefully* clear *a*) that there *is* a choice and *b*) *what* it is.

2. This becomes doubly true because Nixon does *not* want such a choice defined. His haziness on issues may be natural, but it is not accidental. It is his deliberate *intent* to *blur* issues between you and him. *We must not conspire with him in doing this.* . . .

3. This means that your public utterances essentially must be aimed at *your standing in the polls—NOT the presumed preconceptions of delegates*. Obviously the latter can and must be attended to *personally and privately*. But the decisive favorable influence *on* the delegates *will* be the polls. Or as Lloyd Free says: "The Governor is *not* going to win delegates by sounding more and more like Richard Nixon. He cannot out-Nixon Nixon."

The time is upon us for you to sound less and less like a philosopher —and more and more and more like a fighter.

What advertising agencies know about is advertising. There was a remarkable contrast between the pretentious and amateurish advice the Tinker people had to give on political strategy and the simple logic of their actual media plan. It was aimed, they stated plainly, "at effective influence on the national public-opinion polls." It should focus on a number of key markets: "1. Representative of large and movable blocs of delegates. 2. Representative of population segments potentially favorable to and therefore movable by clear and dramatic statements of the Governor's position on the vital issues." They listed sixteen big northern states, with one-third of the population and just over one-half of the delegates to the Republican Convention between them, as "communication targets."

Tinker recommended three complementary assaults on public opinion. The one most directly focused on the key areas was a campaign of sixty-second spot television commercials for early- and late-evening time periods in thirty key markets. These spots would be precisely aimed at the very people most likely to react favorably when questioned about Rockefeller by Gallup and Harris.

Tinker also recommended approximately three minutes a week of national network television advertising for the seven weeks of the campaign. Correctly used, they argued, television "is the most emotionally evocative of all media. Its topicality brings the futility of Vietnam into fifty million homes nightly." Three network minutes a week, they calculated, would bring Nelson Rockefeller into ninety percent of all American homes.

The most original advertising recommendation the Tinker people made—and, in the end, perhaps the most successful—was not for television, but for the oldest medium of all: newspapers. Tom Losee explained the rationale. "People see so much advertising," he said, zapping his head with his hands and making electronic zeroing-in noises. "Fifteen hundred, two thousand messages a day coming in. People think it's bullshit. Political advertising, to get through, has to be simple. It has to be dignified. Not that same old hack political gobbledygook." And so Tinker recommended that Rockefeller insert, in forty newspapers in the chosen key areas, "in referential, documentary black and white, the Governor's position on the key issues. As contrasted to the general nonpositions of Richard Nixon." This was done. And as a final touch, the newspaper ads were bound together in a special supplement in the *Miami Herald* for the opening of the convention, so that each delegate would be confronted with a plain, bold statement of Rockefeller's position, signed in the hand that launched a thousand checks.

The entire media budget came to four and a half million dollars. In round figures, two million of that went on the television spots, one million on the network television, and a million and a half on the newspaper advertising. The advertising started in mid-June, and Losee and the Tinker people originally planned to bring it to a peak, not at the opening of the convention on August 5 but ten days earlier, on the day when the last Gallup interviews were being carried out. "Why spend money influencing people who have already been interviewed?" one of the admen put it. "The whole strategy of our campaign was to influence the polls."

The strategy was clear enough, but what about the tactics? What issues should the spots and the newspaper ads stress? At this point in the development of the Rockefeller media campaign something extremely interesting happened. It may not have affected the result, but it should be a warning against oversimple judgments of how the new scientific politics works. The theory presupposes remorseless pragmatism, unmoved by human emotions or ideological preconceptions: The polls identify the sections of the electorate that can be won; further polling determines which issues should be stressed to attract the winnable voters; and the media campaign then automatically addresses itself to those issues. That is the theory. But that is not quite what happened in Rockefeller's campaign.

The polling on which Rockefeller's media campaign was based had been done in February by Lloyd Free. Using a national sample of Gallup interviews, Free had asked people to say how worried they were about twenty-one problems or concerns he had listed on the basis of earlier polls. Their answers were graded on a four-point scale and used to draw up another list of problems worrying the American electorate, in order of intensity:

1. Vietnam
2. Crime and juvenile delinquency
3. Keeping our military defense strong

4. Rioting in our cities
5. Preventing World War III
6. Prices and the cost of living
7. Drug addicts and narcotic drugs
8. Maintaining respect for the U.S. abroad
9. Government spending
10. Communist China
11. Raising moral standards in the country
12. The threat of international Communism
13. Keeping NATO and our other alliances strong
14. Relations with Russia
15. Improving our educational system
16. Reducing poverty in this country
17. Negro racial problems
18. The problem of ensuring that lower-income families get adequate medical care
19. Air and water pollution
20. The trend toward a more powerful federal government
21. Rebuilding our cities

Clearly, this list reveals an extremely conservative set of priorities in the minds of the voters. The right-wing concerns, numbers 2 through 13, all rate higher than the characteristically liberal concerns, numbers 15, 16, 17, 18, and 21. One would expect a campaign that took this profile of the voters' state of mind as its starting point to stress the need for toughness and preparedness in foreign policy and to put law and order ahead of social reform at home.

The logic of the list, pointing toward a conservative emphasis in the Rockefeller campaign, was reinforced by another consideration. As Free pointed out to Rockefeller at the Memorial Day meeting and on other occasions in private, it would be worthless for him to go after the votes of the poor and the blacks, or even their weight in the opinion polls. (Free was not making this point out of personal predilection. He happens to be a liberal Republican. To him, it was a matter of fact.) The Negro vote, he pointed out, was nine per cent of the electorate, and ninety percent of it was likely to go to the Democratic candidate in November. Not only that: any support that might be won among Negroes or the poor was likely to be won at the expense of support from larger blocs of white Republicans or independents.

There was a third argument that cut the same way. The politicians —people like the lieutenant governor of New York, Malcolm Wilson, and Leonard Hall, an ex-Republican National Chairman—who were in charge of the delegate-wooing side of Rockefeller's operation viewed any emphasis on liberal issues in the media campaign as flatly counterproductive of what they were trying to do.

Yet, the Rockefeller advertisements were not conservative. They were, on the whole, liberal—some of them almost provocatively so. Free's sample might put "rebuilding our cities" as the last of the electorate's concerns, but one Rockefeller ad showed the candidate talking about urban renewal in Harlem and saying, "We have faith in the heart of Harlem, and we have faith in the people who live there." Most "unscientific" of all was a sixty-second film commercial that opened with a drum roll and a shot of a dark, wet slum street. Rockefeller himself read the narration, in that arresting, husky voice of his:

Three thousand black men were among those brave Americans who had died so far in Vietnam.
    One hundred thousand black men will come home from Vietnam. What will they make of America, these men who risk their lives for the American Dream, and come home to find the American Slumber? What will they make of the slums where, too often, jobs are as rare as hope?
    This is Nelson Rockefeller, and I say they deserve more than this. I say they deserve an equal chance. They deserve decent housing. Decent jobs. And the schooling and training to fill these jobs.
    To those who cry, "We can't afford it," I say, "We can't afford not to do it."
    To those who cry, "Law and order," I say, "To keep law and order, there must be—

At this point a black man looms out of the shadows and walks toward the camera, as Rocky says,

Justice and opportunity!

Justice and opportunity! That was not the first thought, apparently, evoked in many a viewer's mind by the sight of a strange black man walking swiftly out of the shadows on a dark street. "That ad was a flop," says Free candidly. "In fact, a lot of people, especially women, didn't like it at all. You see, you couldn't really tell who was coming toward you. It was a little alarming for many people."
    The repercussions were immediate. Professional politicians from various points around the country got on the phone and "squawked like hell," as one of Rockefeller's closest friends puts it: "There was a big playback on that ad about the black soldier." "Our campaign was pretty schizophrenic," says another of Rockefeller's housecarls. "Sometimes our two organizations, the one aimed at the delegates and the other at the polls, were antithetical. If we put out something, say, a full page on the riots, that would appeal to Democrats and liberal Republicans in the northeast, Malcolm Wilson would go out of his mind in the Midwest—and you couldn't blame him." To their credit, the Rockefeller people were unde-

terred. "We had our charter," says Losee, "which was to go ahead and influence the polls. The politicians might scream like hell, as they did about the riot ad. But that was none of our business."

How did this confusion, this tug of war between heartless pragmatism and liberal instinct, remain unresolved so long? This was supposed to be a supremely professional operation of the new, nonideological politics.

But even at the level of pragmatism, Rockefeller faced a dilemma. Cold logic might dictate that he should concentrate his advertising effort on the issues that troubled the people, and that if the people wanted conservative talk, he must give it to them. But an equally unsentimental argument, as we have seen, cut the other way. As both Emmett Hughes and Free argued, Rockefeller could not hope to press his claims as a leader by trying to "out-Nixon Nixon." He must present "a choice, not an echo." And he must be himself.

The second reason for the unresolved dilemma lay in the kind of man Nelson Rockefeller is. He is not a desiccated calculating machine. On the contrary, he is emotional by nature, and, in particular, he is emotionally committed to the very issues that ranked so low on Lloyd Free's list of priorities: rebuilding cities, justice and opportunity for Negroes. "Nelson got tangled up in his emotions," says Free affectionately.

Finally, Rockefeller is a proud man. He might desire the Presidency. He might even, in some hidden corner of his Rockefeller soul, have some difficulty in repressing the thought that he had a right to it. But he was not going to stoop for it.

All of this is relevant to the future of the new scientific management in politics. It is never going to be easy to find candidates who combine the required force of character and intellect with a willingness to accept policies shaped by polls and computers. But a more specific lesson can also be drawn from the "schizophrenia" of the Rockefeller media campaign. It is that the "creative people" themselves will find it difficult to follow a grimly logical course. For one thing, some subjects make better film than others; it is easier to dramatize highly emotional issues of social justice. For another, people with the talent to manipulate the technology of mass media have ideas of their own. "What happened," says one of Rockefeller's political advisers, "was that the executives agreed with the policy indicated by the polls, but then the creative people gathered up the ball and ran with it. What they produced was pretty much what you'd expect from a group of New York intellectuals." Exactly: television films are not made by farmers in Iowa.

How effective were the New Politics, Rockefeller style? The campaign was, of course, extremely expensive. When Rockefeller was in Tulsa in June for the governors' conference, Les Slote managed to find an hour for *la dolce vita.* It gets hot in Oklahoma in the summer, and Slote was relaxing in the hotel pool, a cigar in one hand, a drink within range, with two pretty secretaries in bikinis to apply the sun-tan lotion. A reporter jocularly addressed him as a "cheap so-and-so." "Sir," said Slote, rising majestically from the water in mock indignation, "call this campaign what you will, but never call it *cheap!*" Few reporters were inclined to do so. Speculation rioted. In fact, the total cost was rather less than some of the more awed guesses: in the region of seven million dollars, all told, including the media budget, salaries, transportation, polls, communications, and rent—for the lavish Americana Hotel in Bal Harbor at convention time and for office space in New York and elsewhere. One close friend believes that each of the five Rockefeller brothers agreed to limit his contribution to seven hundred fifty thousand dollars. What value did they get for their investment?

"We actually did influence the polls," Tom Losee insists. Unfortunately, whether he was right or not depends upon which polls you read. The Harris series gives some support to his claim. For example:

May	16–18	Nixon 37	Humphrey 41	Wallace 14
June	10–17	Nixon 36	Humphrey 43	Wallace 13
July	25–29	Nixon 36	Humphrey 41	Wallace 16

May	16–18	Rocky 37	Humphrey 40	Wallace 17
June	10–17	Rocky 36	Humphrey 40	Wallace 15
July	25–29	Rocky 40	Humphrey 34	Wallace 20

In other words, if you are prepared to ignore all extrinsic factors that might have affected the candidates' standings and treat the fluctuations of the figures as a direct result of their media campaigns; if, too, you ignore any effect, positive or negative, that other candidates' media expenditures may have procured; then on Harris's figures it can be said that, whereas *before* Rockefeller's advertising campaign opened both Rocky and Nixon would have been beaten by Humphrey, *after* it Rockefeller led Humphrey by six percent and Nixon trailed him by five percent.

No such conclusion can be drawn from the two Gallup polls for which the interviewing was done between May 4 and 8 and between June 29 and July 3:

| May | 4–8 | Nixon 39 | Humphrey 36 | Wallace 14 |
| June | 29–July 3 | Nixon 35 | Humphrey 40 | Wallace 16 |

| May | 4–8 | Rocky 40 | Humphrey 33 | Wallace 16 |
| June | 29–July 3 | Rocky 36 | Humphrey 36 | Wallace 21 |

As we have seen, all Rockefeller's hopes were pinned on Gallup's third and final, eve-of-Miami, poll. They were to be cruelly disappointed. On July 30, George Gallup released from his sibyl's cave in Princeton the results of the poll conducted between July 20 and 23. In bold type across the whole sheet, the headline read: NIXON OVERTAKES HUMPHREY AND McCARTHY; ROCKY RUNS EVEN AGAINST BOTH DEMOCRATS. The figures showed Nixon seven points ahead of Humphrey at 40–38, where he had been 35–40; and Rockefeller still dead level against Humphrey at 36–36.

Bobby Douglass, an aide traveling with Rockefeller, describes the effect: "It was a terrific blow. We got it in the morning, in Washington. The press didn't catch up with it until we got to Pittsburgh that afternoon, on our way to Chicago. We decided to release our own polls to blunt the impact. But it didn't do much good. Nobody could understand what had happened. There were all sorts of suspicions in the heat of the moment, including the suspicion that Gallup had been got at, which was absurd. The Governor was fantastic. He never winced. He kept his cool, waiting to see what Harris would say. It was about one in the morning [of July 31] when we got advance notice of the Harris figures. You can imagine what an exciting evening that was!"

ROCKY TOPS ALL CANDIDATES, said the headline on the Harris poll when it appeared in the *Washington Post,* on August 1. The same day, Rockefeller headquarters released what they carefully called an Archibald Crossley poll—which was, in fact, done by Crossley for his friend Free and paid for by Rockefeller. It showed Nixon leading Rockefeller by two percent nationally, but Rockefeller ahead in seven out of the nine key industrial states in which everybody realized the election was going to be decided. But by that time, it was too late. The damage had been done.

A flat contradiction between George Gallup and Louis Harris at such a critical moment was a landmark in the history of political polls in the United States. It was the first serious blow to their growing credibility since the disaster of 1948 when they predicted that Dewey would beat Truman. Realizing that the crisis for their profession was too grave for rivalry, Gallup and Harris put out a joint statement insisting that both of their polls were right—at the time the interviewing was done—and concluding, from an appraisal of the two candidates' strength in the big industrial states, that Rockefeller had the better chance of being elected. But what could explain so total a divergence over so short a period? The Gallup interviewing was done between July 20 and July 23, Harris's between July 25 and July 29. Lloyd Free suggested one explanation to Rockefeller: that Gallup's result reflected the endorsement of Nixon by General Eisenhower, still the most admired man in American public life. But Eisenhower's endorsement came on July 18. Could its effect have been at once so great and so short-lived? Privately, the pollsters concede another possible explanation. "Those of us who know anything about statistics know," Free told us, "that in the case of any given random sample poll, there are ninety-five chances out of a hundred that it will come within the limits of probability—that is, within three or four percent of the true figure. It is easy to forget that that is another way of saying that there are five chances in a hundred that it will not." In plain language, one of the polls may have been plumb wrong. Which one?

It scarcely matters. For Rockefeller's whole effort had been staked on his faith that the polls would convince the Republican delegates that he could win and that Nixon could not. The flat contradiction between the two major polls meant that neither of them would convince the delegates of anything—least of all of something they did not want to believe.

The Rockefeller campaign can be seen as a rebellion by one section of the American upper class against the dominance of the middle class in the Republican Party. The candidate and his financial backers sprang from the great dynasties of the American business aristocracy. Their advisers— men like Hinman, Thayer, Hughes, and Free—had risen in the service or at least in the atmosphere of large-scale American corporate enterprise. Their instinct was to challenge the Republican leadership with weapons that had proved themselves in the corporate world—polls, computers, planning, advertisements.

But there is another section of the upper middle class in America that has little to do with the aristocracy of corporate business. Its life intersects with that of the great corporations at many points, but it has very different values. This is the aristocracy of education and intelligence. While the old pols of the Republican Party were being challenged by Rockefeller, in the Democratic Party, the McCarthy challenge was led by the intelligentsia, that also used the tactics and the weapons that came most naturally to it. This is what happened in every state where McCarthy had strength—in California, in New York, in the Middle West, in Oregon and Colorado. But it can be seen with the clarity of a laboratory experiment in the case of Connecticut.

Connecticut is the third smallest of the states in area, but the fourth most densely populated. Four-fifths of its two and three-quarter million people live in urban areas, most of them in the two sizable cities of Hartford, the capital, and New Haven, in industrial Bridgeport, and in the spreading, wealthy, New York suburbs in Fairfield County—Stamford, Norwalk, Westport. It is an industrial state with a high proportion of ethnically conscious first- and second-generation immigrants, and a high proportion of Roman Catholics. So it is not surprising that the Democratic

Party in Connecticut has long been in the grip of a relatively genteel but deeply entrenched machine. And the machine has for twenty years, been in the grip of a Hartford Irish lawyer named John Moran Bailey. Bailey won the chairmanship of the Connecticut party in 1948, and in 1960, thanks to having been the first of all the bosses to come out for John F. Kennedy, he became Democratic National Chairman as well.

Bailey's power was based on patronage—which successive Democratic governors cheerfully allowed him to dispense in return for the thumping majorities he delivered for them at election time—and on his control of the funds raised at enormous dinners to which contractors and others hoping to do business with the state, employees, and ambitious politicians were invited. In Connecticut he was known as King John, and on the national level he established himself as one of the great magnates of the old feudal politics.

On the eve of his greatest battle, Bailey walked alone into the lair of his enemies. It was at a McCarthy party in the Carleton Room of the Hotel America in Hartford, on Friday, June 21, the night before the Connecticut state convention. He found himself face to face with two of his most for-midable adversaries, the playwright Arthur Miller and the novelist William Styron. Someone made introductions, and Miller asked, politely but with a finger pointed for emphasis, "Mr. Bailey, how do you keep all that strength?" Bailey pushed his glasses back on his forehead and took his cigar out of his mouth. "I just keep shaking hands," he said. Miller looked after him as he left. "He's really not the worst guy in the world."

But Connecticut was perhaps the worst state in the country, outside the South, from the point of view of those who sought at the beginning of 1968 to challenge the reign of the old politics. Bailey stood at Lyndon Johnson's right hand. And there had never been a challenge to his right as state chairman to pick whom he pleased to attend the convention. In January, he made the expected pronouncement. "The Democratic National Convention is as good as over," he said. "It'll be Lyndon Johnson, and that's that."

But that was not that. On April 3, Senator McCarthy was hailed by wildly cheering crowds in Bailey's own state as he pronounced the dam-nable heresy that "you only need a strong organization when you don't have people who can make independent judgments. . . . I think Mr. Bailey is like the Wizard of Oz," McCarthy went on. "When you pull the curtain back, there is only a voice."

On April 10, rather more than forty-four percent of the Democrats who voted in primary elections in thirty-one large Connecticut towns—pri-maries that most residents of the state had never realized they could have—were for McCarthy.

On June 22, after a night of tense bargaining and extravagant excitement, almost a third of the delegates to the state convention in Hartford walked out in protest at Bailey's tactics. On August 28, out of the forty-four delegates who were with John Bailey at the convention in Chicago, nine voted for Senator McCarthy.

How was such a rebellion mounted? What sort of people dared to mount it? And how did the old pol respond to this frontal challenge from the new politics?

After it was all over, one of the McCarthyites summed up their strengths and weaknesses accurately, if arrogantly: "We didn't know much about politics, but we were pretty intelligent."

The chief ring-leader of this guerrilla insurrection among the intellectuals was a Protestant theology teacher named Reverend Joseph Duffey. Duffey first learned that McCarthy was going to be a candidate at an ADA board meeting in Washington. Although Al Lowenstein invited him to come to his Democratic Alternative meeting in Chicago, Duffey was not specially keen on going. He had been active in various peace groups, but he found himself disenchanted with the present mood of the New Left: "I guess you could call me a sort of revisionist Marxist, but certainly I had very little sympathy with the Maoists." At the last minute, on an impulse, he decided to go to Chicago on December 2.

To his surprise, Duffey found there were about a dozen people from Connecticut there, and they decided to hold a caucus in the hotel. They were a highly educated, distinctly well-to-do group, and not particularly young: Duffey was 35, and most were older. Perhaps the most experienced was Mrs. Stephanie May. She was on the national board of SANE and had been an important organizer in the campaign for the nuclear test ban treaty. She was a transplanted New Yorker; the whole McCarthy campaign in Connecticut drew heavily on the New York suburbs. The major question at the caucus was whether what was wanted was another peace campaign or a political campaign. Duffey argued strongly that in an election year it must be politics.

A meeting was held on December 10, in Ezra Stiles College at Yale, one of the two magnificent new colleges designed by Eero Saarinen. Yale was the second great focus of the McCarthy movement in Connecticut. Already in the autumn, a Yale Law School student, Geoffrey Cowan, had been in touch with Lowenstein and Curtis Gans. Now he prepared a two-page study of Connecticut electoral law and read it out to the meeting.

There were about thirty people there, a slightly broader cross section than the group in Chicago the week before, but still middle class. There were engineers, accountants, a few clerks, housewives, and teachers. To their great surprise (although most of them were to some extent active in local politics), they found that Connecticut could in effect have a primary.

A new system for selecting convention delegates had been introduced in 1955 but never used.

The unit of local government in Connecticut is the "town." There are 169 "towns," some urban, most rural or surburban. In towns of under five thousand, Cowan told the group, the first round of selection of delegates to the state convention took place in caucuses, which began late in February. Any registered Democrat could take part. In the bigger towns, which was where the regular party had its strength, participation would not be so easy. Delegates to the state convention would be named by the town committee. The only way of challenging them was to pick a whole rival slate, pay a filing fee, get a petition in its favor circulated by a resident of that town, and get five percent of the registered Democrats to sign it.

After the meeting, Mrs. May telephoned Washington and asked national headquarters for some buttons. "Gee!" said the man she talked to. "That's a great idea! I'll have some made."

On January 13, the first McCarthy for President meeting was held at a restaurant in Cheshire, in the middle of the state. By this time Arthur Miller and William Styron had agreed to be sponsors, and Paul Newman had become an enthusiastic supporter.

They still couldn't get any literature out of Washington, so they sat down and wrote their own—biographical stuff about McCarthy, propaganda about the war, and a little leaflet, written by an engineer, called "The System: You Have to Know It to Beat It." They laughed a lot about the number of places in the law where it turned out that things happened "at the discretion of the chairman." That meant Bailey.

In the next few weeks, something very strange happened—the result, perhaps, of the Tet offensive. The insurgents began to be surprised at how much strength they had. Reports came in from one caucus after another in the smaller towns that they had elected delegates who were for McCarthy. And in the bigger towns people were organizing petitions and registering new voters. In New Haven, McCarthy people registered enough Yale graduate students to beat the Barbieri machine; the prime mover there was Chester Kerr, head of the Yale University Press.

On February 17, Senator McCarthy made his first appearance in Connecticut. It so happened, by coincidence, that that was the night of one of John Bailey's big fund-raising dinners in Hartford. It became a trial of strength. The insurgents and the regulars both tried to get as many people as possible to come to their show. In the end, Bailey's gigantic dinner attracted about 1800 people, but there were 2500 at the McCarthy rally in Westport.

Shortly afterward, a McCarthy for President office opened in Hartford on a shoestring. The McCarthy people were mostly quite well off, but they were not in a position to make the big donations that businessmen can afford. What money could be raised in Connecticut was mostly sent out of the state. "We had been discouraged by the national staff from doing anything in Connecticut," Joe Duffey says, "because it looked so hopeless."

In spite of the shortage of money, things began to look far from hopeless. Soon the required number of signatures had been certified on petitions in thirty-one of the larger towns. Now the question was how to turn delegates to the state convention, among whom the McCarthy supporters ultimately numbered 284 out of 958, into delegates to the National Convention in Chicago. The McCarthy camp set up a committee which from April to June met weekly at a restaurant in Hartford to prime Joe Duffey, who went each week to negotiate with John Bailey. At first, there were just nine on the committee: Duffey, Mrs. May, Mrs. Anne Wexler, the vivacious wife of a Westport eye surgeon, and representatives of each of the six congressional districts. But gradually it grew, partly because there was an unquenchable suspicion, not of Duffey's motives, but of his ability to avoid being cheated by Bailey. Duffey realizes now that the insurgents misunderstood Bailey's power. "They thought he was the boss, therefore he could deliver what he wanted. But after I had met him a few times, I realized that he too was locked in by his associates."

(There was another cause of dissention in the insurgent forces in April and May. Many of the McCarthy supporters would have preferred to be for Robert Kennedy, and Kennedy's entrance into the race produced great strains and some suspicions.)

"At the beginning of our weekly talks," Duffey remembers, "Bailey and I were sparring with one another. He would say to me, 'Don't worry, it's going to be an open convention.' I would tell him that we wouldn't be happy with less than half the delegates because after all we had got more than forty-four per cent of the votes in the primaries. And he would tell me, 'Don't worry, if you behave responsibly, we might have no objection to giving you one or two seats on the delegation.' "

"I began to enjoy the stimulation of those Friday night sessions," Duffey admits with some surprise, "and I feel he enjoyed the drama and the competition too: that was one of the reasons why he was in politics. I felt I was learning something about human nature and also about the nature of power. In the beginning we had a certain paranoia and also a certain naiveté about Bailey's power. But as I talked to him, I began to understand that he had power only by exercising it as a broker, by seeing that as far as possible people got what they wanted."

Shortly before the convention, the McCarthy people realized that *they* had something that Bailey wanted for *his* people. In the primaries, almost by accident, they had won some seats on the state committee, as well as at the state convention, and some of the leading figures of the party had been swept off the committee. In particular, there was the case of Miss Katherine Quinn, who had been on the committee for forty years. She more or less ran the state while Bailey was in Washington, and she was greatly beloved. She had, someone said, "been to a thousand wakes." The McCarthy firebrands saw her as a bargaining counter, but Duffey, who had to do the bargaining, realized this could be dangerous. He knew that there were people on the other side who grudgingly recognized the merits of the insurgents' case; who would not go for McCarthy but who would vote for a resolution giving the McCarthy people a fair share of delegates at Chicago in the name of justice. For such people, it was a bombshell that Miss Quinn had been defeated, and if Duffey tried to exploit her fall, he would be a knight in tarnished armor.

Bailey, understanding this, played it for all it was worth. At the state convention itself, his crowd turned up wearing buttons saying "I Love Katie." Duffey tried to take the sting out of this counteroffensive by attempting to put Miss Quinn back on the committee. But Katie Quinn refused to be put back. The McCarthy people had stooped, without conquering. "It may sound absurd," Duffey mused to us, "but I did have the feeling that this was a case where we amateurs were playing the game a lot more crudely than Bailey would have played it."

The McCarthy levies were skillfully trained for the convention by Anne Wexler. They circulated copies of *Robert's Rules,* complexes of draft resolutions, and contingency plans. Quietly, they got fourteen of their people onto the thirty-seven-man rules committee, so that by the time the real business of the convention opened, it was clear that Bailey would have to deal with them. To the regulars, it seemed that someone was getting away with something, and their agony was well-expressed in a heart-felt cry from Robert Killian, state Attorney General:

The rule of the majority [*in which he counted himself*] is the very fabric of our democracy. . . . The Elks have it, the Knights of Columbus have it, the American Legion has it, and gentlemen, as a man who was once a member of that great organization, I can say the Boy Scouts have it. Gentlemen, I recall that the Daughters of the American Revolution abide by the majority rule!

The insurgents had their first meeting with the Bailey forces on Friday afternoon. Bailey offered five seats on the delegation to the national convention, and said he wouldn't budge. Duffey said, "Ten," and they laughed. So then the McCarthy people offered to swap Katie Quinn for seats. There was a horrified cry of "Katie Quinn is not for sale!"

Bailey had sometimes said to Duffey as a joke that the whole thing would be worked out at midnight on the evening before the convention. But it was two A.M. when Duffey received the summons to come to Governor John Dempsey's suite in the Hotel America. "It was like something out of *The Last Hurrah*," he said afterward. "The place was surrounded with strong-arm men, and I couldn't get into the inner sanctum until I had been O.K.'d. Bailey met me and said, 'I'll go to seven or eight.' " Duffey went back to his committee again, and the committee gave him a flat no. What was more, they now wanted him to run against Abraham Ribicoff for the Senate. Duffey called Ribicoff and broke this news to him; Ribicoff was extremely unhappy.

Duffey went back to the Governor's suite at about three A.M. The suite was crowded: the Governor himself was there, and Ribicoff, and what Duffey remembers as "all these hard-eyed men sitting around on beds." At one stage, a drunken woman came to the door. Someone barred her, but she bit the Governor's doctor on the arm, and he was hopping round giving out little moans.

Duffey explained that his people had been prepared for ten seats and that if they got less they would walk out of the state convention. At about four, having tried everything else, Bailey asked Duffey how much he made at the theological seminary and then offered him a job with the National Committee in Washington. "It was for rather a lot of money," says Duffey without resentment.

Duffey went away again, and Ribicoff called to say that the Governor was furious. Duffey told him there was nothing he could do about it, because even if he accepted less than ten seats, his people would walk out. Ribicoff was desperately anxious to prevent an open break, and the next day he actually got up and told the convention that the McCarthy people could have his seat. That still didn't add up to ten, however; so out they walked.

Rather to the Connecticut leaders' surprise, this heroic gesture was not at all appreciated by national McCarthy headquarters. On June 26, the Wednesday after the convention, Joe Duffey saw McCarthy in New York. McCarthy did not seem very interested in the details of the struggle in Connecticut, but he made it quite plain that he wanted those nine delegates. So Duffey wrote a letter to Bailey and called a press conference. He would take the nine delegates, he said, though he reserved the right to protest. He still wonders whether he was right. "If we had held back, we might have got more than those nine seats. We would have put Bailey under tremendous pressure. All the people who were running for office would have pressured him. I still wonder whether, after I talked to McCarthy, there wasn't a failure of my own will and patience. Perhaps the point was that both Bailey and I were locked into a system that couldn't bear so much participation."

Perhaps that was it. "The System—You Have to Know It to Beat It." Or should the pamphlet have been called "The System: You Have to Join It to Beat It"? Joe Duffey and Anne Wexler and their friends achieved a great deal. They brought new people into politics, raised new issues, and shook the assumption that the old pols would always have it their own way.

"There is at least a possibility," says Joe Duffey cautiously, "that things will never be the same again." Just before Christmas 1968, a new Connecticut organization called the Caucus of Concerned Democrats met. Duffey and his friends were all there, and so was the New Left; so was a surprising sprinkling of party regulars. Already some people in Connecticut are hoping that what Duffey calls the "second- and third-generation educated" will be the new backbone of a Democratic Party in the state. Perhaps they will, perhaps they won't. But a New Politics? Certainly the lesson of 1968 in Connecticut would seem to be that the new politicians were successful in exactly the proportion that they learned to play the old game.

Pressure Groups   7

This study by John Denton is part of a larger one tracing the success of Proposition 14 in California in 1964. Proposition 14 was a measure to repeal the effects of the Rumford Fair Housing Act of the previous year. This proposition was supported vigorously by the National Association of Real Estate Boards (NAREB) and the California Real Estate Association (CREA). In reporting the actions of these two organizations, the author came across a much broader spectrum of practices that are contained herein as a case study of the NAREB and its attempts to perpetuate racial segregation through private pressure as well as through public enactments such as Proposition 14. The thin line between public and private actions is sometimes difficult to discern because of the power of private law systems described by Mr. Denton. The student should recognize, however, that one of the fundamental public choices we make is which goods and services will be produced publicly and which privately; this decision is, highly political, of course. The case also illustrates why desegregation is so difficult even when the government is firmly supporting it. Finally, the student should consider the consequences of how firmly entrenched are groups such as the NAREB, the control they exercise over our decision-making markets, and the obvious difficulty of choosing strategies to combat them. Without a doubt, this case delineates the activities of only one among a vast number of private or quasi-public organizations that wield tremendous power in American society and politics.

JOHN H. DENTON

The National Association of Real Estate Boards and the Ghetto System

SEGREGATION AND PRIVATE GROUP LAW SYSTEMS

Innumerable decisions are involved in the choice of residence for Americans. Can these decisions be freely made, or are there constraints and sanctions, imposed by private groups, which dictate that minorities shall live in older city neighborhoods and whites in suburban newer ones?

By private group law systems we mean well articulated, although generally unwritten codes specifying how individuals are to act in given circumstances. Enforcement of such codes will be by those methods that effectively bind us to customary ways of behaving; on the one hand, punishments such as group scorn, ostracism, and noncooperation in business and social activities with those who break the codes; on the other hand, rewards such as social, economic, and political advancement for those who respect the codes. These unwritten codes are often fortified and strengthened by formal procedures and express agreements that make no mention of race but that exist solely to enable members to hold the line against racial intrusion. Illustrations of these more formal kinds of sanctions are membership clubs to which one must belong before being permitted to purchase real estate in a designated area, and buy-back agreements that require owners offering their property for sale to give their neighbors, or the subdivider, or a neighborhood association first refusal. Words are never used to spell out that the purpose of these devices is to maintain segregation, but everyone understands that they will be employed only if an owner breaks the line by selling or renting to a member of an "undesirable" ethnic group. Because a device of this kind—say a buy-back agreement—is seldom openly applied for racial exclusion purposes, it is difficult to find cases illustrating their uses in this way. In such cases the discriminatory intent is usually hidden behind an innocent sounding enforcement of the letter of the agreement. But *House*

John H. Denton, *Apartheid American Style* (Berkeley: Diablo Press, 1967), pp. 37–70. (Abridged.)

and Home, the prestige magazine of the home building industry, then owned by the Luce interests, reported the following in June 1964:

> In Kansas City, Lake Lotawanna Development Company, developer of 1200 lots on an artificial lake, is suing a couple who announced plans to sell a home to a Negro. The Company contends Mr. and Mrs. William Hill violated a deed restriction requiring them to offer to sell first to adjoining neighbors and the subdivider.[1]

To many minority persons the question whether there are private group law systems operating to prevent minorities from breaking out of their ghettos must seem rhetorical. For them the answer is so obviously "yes" that it is inconceivable that it should need explicit proof. . . .

This study will examine some of the ways in which organized real estate, led by the National Association of Real Estate Boards (NAREB), operates a law system that reaches into government, churches, and universities. Organized real estate is allied with reactionary forces in industry, commerce, and banking in its efforts to control private decisions in the real estate market in order to support and preserve the ghetto system. . . .

CUSTOM, CONVENTION OR LAW SYSTEM

Lawyers are possessive about the term "law system." They usually limit its application to those formal codes of conduct operated by judges, lawyers, and public administrators under the power of the government; other behavior control systems are termed "customary" or conventional. The implication is that law is the only control that does not depend on the individual's consent. This does not mean that lawyers do not recognize the power of institutions other than their own but rather, they tend to rely on the self-serving fiction that all other institutions depend on the law for legitimacy and that law has the only real power to bend a man's will to its orders. Roscoe Pound, the eminent law teacher and philosopher said:

> We must not forget that law is not the only agency of social control. The household, the church, the school, the voluntary organizations, professional associations, social clubs and fraternal organizations, each with their canons of conduct, do a greater or less part of the social engineering.

Then, like J. Edgar Hoover, or some other policemen, Pound adds: "the brunt of the task falls on the legal order."[2]

The practical answer to this assertion is given by Karl Llewellyn, eminent legal scholar and teacher:

Rarely, very rarely, we check conduct or embark on conduct or modify conduct, with a conscious eye to the law. When we do, it commonly has to do with fresh-baked law, new law—and it must be that most freakish of new law; new law that for some reason we happen to know about.[3]

Llewellyn is clearly right. We are far more likely to be aware of the rigid segregation code of real estate brokers, mortgage loan officers and institutions, appraisers, and public officials than of any of the state or municipal codes. Californians knew about the Rumford Act because it was fresh law and because California Real Estate Association (CREA) used every available public relations means to create unwarranted fears about that law. In effect, the real estate industry's private law system challenged the law passed by the legislature, the Rumford Act, and forced its repeal, by Proposition 14, so that the industry's control could not be challenged.

The term "law system" is used in preference to "custom" to make sure that the reader understands that the ghetto system is maintained by *force* and does not depend upon the consent of those whose actions are controlled. Of course, most white Americans appear to discriminate "voluntarily" but, where this is not the result of social or business pressures, it often results from fear of "getting out of line." We must recognize that our tendency to observe the law is as necessary for the enforcement of the segregation code as it is for the enforcement of any other law system. . . .

Housing Segregation Is the Foundation of the Ghetto System

The ghetto question is broader than just housing segregation. It has often been pointed out that ghettos result in de facto school segregation and other inequalities in the provision of public services to the various neighborhoods in a community. Not as frequently noticed, but certainly of equal importance, is the fact that the ghetto system results in gross inequalities of economic opportunity. The ghetto dweller is limited not only in his choice of housing, but in the income and investment real estate that he can buy; he is barred from membership in business and professional associations, and his opportunities to enter most types of businesses are extremely limited. For example, service jobs as department store clerks, bank tellers and the like have generally been limited to stores and banks located within the ghetto.

Sociology Professor Leo Kuper, formerly of South Africa and now on the faculty at UCLA, has the following comment on the relationship between racial discrimination and the economic elite:

Race prejudice and discrimination generally protect a structure of privilege in property, occupational opportunity, prestige and other material and social benefits. The link between property and discrimination is particularly close. For this reason, realtors as representatives of property interests occupy a crucial position. It seems inherent in their profession that it should influence realtors to become active agents of racial discrimination in such societies as the United States where the practice of racial discrimination is so widespread and where property owners and realtors are mostly white.[4]

Although NAREB and CREA members pride themselves on being "representatives of property interests," they deny that this leads them to become *active* agents of racial discrimination. Generally, they insist that they do not initiate or encourage racial discrimination and the entire impetus to discriminate comes from property owners. Sometimes, however, they make the contradictory claim that in the sale of single family homes, almost no one discriminates. CREA President Burt Smith has made this claim on a number of occasions and supported it by citing the few discriminatory listings found in CREA's statewide survey of multiple listing practices, reported in the previous chapter [of the larger study]. He reasons that (1) the Unruh Act prohibits agents from discriminating without an owner's written authorization, and (2) the CREA survey shows that owners seldom give such an authorization, therefore, housing "being offered through CREA member boards' multiple listing services is available to qualified Negroes and other minority groups."[5] This could mean that discrimination in the sale of single family homes is practically nonexistent —an *Alice in Wonderland* explanation, in view of what is generally known.

As a test of the genuineness of CREA's claims we need to inquire: (1) Why do most minority people live in segregated neighborhoods? Is segregation increasing or diminishing? Is segregated housing the result of poverty, choice or discrimination? (2) What proof is there that realtors and allied real estate professionals have taken and continue to take concerted action to maintain and strengthen the pattern of segregated housing? (3) If there is evidence of such concerted action why is existing law not effective to prevent realtors and their allies from practicing racial discrimination? The remainder of this study will be devoted to answering these questions.

WHY IS HOUSING SEGREGATED?

Housing segregation was quite general prior to the 1948 U.S. Supreme Court decision in *Shelley* v. *Kraemer*.[6] That case ended court enforcement of owners' agreements to maintain segregated housing. Proof of the need for antidiscrimination housing laws hinges on what has happened since that decision.

The last fifteen to seventeen years have produced little change in the rigorous pattern of racial segregation established by the industry prior to the *Shelley* case. The most comprehensive data about housing segregation are in the many findings by legislative bodies in the states and cities that have adopted open occupancy laws and laws prohibiting broker discrimination. NAREB and CREA contend that these findings are based upon political considerations rather than a careful weighing of the facts. However, such scientific studies as have been made in recent years fully support the legislative findings that housing segregation is the result of discrimination. The conclusion of scholars is that the pattern of controlled housing segregation has not decreased significantly since the *Shelley* decision.[7] The most recent study of this is by Drs. Karl E. and Alma F. Taeuber and has been published under the title *Negroes in Cities*.[8] For this study the authors developed a segregation index that showed that between 1950 and 1960 the average segregation in 109 cities decreased by only 1 percent (from 87.3 percent to 86.1 percent).[9] There were some exceptions to this dismal record and had it not been for these exceptions the average segregation index in the majority of cities would actually have risen. One of the most notable improvements throughout the United States occurred in San Francisco, where the change from 1950 to 1960 showed a decline in the segregation index from 79.8 percent to 69.3 percent.[10] This change is of particular note since the San Francisco Real Estate Board was one of the earliest, if not the earliest, real estate board in the United States to admit minority brokers to board membership. This open policy dates back to the early 1950s and is striking support for the contention that there is a direct correlation between real estate board policies and housing segregation.

The Taeuber study shows that in spite of the *Shelley* v. *Kraemer* decision, the well-established pattern of segregated housing has continued without substantial change in most places in the United States. Dr. Taeuber asks: "What causes segregated housing? Is it the result of poverty? Choice or discrimination?" He concludes:

A summary assessment can now be made of the three factors (choice, poverty or discrimination). Neither free choice nor poverty is a sufficient explanation for the universally high degree of segregation in American cities. Discrimination is the principal cause of Negro residential segregation, and there is no basis for anticipating major changes in the segregated character of American cities until patterns of housing discrimination can be altered.[11]

How Does Organized Real Estate Help to Maintain Segregated Housing?

The history of concerted action to force minority people to live in ghettos breaks sharply with the *Shelley* v. *Kraemer* decision in 1948. Prior to that decision the force exerted against minorities was open and undisguised;

since then it has become covert and hypocritical. Some forms of organized racial discrimination have disappeared, but the *most effective* ones prevail, and new subtle forms beyond the reach of existing law have been developed.

The most direct use of legal power had been by means of zoning ordinances establishing zones or ghettos (for that is what they really were) where members of the minority races were required to live. At one time segregation ordinances, as they were frankly called, were quite common in southern and border states but the U.S. Supreme Court in 1917, in *Buchanan* v. *Warley*[12] outlawed such ordinances. In spite of this decision some states continued to enforce racial zoning. In a 1925 Louisiana case, the U.S. Supreme Court had to insist that *Buchanan* v. *Warley* applied in Louisiana as well as the rest of the United States.[13] As late as 1935 Oklahoma City attempted to enforce a segregation ordinance that was identical in wording to the one overturned in *Buchanan* v. *Warley*. When Oklahoma City claimed that it was required to pass this ordinance by Governor "Wild Bill" Murray, who had imposed martial law and had refused to lift it until a racial zoning ordinance had been passed by the Oklahoma City Council, the Supreme Court of Oklahoma replied:

The initial step in segregation of the races in this locality occurred in May, 1933, when Hon. William H. Murray, as Governor, issued an executive military order declaring a state of martial law to exist in certain areas of the city of Oklahoma City, declaring a "Segregation Zone" for white people and another for black or colored people, and between the two a "nontrespass zone," that the object thereby sought was preservation of the peace and prevention of riot and bloodshed; . . . that the duration recited by the terms of the decree was, until said city, pursuant to request of the Governor, should pass a valid ordinance in lieu of said order. . . .
The city of Oklahoma City was not, as stated in its brief faced with the 'dilemma of allowing martial law to remain in force and effect or adopting such a comprehensive zoning law as to cope with the problem' . . . The substance of this contention is advocacy of the policy of . . . exercising wrongfully police power to defeat illegal martial law, which is but the power of police unlawfully employed.[14]

The rationale for Governor Murray's action in Oklahoma has often been used to excuse culpable action or inaction by public officials in many parts of the United States: "Segregation is the only way to avoid friction between the races." To maintain segregation these public officials often had recourse to "law enforcement versus the law,"[15] i.e., use of police power to frustrate the right of every citizen to equal treatment before the law.

With the failure of racial zoning, recourse was had to private contractual agreements among landowners binding themselves and succeeding owners not to permit persons of designated races and religions to occupy the property covered by the agreement. These private agreements when placed on the public record could be enforced against subsequent owners by lawsuits for damages or by court injunction. Although both of these legal proceedings required the active intervention of legal power, the Supreme Court, in *Corrigan* v. *Buckley,* rejected the argument that this constituted government action within the prohibition of the 5th, 13th, or 14th Amendments.[16] In the years between that decision and the *Shelley* decision the use of racial restrictions became general real estate practice throughout the United States.

Classifying racial restrictions as agreements among property owners is misleading. This is how the practice started, but it was soon taken over by real estate men and it became routine for them to place race restrictions on all their subdivisions. This would take place about the time the subdivision map would be filed and before any lots had been sold. The FHA sanctioned the practice by requiring such race restrictions in all FHA approved subdivisions and even developed a recommended form of racial restrictions. Robert C. Weaver, now Secretary of the Department of Housing and Urban Development, in his book, *The Negro Ghetto,* points out how the real estate industry influenced the FHA.

. . . The financial institutions through which FHA operated and from which most of its key officials in Washington and the field were recruited were the very financial and real estate interests and institutions which led the campaign to spread racial covenants and residential segregation.[17]

The *Shelley* case ended the general practice of filing race restrictions, but it did not outlaw them. Some owners still place such restrictions on the record.[18] Furthermore, there has been an almost complete lack of effort to have existing restrictions removed from the public records.

Every bit as effective as zoning ordinances and racial restrictions were the rules that bound real estate brokers, appraisers, and other professionals belonging to the National Association of Real Estate Boards to discriminate against minority persons. Before 1950, article 34 of the Code of Ethics of NAREB read as follows:

A realtor should never be instrumental in introducing into a neighborhood a character of property or occupancy, members of any race or nationality, or any individual whose presence would clearly be detrimental to property values in that neighborhood.[19]

Under this strange concept of "ethics" a real estate broker selling a home in an all-white Anglo neighborhood to a Negro, Mexican-American, Oriental, or other minority persons risked being deprived of his membership in the local real estate board. Consistent with this Code of Ethics provision, appraisers lowered their estimates of market values for properties in neighborhoods where minority persons had settled. Since mortgage loans and sales prices are predicated on appraised values, the fear of financial loss frequently created a very real panic where property was sold to a minority person. This panic has often been documented in articles dealing with blockbusting and similar techniques used by unscrupulous brokers to create opportunities for profitable purchases by exploiting fears about loss of values when the first minority occupant enters a neighborhood.

The editor of the realtors' newspaper, *Headlines,* Eugene P. Conser, made the following frank comments about the pre-*Shelley,* Realtor Code of Ethics and the decision of NAREB to change the wording:

Thus it was that the Code of Ethics reflected the then widely accepted policy of "separate but equal facilities . . . Reflecting this prevailing sentiment, our Code of Ethics cautioned that a Realtor "should never be instrumental in introducing members of any race or nationality, or any individuals . . ." whose presence would adversely affect property values in a neighborhood.
This prevailing sentiment also took the form of restrictive covenants written into deeds . . . to prevent occupancy by persons of specified national origin and racial and religious groups.
There can be no question but that the restrictive covenant, particularly in its increasingly general application to the Negro race, became recognized by Negro leaders as a major barrier to their ever being able to exercise citizenship rights within the ever-expanding terrain so restricted. *Neither can we as Realtors deny our major responsibility* in spreading this particular method of applying the then existent public policy of "separate but equal." (emphasis supplied)
With the court decision as a guide to obvious change in public policy the Association amended its Code of Ethics to strike any reference to "occupancy" or to "race or nationality."[20]

In the next issue of *Headlines* the editor explained the changed wording in the NAREB's Code of Ethics:

The change made in the Code of Ethics eliminating any reference to "race or nationality" was a milestone that escaped general recognition and was not widely publicized among the real estate boards at the time—1950. Although there is no record of disciplinary action having been taken against a Realtor for "introducing" an ethnically diverse family into a neighborhood, the authority seems to have been generally assumed to be still incorporated in the rephrased Article 5, which read:
    The Realtor should not be instrumental in introducing into a neighborhood a character of property or use which will clearly be detrimental to property values in that neighborhood.
The changed position of the realtor under the revised provisions of Article

5 was more emphatically called to attention in a series of editorials commenting upon all of the articles of the Code, published in 1959, in which, in pointing out that the term "occupancy" had been stricken, it was stated:

> Character or use does not include occupancy. While use refers to employment of property, i.e., residential, commercial, industrial use, etc., and illegal or otherwise objectionable use, occupancy refers to inhabitation of property . . .

This comment was accepted as authoritative, although *it caused inquiry from some boards surprised to learn that Realtors no longer could be subjected to disciplinary action if they assisted minority families in finding homes in "all-white" neighborhoods.* There was no indication, however, that Realtors generally undertook to follow such a policy, the resistance of home owners being at that time almost universally adamant.[21] (emphasis supplied)

This editorial may seem a remarkably frank admission of the way in which realtors established a firm pattern of segregating races. The basis for this frankness which continues throughout a series of ten or twelve editorials in *Headlines* on the subject of discrimination is the specious justification that realtors were simply following "public policy." Here and throughout all the explanations of the firm and long standing pro-segregation policies of realtors, we find that the excuse is that realtors are merely agents, and it is the owners who employ them who insist upon discrimination.

No one will deny that many owners want to discriminate against minority persons, but the question that is unclear is how far this is due to their strong prejudices and how far it is due to the fear of financial loss, reprisals and neighborhood panic that are the direct results of the propaganda of professionals operating in real estate markets. There is ample evidence that both before the *Shelley* case and since, the dominant force in creating and maintaining ghettos is the activity of professionals in the real estate industry. This covers the whole spectrum of specialists such as appraisers, property managers, and mortgage loan officers as well as home builders, escrow, and title company officers, most of whom are members of real estate boards affiliated with NAREB. NAREB influence is paramount in the real estate market. It has outright control of organizations dominating most of the real estate specialties such as appraising, management, consulting, industrial real estate, etc., and it has close working relations with all the other large membership associations covering other real estate specialties.

For the white realtor this pattern has direct financial benefit since it enables him to earn more by dominating all phases of the real estate field. Minority brokers and financial institutions owned by members of minority races are thus excluded from participating in the more lucrative real estate markets and are barred from practicing in the profitable and prestigious specialized area of real estate.

The change in the Code of Ethics has had little impact on the practice of realtors; and throughout the industry it has been recognized that the change in the wording was a mere device to create a better image for the realtor. Realtors continued their discriminatory patterns of behavior and few seemed to understand that a board member who would fight for his rights could now sell to a nonwhite buyer in a previously all-white neighborhood without risking expulsion from the board. Eventually someone who was brought up on charges, fought back and won. For realtors this was such a landmark decision that it was published in the 1959 annotated version of the Code of Ethics. The report follows:

Following Realtor A's sale of a home to Buyer B, Neighbor C complained to the Board of Realtors that its member, A, had violated Article 5 of the NAREB Code of Ethics by selling a home to Buyer B, a non-white purchaser, in a block that contained no other non-white occupants.

The complaint was reviewed in a formal hearing before the board's committee on professional standards. The complainant stated that he was familiar with the NAREB Code of Ethics, and that since Article 5 prohibited action by a Realtor to introduce anything into a neighborhood that could adversely affect property values, Realtor A's action was a violation. He expressed his opinion that the occupancy of the house sold by Realtor A to Buyer B would definitely lower property values in this particular block. Realtor A's defense was that Article 5 relates to the introduction into a neighborhood of a "character" of property, or a "use" of property, that would be detrimental; that his action had not introduced any new character or use of property into the neighborhood; that the property sold to Buyer B had been for residential use previously and would be used exclusively for residential purposes by Buyer B. He pointed out further that the words "occupancy" and "race" which at one time had appeared in this part of the Code were stricken out many years ago, clearly demonstrating an intent to exclude any such considerations from the Article, and that this action was in no way in conflict with the Code."

It was the judgment of the board that Realtor A's defense was vaild and he was found not guilty of unethical conduct.[22]

Mr. Conser admits that many NAREB members were astonished at this decision. This is shown by the following excerpt from one of his editorials previously quoted:

. . . it caused inquiry from some boards surprised to learn that Realtors no longer could be subjected to disciplinary action if they assisted minority families in finding homes in "all-white" neighborhoods.[23]

Cases of realtors disciplined for introducing minority persons into all-white neighborhoods are not often heard of, partly because realtors seldom do it, and when they do, they do not bring suit if they are fined or are ousted from the real estate board. However, realtor Harry Beddoe, ousted in 1956 from the Southwest Realty Board in Los Angeles for selling a home in an all-white neighborhood to a Mexican-American, sought damages against the board. The Superior Court said that it could grant restoration of membership, but not damages. Since Beddoe had not asked for restoration, the court found for the defendant.[24]

There have been many published reports by Negroes of their efforts to obtain good housing in all-white neighborhoods and the difficulties they have experienced in these efforts. Some of this material can be found in the book *Urban Desegregation* by L. K. Northwood and Ernest A. T. Barth,[25] and many other publications, but most of it is found in the literature of Fair Housing Committees throughout the United States that have mounted local projects to test realtor attitudes toward members of minority races. The method of real estate boards has been described by Clement E. Vose in his book *Caucasians Only*:

> The method being employed here in St. Louis . . . is to have the Real Estate Exchange zone the city and forbid any member of the exchange under pain of expulsion to sell property in the white zone to a Negro. If the real estate men refused to participate in the sale, the breaches will at least be minimized to those who deal with each other directly or through . . . a non-member of the exchange who could be easily identified and boycotted more or less by all the people to whom the knowledge comes.[26]

Vose cites instances of disciplining by local boards in various parts of the country, all occurring after the *Shelley* case and some after the change in the Code of Ethics.

Why Is Existing Law Not Able to Overcome the Real Estate Industry's Efforts to Maintain Segregated Housing?

The lines of defense of real estate professionals against the efforts of minority people to achieve equality in the housing market are so numerous they must be examined individually to see the depth and strength of the structures that protect the white realtor in his domination of the real estate market. Perhaps the most notorious of these devices has been the consistent refusal of the local boards affiliated with NAREB to admit minority persons to membership. As a result of this exclusionary policy it has been difficult for Negroes and other minority persons to enter the real estate business. In the first place, most states require a period of apprenticeship as a salesman in the employ of a licensed broker. Since a white realtor could not hire a

Negro without risk of being ostracized by his fellow brokers there was little chance for Negroes to get a start in the real estate business. When a Negro succeeded in surmounting this problem he was still excluded from membership in the board and thus effectively barred from participating in the real estate market except in the ghetto. A 1962 survey reported by the National Committee Against Discrimination in Housing revealed that in most major cities local real estate boards still had no Negro members.[27]

In order to create a second line of defense against the efforts of minority brokers to get the benefits of real estate board membership, white realtors in many communities organized their multiple listing services outside of the regular board structure. The multiple listing service is a broker cooperative whose members are required to share most of their residential listings. In recent years these services have grown rapidly until today the vast majority of sales of existing single family dwellings are handled by them. In San Francisco, the multiple listing service was, until quite recently, entirely separate from the local real estate board. This meant that the San Francisco board's "liberality" in admitting minority brokers to membership was not as significant as it might at first have seemed.[28]

To reduce the pressure from minority brokers for admission to real estate boards, NAREB has even tolerated the formation of a second NAREB, principally made up of Negro brokers. The initials of the second NAREB have the same significance as the first except that the "B" stands for brokers instead of boards. The Negro NAREB, because of its limited membership and exclusion from the general market, is severely hampered in opening housing opportunities and in advancing the business of its members, but white realtors find it useful to point to the Negro brokers organization as "proof" that Negroes also prefer segregated boards.

Much of the success of white realtors in maintaining a discriminatory real estate market in spite of the law is the direct result of (1) NAREB's skillful manipulation of its organizational structure to take full advantage of all available legal technicalities, (2) the power of its allies in related fields, and (3) its ability to penetrate government, the universities and the church to create a favorable public opinion toward realtors. Each of these factors will be reviewed in the following pages.

THE AUTONOMY OF NAREB's LOCAL BOARDS

About thirteen or fourteen years ago NAREB carefully revised its structure and that of its state and local affiliates to give these organizations a seeming autonomy. Two of the most important purposes of this facade were (a) to create a massive barrier against the struggle of minority brokers to gain admission to NAREB affiliates and (b) to enable NAREB and the state organizations to engage in legislative lobbying and political activity without endangering the tax exempt status of the local boards. Most real estate men and many local board leaders do not understand the legal intricacies by which this sleight of hand has been achieved. They need to be educated by frequent explanations such as the following which appeared in a recent issue of the CREA magazine.

BOARDS AUTONOMOUS IN NAREB AND CREA
To a great extent NAREB looks upon member Boards as being auto-nomous. However, there are some basic matters which are not discretionary and not left up to a member Board if it is to remain a chartered Board of the National Association of Real Estate Boards.
A member Board must adopt and uphold the Code of Ethics of the Na-tional Association. The Board's governing regulations (i.e., Constitution & Bylaws or Special Regulations) must not be in conflict with CREA or NAREB's Constitution & Bylaws. It must agree to control and protect the term Realtor within its jurisdiction without creating any inequitable limi-tations on its membership or violation of law. It must have the machinery for enforcing the Code of Ethics, elect officers, hold at least one meeting a year, and pay its dues to CREA and NAREB as a 3-way Board.
Aside from what is mentioned above, a Board is fairly autonomous. The penalty, of course, for failing to live up to what is stated above would be the loss of a charter.[29]

BOARD AUTONOMY AIDS NAREB IN DISCRIMINATING AGAINST MINORITY BROKERS

As a result of this device a court decision requiring one board to admit a minority broker to membership has no effect upon the activities of any other board. In this way the opening of each board has become a long, drawn out legal struggle, expensive and time consuming for the broker who brings the test case and for the civil rights groups that support him. Lawsuits testing local board policy on admitting Negroes are pending in some parts of the United States. One recently settled case in northern California required the Contra Costa Real Estate Board to admit its first Negro member.[30]

In New Jersey the Trenton-Mercer County Real Estate Board recently admitted its first Negro member. This resulted from an out of court settle-ment ending the eleven-year struggle of this broker for admission to the board. In that period she had been rejected six times without being given a reason for any of the rejections.[31]

In Santa Barbara, California, a pro-integration white broker obtained a $7,500 out of court settlement plus membership in the board after he filed an anti-trust suit.[32]

In Los Angeles the American Civil Liberties Union has brought an action on behalf of three Negro brokers to force the Southwest Real Estate Board to accept them as members and to pay a total of $324,000 in damages to them by reason of their exclusion from board membership. In this suit it is alleged that 650 of 700 white brokers and *none* of the 500 Negro brokers practicing in the area has been admitted to the board.[33]

These cases illustrate what could have been accomplished long ago by enforcement of anti-trust laws by elected public officials but it should be noted that the victories discussed above have *all* resulted from actions by private attorneys or attorneys for the ACLU or NAACP. In few cases have district attorneys or state attorneys general taken action, and only recently has the U.S. Department of Justice become concerned. On February 4, 1966, the *Wall Street Journal* carried an article indicating that the Department of Justice has, at long last, begun an investigation of the anti-trust practices of real estate boards. The following paragraphs are from that story:

In recent weeks the U.S. Justice Department quietly has begun questioning Negro house hunters, sympathetic real estate men and civil rights leaders here (Los Angeles) about alleged racial discrimination by local real estate boards. Specifically, the government is seeking evidence that realty board members have "conspired to restrain trade"—the catch-all anti-trust charge —by denying board membership to pro-integration brokers and by keeping Negro families from finding homes in white neighborhoods.

Cases Settled Out of Court

The use of anti-trust laws against alleged discrimination by some real estate agents has been attempted in private anti-trust suits filed under Federal and state laws; in addition to Federal anti-trust laws, nearly all states also have such laws, to prevent restraint of trade within state lines. However, out-of-court settlement of these cases have deprived housing discrimination foes of any legal precedent . . . If real estate agents agree among themselves to steer Negro buyers away from white neighborhoods, this restrains trade by limiting the market open to Negro buyers and by depriving white property owners of would-be Negro buyers; also if agents conspire to keep Negro or white brokers who favor integration off local realty boards, this deprives these brokers of a share of the board's cooperative pooling of house listings and lessens competition . . .

Warning White Buyers

An officer of another realty board near San Francisco says that despite its efforts to halt discrimination, one of its members recently warned white buyers against a neighborhood because a Negro had moved in; another broker on the same board recently boasted to a white buyer, "We have ways of keeping Negroes out of certain areas." Neither broker was disciplined in any way by the board.

One Los Angeles area board called a broker on the carpet last fall because he did comply with [the NAREB revised code of practices that allowed free movement of minority groups into whatever neighborhoods they desired; the code was adopted by all but three of California's 177 boards]. Later, this board disbanded its equal-rights committee, set up under this provision of the code; asked why, one board member claimed "we have no problem of discrimination here."

One white broker who brought two Negroes into white neighborhoods reports his business referrals from other realty board members dropped off so sharply he left last July to join an aerospace firm. Another says he has been denied access to his board's local listings of homes for sale because of his outspoken views against discrimination. He adds that he currently has two lawyers preparing an anti-trust suit against the board.

There are some 83,000 realtors in the U.S. They are real estate brokers who are members of local units tied to the National Association of Real Estate Boards (NAREB). Although these real estate agents make up only about 24 percent of all real estate brokers in the nation, a NAREB official once estimated they handle 90 percent of real estate transactions. Realtors generally insist they be called by that name rather than real estate brokers.[34]

As a result of the Department of Justice's investigation the Southwest Realty Board admitted its first Negro member. But success by one Negro broker will not necessarily help others to gain admission even to the same real estate board.

No board acknowledges that an applicant has been refused membership because of the color of his skin. Instead, boards rely on vague generalizations about lack of experience or ability or character. For example, the reasons advanced in one of the cases cited earlier were that "he was slow closing deals; he once failed to split a commission with another broker, and he once wrote a check with insufficient funds." (The board later admitted that the check had been made good.)[35] Thus the issue on appeal will never hinge upon the right to exclude a person by reason of his race or color, but rather on the genuineness of the reasons offered for denying admission. Since these reasons raise questions of fact, the decision will not be a legal precedent that can be relied upon by other applicants seeking to force their admission to other boards.

The relationship between board membership and the opportunity to earn a living as a real estate broker cannot be overstressed. Not only do board members have many more opportunities to obtain listings and make sales (the *Wall Street Journal* estimated that board members do 90 percent of the real estate business)[36] but membership in a real estate board also makes a broker eligible to work toward professional designations and memberships controlled by NAREB. The following are examples:

American Institute of Real Estate Appraisers. The most powerful organization of appraisers, whose members are recognized by courts, official agencies, and mortgage lenders as the top experts in appraising. After admission to membership, a realtor may use the designation M.A.I. No other appraisal designation carries the same weight. The Institute publishes a journal which is the closest thing to "learned" of any publication by a real estate organization.

Institute of Real Estate Management. This is the only national organization for brokers specializing in real estate management. It awards the designation C.P.M. (Certified Property Manager). Its members are also recognized by lending agencies, government officials and the courts as expert real estate managers.

National Institute of Real Estate Brokers (NIREB). This organization produces a variety of aids for brokers in selling, running their offices, training their personnel and every conceivable aspect of real estate business technique.

These are but a fraction of the advantages of which minority brokers are deprived by being denied membership in a NAREB board. There are many other NAREB-controlled organizations and committees that can be useful to a broker in developing his business. NAREB tries to blanket all aspects of real estate and starts a captive organization whenever its officers sense that a real estate specialty is developing. For example, the Society of Real Estate Counsellors has been started in recent years—not to obtain members, since membership is by invitation only—but to preempt the field and prevent any other organization from attempting to organize those who want to specialize in real estate consulting.

An example of the way in which NAREB and CREA jealously guard against the formation of competing organizations occurred in Los Angeles in 1962–63 following creation by a group of brokers of an organization for specialists in property exchanging. This association established the designation C.P.E. (Certified Property Exchanger). A few months after organization, the members were put under severe pressure to affiliate their association with CREA. This pressure can take many forms, including the threat to form a competing group within CREA and thus to drive the independent organization out of business. In the case of the property exchangers the pressure was effective and they affiliated their organization with CREA.

Membership in one of NAREB's local boards also affords a broker the privilege of calling himself a "Realtor." Although the term has been widely advertised by NAREB, the public generally considered it a synonym for real estate broker, until opponents of Proposition 14 popularized the scornful paraphrase of the inevitable query by the racist: "Would you want your daughter to marry a Realtor?"

REAL ESTATE APPRAISAL STEREOTYPES ABOUT "MIXED" NEIGHBORHOODS

Another defense against minority penetration of the real estate market has been the notion that mixed neighborhoods have unstable values. Real estate brokers and property managers support this stereotype by encouraging and hastening the change-over to minority ghettos of neighborhoods with some nonwhite occupancy. In real estate, the term for neighborhoods that have experienced some minority entry is "transitional." This originally meant an aging residential neighborhood; it is now a polite way of saying "minority penetration" and is a red flag for other brokers, appraisers and for mortgage lenders. Many financial institutions do not lend on property in "transitional" neighborhoods, and some that do charge higher rates and lend at a lower proportion of the property's value than would be the case in other neighborhoods. Municipal authorities often abet segregation by reducing the services provided to these neighborhoods. Housing codes are not enforced and landlords are permitted to milk their properties; then streets are neglected, and trash pick-up is reduced; finally, the neighborhood becomes an eyesore and the city then declares that the minority slum dwellers must be removed through urban renewal so that middle-class whites can be coaxed back.

The doctrine that minority entry means declining real estate values was developed by NAREB and became one of the cornerstones of appraisal theory and practice. The Appraisal Institute, created by NAREB, explicitly taught this in its texts until about 1950. Thereafter its texts used euphemistic terminology such as that now found in the Realtors' Code of Ethics, but in its classes the doctrine was generally still taught throughout the entire decade of the fifties. Even today it is a cardinal principle of appraisal practice, even though the concept may hide behind some word such as "transitional" that will be entirely clear to all those "in the know." Stanley McMichael, a NAREB power and a prominent real estate text-writer, said in his book, *Real Estate Subdivisions*:

That the entry of Non-Caucasian into districts where distinctly Caucasian residents live tends to depress real estate values is agreed to by practically all real estate subdividers and students of city life and growth. Infiltration at the outset may be slow but once the trend is established, values start to drop, until properties can be purchased at discounts of from 50 to 75%.[37]

The same sentiments were repeated in McMichael's *Appraisal Manual* and in the text by Arthur A. May, entitled *Valuation of Residential Real Estate*.[38]

Data from which these so-called appraisal principles were deduced were observations that minority races moved into neighborhoods of declining values. But the supposedly expert observers were not keen enough to see that the declining values were the reason for the minority entry, not the other way around. As a matter of fact, substantial minority entry usually resulted in rising property values as minority persons competed with each other for the relatively scarce housing available to them. Very carefully conducted studies have documented these facts.[39] But in spite of these studies, appraisers continue to downgrade integrated neighborhoods. This results in fear verging on panic when property owners discover minority persons looking at property in their neighborhood.

In the notorious Deerfield case (1959) the insidious poison about property values declining was a dominant theme. The Deerfield case involved an attempted development of an interracial subdivision in the Chicago suburbs—51 houses selling for over $30,000 of which 10 or 12 would have been sold to Negroes. The citizens of Deerfield drove the developers out by reviving a defeated park proposal and choosing the site of the interracial subdivision for the park. The Deerfield Village Board of Trustees kicked off the campaign to run the developers out of town by the following statement:

The Board of Trustees of the Village of Deerfield is making a detailed study of the proposed sale of homes in the Progress Development subdivision on a so-called integrated basis. It is evident from the great number of telephone calls and visits to members of the Board and to the Village Hall that the people of the community are gravely concerned. The people are demanding that action be taken to maintain their property values. . . .[40]

This was a major argument of those who oppose housing integration on the ground that they are concerned solely with protecting the right of property owners to do exactly what they will with their property. Here the owners of a small tract of land were prohibited from doing with their property what they had planned and undertaken to do. The interracial subdivision was actually under construction when the condemnation was voted. The owners were literally driven off their land solely because they wanted to develop it as an interracial subdivision.

It is important for the reader to understand why condemnation provides segregationists with the most powerful legal tool yet devised for allocating residential space on the basis of race. Its use in this regard is not confined to a Deerfield-type condemnation, but also to highway condemnations, urban renewal and slum clearance and other governmental "improvement" programs. As a general rule, courts will not interfere with the decisions of an official body to order condemnation of private property for a public purpose. The court will normally not consider the motivation of officials in choosing a location to be condemned, and barring outright fraud will accept the decision of public officials on what constitutes a "public purpose." Thus, highways can be built through minority neighborhoods or used as segregation walls to delineate neighborhoods, and urban renewal can be employed specifically to prevent the dispersion of minority people and force them back into the densely populated ghettos.

BANKING AND MORTGAGE LENDING INSTITUTIONS SUPPORT NAREB's HOUSING SEGREGATION EFFORTS[41]

Although Earl Schwulst, former President of the Bowery Savings Bank of New York, and other prominent leaders of lending institutions have insisted that there is no more financial risk in lending to a member of a minority racial group than there is in lending to anyone else,[42] the industry often evaluates loans on the basis of the race of the applicant. Most banks claim that they will lend to qualified Negroes in all-Negro neighborhoods; but what they really mean is that they will make FHA insured or VA guaranteed money available for *new* all-Negro subdivisions. Their interest in these loans is based on the extra profit they make by charging high discounts and then selling these loans to the government-owned Federal National Mortgage Association, often at full value. For years the government has offered special inducements to the mortgage banking industry to make money available for Negro housing, and the industry has not hesitated to take advantage of these special inducements to make extra risk-free profit. But many banks still refuse to make loans to Negroes in an older Negro neighborhood, no matter how well kept the housing, or how adequate the income of the applicant.

The mortgage banking industry also draws the line at lending to minority applicants entering all-white neighborhoods. Eunice and George Greer, in a recent issue of *Daedalus,* document this continuing segregation policy of mortgage bankers:

In recent testimony before the Commissioners of the District of Columbia, the President of the Mortgage Bankers Association of Metropolitan Washington stated bluntly that "applications from minority groups are not generally considered in areas that are not recognized as being racially mixed." A study by the Chicago Commission on Human Relations found that such a policy was pursued by almost all lending sources in that city. Voluminous evidence from both social research surveys and testimony before legislative and executive bodies indicates that the same is true of most real estate boards in cities throughout the country.[43]

When President Kennedy issued his Executive Order on Equal Opportunity in Housing on November 20, 1962, the Mortgage Bankers Association was quick to react to what its President, Dale M. Thompson, called a "competitive disadvantage" under the new order.[44] The executive order directed that necessary and appropriate action be taken to prevent discrimination in housing and related facilities owned or operated by the Federal government or assisted by the government through loans, advances or contributions, or loans insured or guaranteed by the government. The order included funds provided for slum clearance.

In real estate finance, the effect of the President's order was limited to the mortgage lending institutions engaging in FHA and VA loans, and did not cover conventional (i.e., non-FHA or VA) loans by commercial banks, such as the Federal Deposit Insurance Corporation (FDIC) members, or savings and loan associations, such as the Federal Savings and Loan Insurance Corporation (FSLIC) members. These two groups are the major source of conventional mortgages in the nation, and in a typical year will make 70–85 percent of all home loans. Thus, the largest segment of the home mortgage market was not subject to the nondiscrimination requirements imposed by the presidential order. Furthermore, since the order had no effect on loans made prior to November 20, 1962, a vast amount of FHA and VA backed housing was exempt from its provisions.

This was a clear gap in coverage, and produced a concomitant limitation on effectiveness of the order in reducing discrimination in the nation's housing. Advocates of fair housing were quick to point out this gap, and to recommend that the order's provisions be extended to cover FDIC and FSLIC institutions. And, in so recommending, the supporters of fair housing found themselves unexpectedly allied with the mortgage banking industry.

The Mortgage Bankers Association did, in fact, suggest that the executive order be extended to cover FDIC and FSLIC institutions. This was not, however, the result of a sudden wave of brotherhood among the industry's members, but stemmed from fear that the order would drastically curtail the business of members of the Mortgage Bankers Association who deal almost exclusively in FHA and VA mortgages.[45] In effect, the Mortgage Bankers Association was admitting that discrimination was general in the mortgage lending industry, and they complained bitterly that it was unfair to stop only their part of the discrimination. They were afraid that they would lose business if they could no longer engage in the "regular" discriminatory behavior of the mortgage lending industry.

If the Executive Order is to have any effect, it must be extended and its enforcement provisions strengthened. Experience to date shows that its effect has been much below what had been hoped for by advocates of fair housing. Trends in Housing, published by the National Committee Against

Discrimination in Housing, indicated in a review of the first year under the executive order that "little had happened—good or bad" and that relatively few minority group families had been benefited by the antidiscrimination order.[46] While the fearful results predicted by the mortgage banking industry have not come to pass under the order, neither has a great deal been achieved in the way of fair housing.

A full review of changes in mortgage lending practices across the country would undoubtedly show that discrimination by lenders has decreased in the last twenty years, but the degree of improvement has been small in comparison with the increased numbers of minority people in our urban centers who need mortgage money on a nondiscriminatory basis.

THE SEGREGATION ACTIVITIES OF FEDERAL, STATE AND LOCAL GOVERNMENT

The penetration of government by pro-segregationists is too long a story to be told in one chapter or even in one book. Some of it has been told by Robert Weaver, Secretary of the Department of Housing and Urban Development; some by Charles Abrams in his book *Forbidden Neighbors,*[47] and some in the series of books that came out under the aegis of the distinguished Commission on Race and Housing. Much of it resulted from the influence of realtors who had become public officials in the FHA, the Public Housing Administration, the Veterans Administration, and the urban renewal programs. Its influence is shown in policies on deed restrictions, appraisal practices, housing for minorities, and integration in government-owned housing, in public housing, and in the employment policies of these and other government agencies.

On the state and local level the most obvious examples of the effect of the pro-segregation attitudes of public officials were the refusals by state attorneys general and local prosecuting attorneys to take any steps to enforce anti-trust laws against the racist policies of local real estate boards. These public officials also generally ignored violations of state public accommodations laws. Hiring policies in the state house and in city hall also reflected the segregation syndrome that Negroes were to be employed only for menial tasks.

At the local level, it is in the planning and execution of urban renewal programs that the real estate industry has had the best opportunity to influence public officials to adopt policies that promote housing segregation. City politicians sell urban renewal programs to community influentials on the theory that Negro dispersion can be stopped and that segregated white, upper income enclaves can be created from core real estate occupied by minorities and poor whites. Although it was not his purpose to point this out, Martin Anderson, in the book *The Federal Bulldozer* has documented the way in which local urban renewal programs function to increase housing segregation and to create barriers that isolate the Negro slums from other parts of the city. Anderson estimated that, "The federal urban renewal program eliminated 126,000 low-rent homes . . . and replaced them with 28,000 homes, most of them in a much higher rent bracket. Thus, the net effect of the program has been to aggravate the housing problem for low-income groups and to alleviate it for high-income groups."[48] Most of those displaced have been minority people who are thus forced into denser occupancy of segregated neighborhoods outside the immediate thrust of the "bulldozer."

In addition to destroying the housing of minorities, urban renewal programs also destroy minority-owned businesses. Anderson estimates that up to 1959 one hundred thousand small businesses had been forced to move, with the resultant liquidation of between 25 and 40 percent. He also estimates that in the next decade more than twice as many small businesses will be forced out of their present locations by urban renewal programs.[49] No count is available of how many of these businesses were owned by members of minority races, but the proportion must be substantial, since neighborhoods of heavy minority occupancy are almost the only places where minority businessmen can get a start.

Urban renewal, in most communities, is class war, and most of the casualties are members of some racial minority. Raymond Vernon, former director of the New York Metropolitan Regional Study, is cited by Martin Anderson on the subject of "who wants urban renewal?" Vernon speculates that:

The main stimulus for urban renewal comes from two elite groups—the wealthy elite and the intellectual elite. Both groups have strong economic and social attachments to the central city. And they are in a position to attempt to maintain these attachments despite the desires and wishes of the non-elite. Members of these elite groups include *financial institutions,* newspapers, department stores, *owners of downtown real estate,* academic intellectuals, city planners, city politicians and others who have a strong stake in the maintenance and improvement of the city as they see it today.[50] (emphasis added)

Most urban renewal programs cannot get off the ground unless they are supported by the local real estate board. The support of the local board generally indicates that the planning supports the interests of the downtown real estate owners and the segregation policies of the real estate industry. An excellent illustration of the way in which the interests of these two groups mesh has been revealed in a lawsuit filed in the U.S. District Court for the Northern District of Illinois entitled *Green Street Association and Others* v. *Richard J. Daley and Others*. The complaint in this action is signed by more than a hundred Negroes who either own or lease residential or business property in a Chicago neighborhood called Central Englewood, which was scheduled for clearance under the urban renewal program. The plaintiffs claim that the plan for this project calls for the demolition of 600 dwellings of which four-fifths were classified by the 1960 U.S. census as standard housing (i.e., not blighted). Of the 525 families to be removed 85 percent are Negro. Although all homes in the project are to be cleared, not so with the large business establishments located there, since in the words of the complaint, the purpose of this project is: "reclaiming and re-establishing the commercial trade and business of white customers for the Central Englewood area."[51] The complainants claim that the prime movers behind the renewal plan are Sears, Roebuck and Co., Wieboldt Stores, Inc., and the Chicago City Bank and Trust Company. The complaint further stated that the Central Englewood clearance was the first "conservation" program in the city of Chicago, and possibly the first in the United States, "designed to convert residential property to a nonresidential use solely for the benefit of commercial interests. Said plan provides for the clearance of approximately 18.1 acres of land devoted to residential use, which land shall be converted into sixteen (16) parking areas and streets, thereby decreasing the total area used for housing in the project area to 3.2 acres."[52]

The effect of a program like this in compressing minorities into more densely packed ghetto areas is clearly shown in the following allegation from the complaint:

According to the defendant, department of Urban Renewal's own estimate, as set forth in the Urban Renewal Plan, 75 percent of present home owner-occupants in the area will be unable to purchase homes in other areas that are "not less desirable in regard to public utilities and public and commercial facilities" and that are "decent, safe, and sanitary . . ."[53]

Unfortunately, this could be an accurate description of what has been happening to most owner-occupants of ghetto homes not only in Central Englewood but wherever they are displaced by urban renewal. Government acceptance of the real estate appraisal theory that homes in "transitional" neighborhoods or in minority ghettos are worth less than similar homes elsewhere guarantees that the owners of those homes will not receive enough to replace them.

The influence of NAREB and its pro-segregation ideas can be found at every level of government—from the village zoning board to the top level offices of federal programs for transportation, housing, urban renewal and many other purposes.

NAREB's Fight for Respectability

More than 85 percent of the real estate agents spend almost all of their time selling single family homes. The remaining 15 percent do everything that can be called real estate except the selling of single family homes. The editors of *Architectural Forum* in a book entitled *Building, U.S.A.* say:

In an overall sense a real estate man today can be anybody with a skill in the use and development of land and airspace, provided he puts that skill to work as a major source of profit . . . in the course of his business and depending on how wide a swath he chooses to cut he may buy, develop, plan, assemble, lease, manage and sell all kinds of land and buildings either for himself or his client . . . yet a common denominator does exist. To a real estate man land and buildings are commodities. There are things to buy and sell, to speculate in for a short time or to invest in at longer range. Whatever functions these physical units perform there is only one that really matters to real estate men: that they return a profit.[54]

It is the top 15 percent of the industry that provides the leaders who run the trade associations that make the policies for the entire real estate industry. Often these men are prominent not only in NAREB and one of the state organizations, but also in the Mortgage Bankers Association, the various associations of home builders or the Urban Land Institute and, these multiple roles constitute a kind of interlocking directorate that tends to produce one effective industry voice.

These industry leaders serve the business and industrial elites, but are not part of them. Few real estate men have inherited great wealth or an established role in the business community, and their educational level is generally well below that of others in the same income class.[55] Real estate men gain little prestige from the business they are in. The image of real estate men as expressed in *Building, U.S.A.* is:

the tribe, known variously as land speculators, town jobbers and just plain real estate men has shown great daring and imagination, though there has always been serious questions as to its exact degree of civilization.[56]

For many years NAREB has concentrated on improving the image of real estate men. This effort has taken three distinct paths: (1) a search for leadership roles in public policy questions; (2) a campaign for academic acceptance of real estate as a field of knowledge worthy of being studied at the college and university level; and (3) a long-range goal of acceptance of real estate men as professionals with public recognition of a status comparable to that enjoyed by lawyers, dentists and doctors (all important clients of the realtor).

It often happens that in pursuing one of these goals NAREB tends to lose ground on one or the other of its objectives. Its sponsorship of Proposition 14 was just such a case. This clearly established NAREB and CREA in leadership roles far beyond anything that the industry had ever been able to achieve.[57] But leadership in the brassy self-serving campaign for Proposition 14 adversely affected the realtors' professionalization goal and probably damaged their campaign for greater academic acceptance of real estate.

NAREB AND AMERICAN COLLEGES AND UNIVERSITIES

What group or groups have a real influence on educational policies in colleges and universities? It is popularly believed that liberal faculties exert a profound influence on their institutions' public policy positions, but while many tenured faculty members may be liberals their power in American higher education is negligible. They appear to have power because they are not fired for their utterances and the positions they take on public issues, but this has nothing to do with power to influence educational policies, or the real stance of institutions of higher learning on public policy questions. Academic senates make great pretense of having control of the educational programs at some of the large institutions, but if this power were real, half the courses taught in schools of business would be thrown out. Ultimately, power in American higher education rests in other groups, and the real estate industry is prominent among those groups.

Long before NAREB's current campaign against open occupancy in housing, it had succeeded in a massive penetration of the world of higher education. Although some realtors are to be found in ultra-rightist attacks on higher education, they know better than most of their fellow travelers the falsity of their claims. They have real estate professors on every major campus of the United States; and realtors sit on many kinds of university boards and committees close to the real power in American higher education.

The campaign of the real estate industry to gain academic acceptance began in the twenties. It paralleled the efforts of chambers of commerce and many other trade associations to gain acceptance in the academic world of the principle that business subjects were worthy of being taught at the undergraduate level in colleges and universities. NAREB, however, mounted a more massive effort than most other individual trade associations and has undoubtedly achieved greater success than most in getting specific courses included in curricula and gaining acceptance of real estate as "major" field of study.

The vast majority of the state universities in the United States have yielded to NAREB's blandishments, as have most lesser state supported institutions. Only the better private institutions and a few state institutions have withstood pressures of one kind or another to include real estate in their curricula. As a result, many institutions have as many as eight or ten real estate courses in their business administration curricula, and most schools of business administration offer a major field of study in real estate. In some cases success in getting real estate courses accepted at these institutions has resulted from political pressure through the state real estate commissioner, an appointee of the governor, who in many states takes a major role in the political fundraising for his governor.

NAREB's pressure has always been accompanied by various kinds of financial inducements, such as scholarships for real estate students, donations for a real estate "chair," and in California by the establishment of the Real Estate Research and Education Fund. Moreover, acceptance of real estate as a field of study had an extra payoff for the industry. Because real estate practice is a maze of petty details, not readily susceptible to organization in a theoretical framework of value in undergraduate education, few of the faculty at most institutions were able to teach the real estate courses that proliferated on their campuses. This resulted in the bonanza for NAREB and its local affiliates that industry leaders were called on to do a great deal of the teaching in this new field.

Business leaders are almost unanimous in affirming that most business administration courses mean little or nothing to the graduate when he enters the business world. Academic researchers agree with the business leaders, but go further: neither the content nor the methodology of most business courses add anything of significance to the intellectual development of undergraduates.[58]

In spite of the general agreement about the undesirability of most business administration courses and especially real estate, insurance, and other highly practical courses in undergraduate curricula, these courses persist and multiply. No one has demonstrated that any purpose is served by these courses, except to gain campus acceptance for the ideas and attitudes of industry spokesmen and to throw about industry leaders the prestigious robes of academe. NAREB's acceptance in the academic world also created an important distinction between members and nonmembers of that association. Universities and colleges using practitioners as full or part-time real estate faculty generally take the advice of the local real estate board in making their selections, with the result that minority real estate brokers and lawyers are excluded from this profitable and prestigious connection with American institutions of higher education. Thus, it is highly probable that until recently no Negro had ever had the opportunity to lecture on real estate at any state-supported college or university anywhere in the United States.

Under pressure from CREA, the California legislature in 1949 established the Real Estate Research and Education Fund to stimulate the university and the state colleges to undertake research and teaching in the field of real estate. At first the amounts available from this Fund were relatively small but in 1956 the legislature increased real estate license fees and allocated 24 percent of these fees to the Fund. From the $100,000 received in 1956, the university share of the annual appropriation increased rapidly until it reached about $300,000 per year by 1960. Thereafter it continued at about that level until recently when the level of support was somewhat reduced.

To administer the money received from the Fund, the university's president created a Real Estate Advisory Committee. This committee is composed of university representatives, the state Real Estate Commissioner and representatives of CREA, with CREA having a clear majority of the membership of the committee. Although money received by the university comes from the license fees paid by all real estate licensees, CREA was given a proprietary interest in the industry seats on this committee. This gave CREA a powerful voice in the university's decisions about what real estate education to offer, and what real estate research to undertake. It is impossible to overemphasize the significance of this remarkable concession to CREA. While it is true that trade associations and business groups exercise enormous behind-the-scenes influence on educational policies in most institutions of higher learning, nowhere else in the United States can one find a trade association in the public position of advising a university president on educational and research policy in the subject area in which the trade association operates.

CREA's penetration of the supposedly liberal University of California paid it rich rewards. The University established real estate courses in its School of Business Administration and created the real estate research program at the Berkeley and Los Angeles campuses. In its Extension Division the University created the most comprehensive real estate curriculum in the country, and the University Senate established a Certificate in Real Estate to be awarded upon successful completion of a specified core of the extension courses. These courses were all taught by members of CREA, and the program still carries the legend, "In Cooperation with the California Real Estate Association." Until recently, no non-CREA broker, and no member of a minority race, had ever taught in any of these many classes offered in seventy or eighty locations throughout California.

In recent years the CREA, through the financial cornucopia of the Commissioner's Real Estate Education and Research Fund, has involved most of the seventy or eighty California junior colleges and the four-year state colleges in gigantic programs of real estate education. CREA members often become regular faculty members of junior colleges in order to teach these courses, which are offered free to any resident of the junior college district.

The University's Certificate in Real Estate gained wide acceptance in the industry and has become a symbol of educational achievement in the real estate field. Since these are continuing education courses not intended for undergraduates, but rather for post-licensee training, they do not represent the same compromise with educational ideals that occurs when real estate courses are taught as part of the curriculum of a school of business administration, or where it is part of the undergraduate work offered in junior colleges or state colleges. For this reason these courses were very properly accorded educational standing in the world of adult education. Individuals who had earned the certificate formed an association of alumni called The Real Estate Certificate Institute, and used the initials RECI to indicate the special training that they had successfully completed. At the time of its founding, about twelve years ago, CREA assumed that this organization (RECI) would become one of its many allied organizations operating in real estate. But CREA discovered, to its dismay, that some of the early certificate holders were Negroes. As a result the RECI remains today an independent organization.

Not surprisingly, other state real estate associations are awed by the power of CREA in California higher education. Many have importuned their legislatures to set up a fund comparable to California's Real Estate Education and Research Fund but success has attended very few of these efforts.

NOTES

[1] *House and Home,* June, 1964, p. 18.

[2] Quoted in Georges Gurvitch, *Sociology of Law* (New York: Philosophical Alliance and Book Corp., 1942), p. 165.

[3] *Jurisprudence* (Chicago: University of Chicago Press, 1962), p. 401.

[4] "Sociological Aspects of Housing Discrimination" in *Race and Property,* John H. Denton, ed. (Berkeley: Diablo Press, 1964), p. 126.

[5] *California Real Estate Magazine,* April, 1966, p. 9.

[6] 334 U.S. 1.

[7] See generally Davis McEntire, *Residence and Race* (Berkeley: University of California Press, 1960).

[8] Chicago: Aldine Publishing Co., 1965.

[9] *Id.* at 44.

[10] *Id.* at 40.

[11] Karl E. Taeuber, "Residential Segregation" in *Scientific American* (August 1965): 9.

[12] 245 U.S. 60.

[13] *Harmon* v. *Tyler*, 273 U.S. 668

[14] *Allen* v. *Oklahoma City*, 175 Okla. 421 (1935).

[15] The title of an excellent book by Alan Barth detailing abuse of power by public officials. New York: Collier Books, 1961.

[16] 271 U.S. 323 (1926).

[17] New York: Harcourt Brace and Co., 1948, p. 70.

[18] See *Trends in Housing* (March–April 1961): 8, for an account of their use in two Washington suburbs, Summer and Spring Valley.

[19] See *Realtors Headlines,* March 8, 1965, p. 2.

[20] *Ibid.*

[21] *Realtors Headlines,* March 15, 1965, p. 2.

[22] Committee on Professional Standards, NAREB, *Interpretations of the Code of Ethics,* 1963, p. 38–39.

[23] *Realtors Headlines,* March 15, 1965, p. 2.

[24] Beddoe then had the choice of appealing the decision or forgetting the matter. He did not appeal and subsequently he became the member of another realty board.

[25] Seattle: University of Washington Press. 1965.

[26] Berkeley: U.C. Press, 1959. (Quoting Gerald Seeger, St. Louis attorney for white property owners in the restrictive covenant cases.)

[27] *Trends in Housing* (January–February 1964): 5.

[28] See Pearl J. Davies, *Real Estate in American History* (Washington, D.C.: Public Affairs Press, 1958).

[29] *California Real Estate Magazine* (May 1966): 8.

[30] *San Francisco Chronicle,* May 11, 1966, p. 10.

[31] *Trends in Housing* (January–February 1966): 8.

[32] *Ibid.*

[33] *Ibid.*

[34] *Wall Street Journal* (San Francisco edition), February 4, 1966, p. 1.

[35] *San Francisco Chronicle,* April 23, 1966, p. 11.

[36] *Wall Street Journal* (San Francisco edition), February 4, 1966, p. 1.

[37] New York: Prentice Hall, 1949, p. 204.

[38] Arthur A. May, *Valuation of Residential Real Estate,* 2d ed. (Englewood Cliffs, N.J.: Prentice-Hall, 1953), p. 74.

[39] See, e.g., Luigi Laurenti, *Property Values and Race* (Berkeley: University of California Press, 1960).

[40] Quoted in Harry and David Rosen, *But Not Next Door* (New York: Avon Books, 1962), p. 38.

[41] *The New York Times,* September 3, 1966, p. 8.

[42] Quoted in Robert Pitts, "Real Estate Valuation and Finance" in *Race and Property,* John H. Denton, ed. (Berkeley: Diablo Press, 1964), p. 106.

[43] "Equality and Beyond: Housing Segregation in the Great Society" in *Daedalus* 95, No. 1 (Winter 1966): 86.

[44] *The Mortgage Banker,* December, 1962, p. 26.

[45] *Ibid.*

[46] *Trends in Housing* (November–December 1963): 1.

[47] New York: Harper and Bros., 1955.

[48] Cambridge, Mass.: M.I.T. Press, 1964, p. 67.

[49] *Op. cit.*, pp. 68–70.

[50] *Op. cit.*, pp. 218–219.

[51] P. 7 of the complaint.

[52] P. 22 of the complaint.

[53] P. 27 of the complaint.

[54] New York: McGraw-Hill, 1957, pp. 12–13.

[55] See generally *Real Estate Education and Research Needs in California* (Sacramento: State Dept. of Education, 1959).

[56] P. 11.

[57] In Arizona the realtors had a comparable leadership success when they were able to win an initiative campaign to add a section to the Arizona Constitution permitting realtors to draw basic real estate instruments. The realtors won this campaign by a margin of more than three and a half to one, following an Arizona Supreme Court decision which held that these basic real estate documents were legal instruments and could only be drawn by lawyers. See Robert Riggs, *Vox Populi, The Battle of 103* (Tucson: University of Arizona Press, 1964).

[58] See generally R. A. Gordon and J. E. Howell, *Higher Education for Business* (New York: Columbia University Press, 1959) and F. C. Pierson, *The Education of American Businessmen: A Study of University-College Progress in Business Administration* (New York: McGraw-Hill, 1959). Findings summarized in Leonard Silk, *The Education of Businessmen* (New York: Committee for Economic Development, 1960).